It Can Always Be Worse

(Never Give Up!)

My Life

By Link Piazzo

For information about permission to reproduce selections from this book, write to:

Link Piazzo
Sportsman's Corner
401 Vine
Reno, NV 89503

Published by Nationwide Marketing.

Art Director: Mark McKinnon. Typographer: Tony Ochoa. Editor: Mike Sion.

Printed in the United States of America.

Library of Congress Catalog Card Number: 99-74257

ISBN# 0-9652694-8-5

02 01 00 99   10 9 8 7 6

Contents

Acknowledgements

In this book I have mentioned many individuals whose lives have impacted me in a major way. Some were mentioned more than others. And then there are people whose names I should have mentioned, but didn't get around to. That's the problem with writing a big, fat book: after awhile, you try to cut back.

Following is a list of people I especially want to acknowledge, whether their names are in the following pages or not. Some of these fine folk are gone; others are, fortunately, still with us:

The Rev. Brewster Adams, Bud Beasley, Norman Biltz, Ty Cobb Sr., Newt Crumley Jr., Ben Dasher, Joe DiMaggio, Lefty Gomez, Joe King, Jake Lawlor, Dick Kirman, Rollan Melton, Jack Threlkel, Eddie Questa and George Wingfield Sr., etc., etc.

I must especially mention my good friend Jim Wood. Through past experiences and conversations with him, he inspired me to write the book.

Preface

A person who has lived as long as I forgets so many events of his life. But if compelled to dig up memories — to sort through old files and diaries and scrapbooks of newspaper clippings — he can become amazed at how much he's seen and done, how much he's experienced, how much he's enjoyed and simply endured. Inevitably, he can reach the conclusion that what he has is the substance for a book.

When I embarked on this project shortly before my 80th birthday, my wife, Helen, wondered what purpose my autobiography would serve. After all, we don't have many close family members. We have only one living child: our son, Craig. Would this narrative serve as an interesting recollection for just one solitary reader? Of course, my older brother, Chet, is still around, and my sister, Melba, and my wife and I have nieces and nephews. So this book would serve as a family history for them, as well, plus interesting reading for my close friends. Still, however, a limited audience.

But my intent with putting my life down in words is more than to produce an heirloom for the Piazzo clan. It is to leave a legacy for the Reno community, as well. For my generation, born in the early part of this century — and which weathered the Great Depression and fought World War II and then built the country into the thriving nation it remains today — is slowly passing away as this century draws to a close. When we go, so do our accumulated knowledge and memories. If we don't leave chronicles behind, we rob subsequent generations of records of local history and, perhaps, whatever nuggets of wisdom we have accrued. At the moment I am writing this, folders and files of handwritten notes and black-and-white photographs have formed a small mountain range on my desk. Frankly, I'm surprised how much I've done in my lifetime! Leafing through my private papers clears the cobwebs in a hurry. Memories come flooding back of incidents about which I had forgotten completely, and the details return to my consciousness with heartening clarity. There are so many anecdotes! Like the time in 1968 when Roy Rogers, the famous singing cowboy and movie star, came into Chet's and my store, the Sportsman.

I showed up at the store and someone said, "Roy Rogers was in here looking for you." I'd never met the man, although, of course, everyone knew who he was. I couldn't figure out why he'd visit me.

The next day I came in and someone said, "Roy Rogers was in here again." I shrugged. The third day, I came in and there he was. He said, "Link, a friend of yours, Gordon

McEachron, said to look you up while I was in Reno." McEachron had been head football coach at the University of Nevada, and a close friend. He'd retired in Apple Valley, Calif. That's where Roy Rogers lived, and the two became friends. Rogers had told McEachron he was coming to Reno for a nightclub appearance with his wife, Dale Evans, at Harrah's. McEachron had told Rogers to look me up.

Rogers was holding a model 12 shotgun. "I need to repair this gun," he said. I had several of the model in stock and knew the gun real well. It had a dented magazine. I guessed what had happened. "What'd you do," I said, "put this in a dresser drawer?" That was a common way guys tried to straighten out their barrels, jamming the front into a drawer; but you're supposed to remove the magazine first. He looked at me with surprise.[1]

We chatted a bit. I asked what he was going to use the shotgun for. "Well, I'm going to shoot in the big shoot here, the Golden West Grand," he said. That was a tournament at a range off Pyramid Lake Highway.

"How good are you?" I asked.

"Well, I'll shoot a 97 or better," he said.

"I'll tell you what," I said. "If you shoot a 97 or better, the magazine's free." The magazine cost $2.50 — about $40 today.

Rogers left town and I forgot all about our deal. Then I received a letter. I still have it framed in my shop. It said, "Dear Link: Since I didn't hit the 97 I guess I owe you $2.50 and a check is enclosed. I would like to tell you what a genuine pleasure it was to meet you and thank you sincerely for your kindness."

I wrote back: "Tell your bookkeeper to take the check off the books because I'm keeping it as a souvenir!"

Just a bit of color from my life, just a little story showing the way people think and act. There have been a ton of incidents like these in my life.

Funny how they start spilling forth from the memory banks, once you get started.

SOME OF THESE OLD memories started coming back to me several years ago, after I was asked to be one of the subjects featured in *War Stories, Veterans Remember WW II*, a project by the University of Nevada Oral History Program, published in 1995. Twenty-one men and women were interviewed about our combat or support roles during that conflict; small portions of the interviews were transcribed. I had been a pilot on a B-25 in the Pacific Theater, and flown 67 combat missions. I'm still amazed, when I think about it, how I even survived.

But that's been a pattern in my life. *Near-misses.* I should have been killed a number of times — not only during the war, but before and since. In all, I guess I should have been killed 30-odd times. Yet, here I am.

I did pretty well to help shorten the war. I thought the good Lord was bringing me back to base safely after every mission so that I could do something astronomical to end the war. That never did happen, so I couldn't understand why I kept returning from my missions intact. There even were cases where I was getting shot at and we were losing engines, and bullet holes were filling the plane, even right above my head — yet, I was never frightened! At any time! I figured, what the hell, I'd get killed today instead of tomorrow, that's all.

I still have the bullet that my crew chief dug out of the aluminum frame in the cockpit right above where my head had been.

---

[1] "C.G." was inscribed on the end of the pistol grip. "What'd you do, steal the gun?" I asked, jokingly. Rogers explained Clark Gable had given it to him.

My bomber had been shot up by camouflaged Japanese guns in a village after I'd knocked out a lot of trains and trucks in a mission over the Philippines. I'd lost my right engine, the Plexiglas canopy was shot out, and gunfire even had ripped off the end of the bomb bay tank — spurting out fuel which, miraculously, extinguished the cigarette my radio gunner, Harry Hall, of Canton, Ohio, had been smoking. Had the gas gushed a few feet from him, the fumes would have ignited and exploded the plane.

We landed nearly out of gas, the plane riddled by about 100 bullet holes . . . and there was that .25 caliber, metal-piercing bullet, which, had it not been spent when it reached the cockpit, would have taken my head off.

The crew chief extricated it and put it on a chain for me. I wore it around my neck for a time, and in the early days back home after the war, whenever things got a little bit tough, I'd take it out to remind myself, "Things aren't very tough. That bullet should have killed me."

For whatever mysterious reason, I've always made it through such situations. I can only credit the good Lord upstairs.

YES, IT'S FUNNY, ONCE you get going, how many stories spill out of you. What's sort of sad is how quickly each of us becomes forgotten once we've left this world, including those who have played significant roles in their communities' development.

Norman Biltz — who became a very dear friend of mine — had been instrumental in bringing some of the wealthiest Americans to make their homes in Nevada, including "Major" Max Fleischmann, scion of the Standard Brands fortune, who took up residence in Glenbrook on the northeast shore of Lake Tahoe.

Biltz had arrived in Nevada in 1927. A couple years after the stock-market crash of 1929 and the ensuing Depression, he and several other Nevadans orchestrated a crafty plan to populate the state with 75 millionaires whose fortunes remained intact, luring them with Nevada's lack of a state income tax and freedom from harsh sales, gift and inheritance taxes. In addition to Fleischmann, automaker E.L. Cord, the family of newspaper mogul E.W. Scripps, a number of Hollywood stars and tycoon Cornelius Vanderbilt III moved to Nevada. The state benefited from their presence.

And Biltz, himself, ended up benefiting greatly.

He owned lots of acreage near Lake Tahoe and was a partner with other major landowners. They sold property to the newcomers to build estates on. Biltz became a multimillionaire himself, and *Fortune* magazine eventually dubbed him "The Duke of Nevada." It was a pleasure for me to meet and know the man. I would visit him once in awhile in his office. One day he told me, "You know something? I just figured out, I have 72 partners!" Sometimes he'd loan money to farmers and take part of their business. He'd have enterprises here and there, such as a little restaurant in Lovelock. I said, "You're pretty smart. You've got 72 partners but you're not doing the work. They're doing the work." Yes, he was a sharp man.

In 1973, Biltz and I served on the same jury in Carson City. A woman was suing the owners of a movie theater after falling down its steps. One day we'd carpool together in his car; the next day, in mine. I knew Biltz was drinking a little heavily. One particular day he was driving. I said, "Norm, what are you trying to do, get these distilleries working overtime?"

I'll never forget his answer. He turned and looked at me and said, "Link, what else is there?"

I did not realize he had terminal cancer. He knew he was going to die. So he was drinking a little bit. But he still performed very well as a juror.

Shortly after, he committed suicide.

A few months later, I was having lunch with friends at the Holiday Hotel downtown. There were about eight of us at the table, plus a full table of familiar faces next to us. Someone at the other table called over. "Link, we can't remember this guy's name. He always wore a sport shirt. He was an alcoholic. And he committed suicide."

"For Chrissake!" I said. "Don't you guys remember Norman Biltz?!"

What a poor way to describe this great man!

"Oh, yeah, yeah, Norman Biltz," they said.

This proves a point. Six months after I'm dead, they're going to say, "Link who?"

But perhaps this book — and whatever wisdom and compelling history it contains — will live on somehow; at least for those who pick it up and pry into its pages.

AFTER ROLLAN MELTON, THE *Reno Gazette-Journal* columnist, heard I was thinking about writing my life story, he said, "Oh boy, this is going to be a best-seller." I said, "Oh no, I'm going to have this printed on real thin paper so when they take it to the bathroom they can use it for toilet paper!"

But I don't know. Perhaps readers will get something out of this book. I hope they do. For I have always spoken out about what I believe is right. It's been one of my pronounced traits, along with grim determination, stubbornness and sentimentality.

A longtime politician from Reno, a popular man who has been powerful in state politics for three decades and is a good friend of mine, was having coffee with me one morning. He remarked, "God, you're outspoken!" I said, "Oh, sure, I don't have to shake hands with people I don't like and I don't have to kiss babies like you politicians. I'm not running for office. I simply tell the truth. If you don't like it, the hell with you."

My mother, Emma, taught her children this. There was no gray area with her. She told us to just tell the truth and don't ever lie, and if people don't like it, that's too bad. Fortunately, my blunt candor has never gotten me into too much hot water, although it nearly has on several occasions.

During my military service, toward the end of the war, my group was stationed on the island of Luzon in the Philippines. My group commander called me in one day. There was a brand-new warplane, the A-26, being shown down in Mindoro. Since I had flying time on the A-20, the commander ordered me to Mindoro to check out the new A-26 and produce a report on whether the military should buy it. I was happy to undertake this mission, since we'd been flying tough combat missions out of Luzon over Formosa, the tiny island that the Japanese had fortified with 1,600 gun emplacements. We were losing planes and crews daily over Formosa. Feeling like it was a vacation, I took a navigator and engineer and flew my B-25 to Mindoro.

I checked in with the major there, and he introduced me to the man from the airplane factory. The major truly was a miserable bastard. When I requested permission to take the A-26 to my outfit and show it to them, he'd said, "Under no circumstances!"

One day, returning to Mindoro from a test flight, I found the airfield socked in with fog. I couldn't land. I told my navigator, Bill Eakin of Allentown, Pa., to make sure he got the name of the man in the control tower and the precise time, to the second, that we radioed him. We continued on to Clark Field on Luzon; it, too, was fogged in. I had my navigator record the information, and we continued on to my outfit at Lenguyen Gulf.

The next day, I flew the A-26 back to Mindoro. The miserable major laid into me, ignoring my explanations. I got mad.

"Major," I snarled, "if you ever have guts enough to come up there where they're fighting the war, you might have to borrow an airplane from me, you chickens— so-and-so."

He sought revenge, writing a heated report about my "insubordination." The report made its way up the chain of command to Gen. Douglas MacArthur's office, then back down the chain to our base. The last sentence read: "reprimand mandatory." It was signed by MacArthur's office and everyone else on the way down the command.

What saved me at the court-martial hearing was that I'd had the presence of mind to have my navigator scrupulously record the names of the men in the control towers where we couldn't land, and the times when we'd radioed them, right to the second.

The case was dismissed. I avoided a court-martial — which would have been a lousy thing to have happen after so much combat action and brushes with death.

The end result is that if you do what's right, you'll probably come out OK. Of course, I thank God I'd had sense enough to have my navigator write down the names of the guys in the control towers and when he'd called them. The court-martial board had researched these facts.

ALL MY LIFE I'VE been a risk-taker. During the war, there were times I did go against regulations. After the atomic bombs were dropped on Hiroshima and Nagasaki in August 1945, I took my B-25 crew and some photographers on an unauthorized, secret mission to check out the damage. I had to smuggle the photographs home. I guess it was worth it; 50 years after the fact, I was asked to donate prints of the photographs to the George S. Patton Museum. I did.

I can't answer why, out of my parents' five children, I've been the one who's taken the most risks. All I know is that if you don't take a risk you're never going to succeed — in *anything*. I get a kick out of the guy who's just sitting down, saying, "Oh God, I'm not succeeding." But he's not making any effort, either!

When I was 19, my brother, Chet, and I started our sporting goods store. In the midst of the Depression, no less. After the war, I took business risks as a developer. It's a trait I inherited directly from my father, Santino. He was the first of his parents' children who left Piazzo, Italy, to come to America to seek a better life.

In life, I've also been very stubborn. You have to be stubborn if you want to succeed. You can't let anybody derail you from your objective. You better be stubborn and stay with it, in business or anything. There always will be nay-sayers, and it's easy to sabotage yourself, to listen to someone telling you, "Oh, that's too tough."

In life, I've been very sentimental, too, especially concerning family and friends. I've been a member of many civic and social organizations. Tradition means a lot to me. It's how communities move forward. And societies, and nations.

Talk about sentimental. In 1988, I was awarded the Distinguished Flying Cross — 43 years after I finished my military service. It was presented to me at the Reno Rotary

Club. I was given a standing ovation. I was asked to speak. I started to say a few words, but all I could think about were my buddies who had not made it. We had become so very close. I couldn't speak. I choked up.

When it was over, two or three veterans came up to me. One said, "I know why you choked up. You were thinking about your buddies." I said, "You're not kidding!"

For whatever reason, they didn't make it home.

But I did. And it's been a terrific life.

SO MUCH OF LIVING has to do with having the proper attitude. On Dec. 11, 1998 — as I was writing this book — I turned 80. But inside, it doesn't feel that way. Eighty is just a number. I'm going to go on living the way I do until I die. To the fullest.

A friend of mine — I won't say his name — got up during our weekday morning coffee klatsch at the Gold-N-Silver Inn in Reno, and, limping, gingerly set his cup down. I took him aside and said, "What the hell's the matter with you?" He said, "I got a leg that has a little pain." I said, "So what? Quit limping!"

He looked at me like I was crazy, for he had taken the opposite attitude. I believe most infirmities are deeply affected by mental outlook. I've had both hips replaced, but I don't walk awkwardly. I had my prostate removed, and a double-hernia. But I do not limp!

I learned this rectitude from my mother. When I was a little kid, a neighbor walked gimpily one night into our kitchen. My mother asked, "What are you limping for?" "Oh Mrs. Piazzo," he said, "I lost a toe on my right foot." She said, "Well, why do you think God gave you 10 toes? Can't you get along with nine?" That was my mother, see. She said, "Quit limping and get along with nine toes!"

They talked for about a half-hour. Then our friend got up and walked out — without limping!

My mother had no sympathy for those who cater to their ailments. When she was 10, she fell into a fire and lost two fingers and part of her left arm. But she did more work with eight fingers than most people do with 10. It's mental.

I had only a high school education when I endeavored to become a pilot during the war. The other cadets had college educations. But I knew that's all they had over me; when it came to flying an airplane, we were equal. And I became a better pilot than most. It wasn't squeezing the most out of my potential; it was putting the most into an opportunity. Not merely "playing the cards you're dealt," as the saying goes, but playing the hell out of that hand at the poker table of life. Getting the hell into the game.

When Chet and I opened our store, back in 1938, it was tough. We worked 14 hours a day, seven days a week. But we persevered, and we made the business work and grow. Today, the Sportsman is the oldest business continuously run by its founders in Nevada.

Along the way, I've contributed to the community, raised a son who is a success, been married 54 years. And I've even been able to give something back to my ancestral home, helping restore a church in the village of Piazzo, Italy. It's been a great life.

One phrase I like is, "Success is living your life on your own terms." My own terms have been hard work, long hours, truthfulness, not being afraid to speak my piece, and taking risks when it was warranted.

There've been a few regrets, some that still eat me up inside. But you just have to keep going. Why nurture regrets?

What I hope readers will get out of this book is that you should live your life on your own terms. Persistence is paramount. Never give up. Ever. Too many people do. I don't advocate that people go out and violate regulations — or the law. Just be honest, and unafraid to speak the truth. Then you'll succeed. And that's the enjoyment of life: succeeding.

I've really enjoyed life. You dig into something, work your brains out and succeed, that's where you get satisfaction.

I hope this book proves as satisfying to readers as it has been for me to write it.

— Link Piazzo, Reno, Nev., March 1999.

Creating a Buzz

It was July 1943. I was 24 years old, and I was hot stuff. I'd just gotten my wings — I was a second lieutenant in the Army Air Corps, a pilot of a B-25, destined for the Pacific Theater and the war with Japan.

Mather Field in Sacramento was only a 45-minute flight from my hometown, Reno. So what the hell — we were still only flying training missions, what we called "navigation missions." I turned to my co-pilot and said, "Would you like to see my store?"

He started to laugh. "In Reno?" he said.

The Biggest Little City wasn't on our mission this day. But there was nothing better to do. And like many of the other pilots, we figured we were going to get killed anyway in the months ahead. Might as well have some fun now.

"Yeah, OK," he said.

We flew over the Sierra Nevada and then toward the Truckee Meadows, the greenbelt nourished by the Truckee River wending down from the mountains and out into the high desert. I zoomed over Reno and dipped down, coming in from the south over Virginia Street, the main drag, with its Reno Arch and world-famous Harolds Club. To those in the downtown buildings or on the sidewalks, the bomber's 54-foot length and 67-foot wingspan must have created the image of a monstrous, glittering aluminum bird in the sunny sky. Not to mention a frighteningly noisy one. The bomber's two Wright R-2600-9 Double Cyclone, 14-cylinder, 1,750-horsepower engines were creating a buzzing drone that was entirely unexpected at the noon hour in the casino core.

As I blew by at 220 miles per hour, 10 feet over the buildings, windows shattered, gamblers spilled drinks, tools rattled off hooks in hardware stores, and in the garage of the local bus company behind my sporting goods store, a bus engine weighing more than a ton shook off its shelf and crashed to the floor.

None of this, however, was known to me up in the cockpit of my B-25, which I navigated with the ardor, if not yet the skill, of Col. Doolittle. I just wanted, after all, to show off my store. And to say hello to my mother down in the old neighborhood. I had no idea what havoc I was causing below.

I dipped into the downtown corridor. The St. Francis Hotel, which my mother, Emma, owned, was below us, on the right, with the Sportsman Sporting Goods Store that my brother, Chet, and I owned, on the ground level. Our sisters, Olga and Melba, were managing it while Chet and I were in the service. I could see the 20-foot storefront;

something was displayed in the window. Just a flash as we raced by and veered up.

KOH radio station was one block north of my store — between Fourth and Fifth streets, on the east side — and the station's great big wooden telephone pole, painted silver, rose higher than my altitude. It towered at least 100 feet. I looked up after showing the co-pilot my store, saw the pole and hit the left rudder. I missed the pole, no problem, really, except that Brewster Adams Church was on the corner of Fifth and Virginia, across the street. I had to miss its steeple, too. I did.

I veered northwest, over our neighborhood. I dipped down and buzzed our block, 10th and Bell streets, circled, then buzzed again. My mother and Aunt Mary — Lalla Mary — came out into the front yard in the long dresses they always wore. They were waving white dish towels. They knew it was I. They figured nobody else was stupid enough to buzz the neighborhood.

J.C. Penney Company was on Sierra Street. My girlfriend, Helen Galbraith (who later became my wife), worked there. I buzzed that, too. In all, I made two or three swipes over the town in five minutes, then headed back to Sacramento. Mission accomplished.

MEANWHILE, UP AT RENO Army Air Base in Stead, north of Reno, trouble was brewing. This base was home to an air transport command, and Reno residents had been complaining about the transport planes flying too low over the city. Of course, none of these planes had buzzed the town as I had just done. The colonel who commanded the base already was sore about being a target of public criticism. And now, some smartass flyboy in a B-25 had buzzed Reno, and a citizen had called his base to complain.

The caller had easily read my plane's number painted on the B-25's tail. The colonel phoned Mather to find out if it was one of that base's planes, and who the hell the pilot was. He obtained this information and was all set to call my commanding officer at Mather. But he never made the fateful call.

It just so happened that a woman was visiting the colonel in his office. The woman was Eva Adams, an aide to U.S. Sen. Pat McCarran of Nevada. She had overheard the colonel's phone conversation, and learned that Link Piazzo was about to be reported. Eva knew my older sister, Olga. They had been very, very close in school. Eva decided to intervene on my behalf.

"I want you to call back," she told the colonel, "and squash this whole thing. It happens to be a family friend of mine." She told the colonel that Link Piazzo was a patriotic young man readying to fight for his country in the Pacific Theater. "Let's not get him in trouble over this little incident," she said.

The colonel grudgingly obliged. And so — completely unknown to me — my rear was saved that day. I probably would have been grounded — at the least.

I CAME HOME ON leave some days later. That's when I learned what damage my little fly-over had done.

Thank God, no one had been hurt or killed. There were no heart attacks, and the falling bus engine had not maimed any unsuspecting soul who happened to be in its path.

In fact, the people of Reno had been delighted by my escapade. Former Gov. Dick Kirman owned Bradley's Wholesale Hardware Store on the corner of Plaza and Virginia streets, a half-block south of my store. He used to stop in, even when he was governor. He was a dear friend of mine. When I came home on leave, he popped into the store and said, "Oh, God, that was terrific. You rattled all the tools off our walls."

The Ferrari family lived at the end of 10th Street where it dead-ends into Washington Street. It turned out that I broke the windows in their house. They were happy about it, though. Hell, Link buzzed the neighborhood.

Buzzing one's hometown was common back then, at least among the crazy pilots like me. Heck, we just felt like coming over for a brief visit.

It wasn't until after the war that Olga informed me about Eva Adams' quick and decisive intercession on my behalf. I had simply landed that afternoon at Mather, and nothing else had transpired. My co-pilot told his roommate about our Reno escapade, and that was the end of it.

I went on to fly 67 combat missions in the Pacific, earning 13 medals, including the Distinguished Flying Cross, and doing my part to shorten the war. Adams, incidentally, went on to serve as director of the U.S. Mint.

And as for the people in my old neighborhood . . . well, the day of my buzzing left a lasting impression.

Early in 1998, a man in his 60s came into the store. "My name is Manfredi," he said.

"I was just a little kid when you buzzed our neighborhood."

Santino's Walk to Reno

On a wall in my office I keep a framed photograph of the village of Piazzo — which is in the province of Genoa (Genova in Italian) in northern Italy — along with the insignia of my family's ancient coat of arms. The photo shows a very pastoral farming village in the foothills of the Alps. For centuries and centuries, the villagers have lived off the land, self-sufficiently, working the fields with their oxen, raising vegetables and hazel nuts and dairy cattle without need of venturing away from their little world nestled between Genoa and Milan. In fact, the village hasn't changed much to this day, as I have witnessed on four trips spread out over six decades. There are two or three very large homes — villazantis occupied by rich Genovese during the summer. Paved roads have replaced muddy streets and oxen finally gave way to more modern farming methods. But, on the whole, the people remain the same: poor, proud and hard-working.

In the photo's background one can see the remnants of the stone castle that one of my ancient ancestors stormed, single-handedly, circa 1100 A.D. The rubble lies in open terrain, a distance equivalent to a couple city blocks from the village proper. For me, the ruins represent much more than a reminder of Europe's feudal past, when counts and marqueses and dukes and kings lorded it over the poor, earnest masses, who obediently gave up large shares of their crops in tribute to these rulers. For me, the remains of the castle outline the beginning of my family's recorded history.

In that region, there was a marquese in a castle on just about every hill. The one ruling my ancestral village apparently was crueler and greedier than most. One day, my ancestor apparently grew so fed up with the status quo — of the impoverished villagers like himself having their goods taken by this nobleman — that he stormed the castle and killed the marquese. Then, like Robin Hood, he distributed the slain ruler's wealth among the villagers.

Ever after, the village has been known as Piazzo.

My father, Santino, was born and raised in this village that bears our family's name, on Oct. 13, 1878. He wanted a better life for himself, but like many young men he was compelled to serve in the Italian army. He vowed that when he received his mustering out pay he would strike out for America. And so he did.

Santino arrived at the immigration center on Ellis Island in New York Harbor in 1905, one in the huddled masses who spoke no English and had next to no money. He gave what he had in his pockets to a ticket agent and boarded a train for San Francisco, where he had a friend. Welcome to America: his ticket ran out in Portola, Calif., a good 200 miles or more from the city. It was the middle of winter. Snow covered the ground. There must have been other Italians on the train, for somehow Santino was able to inquire where the nearest town was. He learned it was Reno, 42 miles away.

Santino was short and stocky, and blessed with a tremendous attitude. I remember him saying, "Walking to Reno, I was very fortunate. When the soles of my shoes wore out, I could find cardboard on the side of the road." I'm not sure where he took shelter at night, but two days later he arrived in Reno, the little town by the Truckee River.

Across northern California and northern Nevada, Italian immigrants were beginning new lives at the turn of the century. Italian farms dotted the Truckee Meadows. In quick fashion, Santino met an Italian who helped him get a job with Verdi Lumber Co., about 10 miles west of Reno. The job was delivering lumber by horse and wagon for the princely sum of $1 a day. This was the toehold Santino needed. Always gregarious, good-natured and entrepreneurial, he struck up a strong relationship with the company owner. Santino arranged for Italians in the community to buy lumber on credit. This set a pattern: for the rest of his life, in whatever business endeavor he was engaged in, Santino Piazzo would extend credit and make personal loans to countless Italians, helping them start businesses, construct homes, build lives.

Often, he would lend money to people. They'd say, "Well, I'll give you a note." He'd decline. "No, what do I want a note for? If your word's no good your signature's no good. All I want is your word."

He made many friends.

In time, enterprising Santino quit the lumber company and began his own business.

He knew how to talk to people; he liked them, and they liked him. He had an honest face. He liked to see people succeed. He became a merchant, buying crops from local Italian farmers and selling them in California; and buying goods from Italians in California and selling them in Reno.

Santino had great vision. I don't think he realized the vision that he had. Coming from Italy, the common person had no chance to succeed. All the land had been taken centuries and centuries ago. Santino came to America and saw nothing but wide-open opportunity. Let's buy and build!

Santino also had the get-ahead work ethic. He embraced his adopted country with all his soul. When he arrived, he could not speak, write or read English. He had no friends or money. In Reno, however, he would go every chance he got to the silent movies, paying his dime as soon as the theater opened and sitting through three or four showings. He taught himself to read English by deciphering the subtitles. Can you imagine that?

Santino thought America was the greatest country in the world. I remember as a boy how other Italians would stop by the house. "Santino," they'd say, "we want you to join the Sons of Italy." "Oh no no," he'd say, "you join American clubs. We are Americans."

From Day One, Santino Piazzo was committed to realizing the good life in America. Eventually his younger brother, Graziuso, came to Reno, too. This turned out to be lucky for my father.

IN RENO LIVED AN Italian, Tony Minetto. He knew the Pizorno family of northern Italy, and sponsored three of the Pizorno children — two girls and a boy — to come to Reno. One of the girls was named Emma. Santino fell for her. But he had to convince Minetto — her de facto guardian — to win her hand in marriage. "You can't marry her until you have $750," Minetto said. He believed $750 was needed to support a wife.

That was a small fortune in that day and age. Santino ended up borrowing the sum from his brother. And so he and Emma married. They honeymooned by renting a surrey and picnicking at Steamboat Hot Springs in the south Truckee Meadows.

My father and mother already had three children — Louis, Olga and Chet — and in 1918, just before I was born, my father purchased a 42-acre ranch for $2,500 in northeast Reno, just north of the current campus of Bishop Manogue High School, a few blocks east of the University of Nevada campus. He had a farmhouse and equipment, and a few cattle. The land was very, very rocky. The Western Pacific Railroad lay tracks running by the property, and workers dumped loads of rocks down the embankment. My mother worked day and night clearing rocks from the soil, carting them off with buckets, with my dad helping out in his spare time. They wanted to grow crops.

My father and a friend, Fred Oliva, built a road up to the ranch using horses and a fresno — a big scooper drawn by horses. They cleared the road to the top of a hill, past the

My father's father, Giacomo Piazzo

present campus of Manogue, and named it Surprise Valley Road. Today, it's known as Valley Road. It's probably in not much better condition, with its cracks and potholes, than it was in my father's day.

I was born Dec. 11, 1918, on the ranch, on a day so cold, my mother said, the water in the wash basin froze. I was delivered by Delle, a midwife hired by all the Italian families in the area. She charged $5 for her services, which included staying at the home for one or two weeks, cooking one meal a day for the family. Delle was heavyset, gray-haired, and very nice. She delivered my younger sister, Melba. Yes, we Italians were a tight-knit community.

My sister, Olga, was the one who named Chet and myself. Chet was born 20 months before me. She named each of us after a U.S. president. Chet — Chester — was named for Chester Arthur. She named me Lincoln. For years I believed my middle name was Emilio. But it turned out no middle name was included on my birth certificate. Sometimes my middle name or the initial "E" still shows up on official documents. But my true legal name is Lincoln Piazzo, with the z's pronounced the Genovese way, with the "z" sound, not the "ts" sound as in "pizza." But I digress.

My memories are few of the ranch. I remember the two horses, Molly and Nig, and the dog, Happy. I remember Happy had a habit of running alongside the train, barking. One time, train workers shot steam at her, which probably ended her habit. In 1922, before I turned 4, my parents sold the ranch. Despite their hardy efforts, the soil just was not conducive to farming. They had improved the property, and my father sold it for $9,500 — a $7,000 profit in four years, terrific for that time.

My father had bought property in northwest Reno, and had a brick house built. This is where our family moved, to 609 W. 10th St., at the intersection of 10th and Bell streets. By this point my father had widespread business interests.

He'd bought a truck, and would buy garlic, onions, potatoes and other produce from local Italians who owned "truck farms" — small farms that raise vegetables. He'd sell the produce to markets not only in Reno but in northern California, as far off as San Francisco. On the return trip, he'd bring grapes back to Reno. All the Italian families made their own wine. He knew all the Italian farmers in the region. He also would bring back California produce the Reno markets wanted, such as melons. He often bought crops at a good rate from distressed areas in California, and sold them not only in Reno but in Portola and Quincy, Calif. He would be gone from home for three or four days at a time.

Long hours didn't mean anything to Dad. He drilled that into his children, too. Santino simply was a worker. He'd make his long drives winter or summer, often on little sleep. And buying and selling produce was just one of his enterprises. My mother never knew the extent of his business dealings. She had her hands full keeping the home fires burning, raising us kids, with little to no idea of what my father was up to at the moment.

In the course of his travels across northern Nevada, my father would come upon dilapidated buildings or struggling businesses in towns such as Winnemucca and Elko, and he'd negotiate to buy the property. He'd make a down-payment — business was conducted then on a handshake, not by written contracts — and expand his budding empire of holdings. His vast interests came to include half-ownership of a restaurant in Lovelock, 83 miles to the east, and a potato farm in Beowawe, more than 300 miles away, across the deserts of northeastern Nevada. Father even had a half-interest with Louis Damonte in a potato grader — a large apparatus with big holes in containers at three different elevations. The device was kept south of Reno at the Damonte Ranch. Potato farmers would pay to use it. My father and Damonte would haul the grader to the different ranches. Potatoes would be dumped in the top; the larger ones would stay at the top, while others would fall to their level, or grade. Then, separated by size, they would be sacked up. My father and Damonte would take their payment in sacks of potatoes.

My father was beginning to prosper, though he never felt rich. He'd take his profits and pay off his debts. He was interested in developing Reno. He saw nothing but opportunity in the sagebrush-filled acreage on the outskirts of the little town. In 1923, when I was nearly 5, he and a partner each put $300 down as an option on rocky property south of California Avenue and west of Arlington Avenue. The two lost their investment. They couldn't sell the lots, which were priced at $25 apiece. I remember my father saying, "Nobody wants to build on those rock piles." Ironically, this area — Newlands Manor — in old Southwest Reno is some of the most expensive property in the city today.

He was more fortunate with property he developed with an Englishman, a Mr. St. George, in northwest Reno, where he sold lots for $20 on up. Then, in 1925, my father bought the Frankovich home on the east side of the 300 block of North Virginia Street, just north of the railroad tracks and Commercial Row, between Plaza and Fourth streets. He knocked the house down and built the three-story St. Francis Hotel. This was a major undertaking. He had to borrow $25,000 from family friends, the Farettos. There was no legal gambling in Reno then; that wouldn't come until 1931, in the harsh years of the Depression, as a kickstart to the state's economy. I believe my father simply must have had great vision to buy and build property in what would become part of a thriving commercial core in Reno.

On the ground floor of the hotel he set up my oldest brother, Louie, in a store he named the Model Fruit Market. Thus, my father was able to sell much of the produce he bought in the local valley through this new family business. He always was thinking business, business, business. He had an amazing mind for details, and possibilities. Again, he simply had great vision. He also had an enormous industriousness. One of his sayings has stuck with me my entire life: "When you go to work for somebody, you go 15 minutes early, and you stay 15 minutes late, and you work as hard and as long as you can." He drilled that into his kids.

There were no allowances in those days, but plenty of chores for us kids. My mother put us to work on all sorts of tasks: chopping wood, mowing lawns. She was the head of the household as far as we children were concerned, because our father was gone so much on business. She was the disciplinarian. What I remember of my father is how popular he was, how other Italians would show up, wanting him to join this or that ethnic club, and how he'd always decline, insisting they assimilate quickly as Americans.

Mom's father, Vincenzo Pizorno.

He also involved himself in state politics, eventually managing the successful gubernatorial campaign of Fred Balzar. Balzar was from an Italian family who had dropped the "e" from their name to Americanize it. Balzar was smart enough to know that my father knew a great many Italians, and could deliver their votes. He was right. My father had helped out so many families, he had a great deal of influence.

I remember one trip I took with my father when I was 7, after Balzar had become governor. Dad got into the Model T Ford, and told me to jump in. I had no idea where we were headed. I was thrilled just to be accompanying him. We drove south on Virginia Street and into the valleys south of town. My father pulled up at the Pagni Ranch, which belonged to an old friend of his.

It was spring. Up at Sky Tavern, about 15 miles up the Mount Rose Highway, was a little state-owned lake, Grass Lake, that was used for irrigation in the valleys below. A ditch ran down. The lake recently had erupted and flooded the farms miles below in Pleasant Valley. Here on the Pagni Ranch, the topsoil had been washed away. Great boulders stood all over the land. It was a disaster for Mr. Pagni.

Our next stop was Carson City, the state capital, another 20 miles south. My father pulled up to a very large, white house. I had no idea this was the governor's mansion. Soon we were walking upstairs, and then were sitting in a very large room. Balzar was at a big desk. I sat next to the wall, seen but not heard. My father sat across from Balzar.

They talked for awhile. Then my father began pounding on the desk. The objects on the desk began jumping. This frightened me. They talked for another five minutes or so. Then my father began pounding the desk again.

Later, he put me back in the Model T and we drove home. A few weeks later, the two of us went back to see Mr. Pagni. On the farm was heavy equipment removing the boulders and putting in topsoil. Evidently, my father had won his argument with the governor. I didn't learn until years later that my father had persuaded Balzar to restore Pagni's ranch, given that it was a state-owned lake that had erupted and caused the extensive damage.

That was the way my father was. He'd help anyone who was a friend of his. In fact, through loans for homes or to start businesses, he helped out a great many people in the Truckee Meadows who later became very successful themselves.

AFTER CHET AND I opened our sporting goods store downtown, for years people would occasionally stop in with the same story. "Are you Santino's sons?" they'd begin. "I want you to know that your dad lent me $500 to get into (whatever kind of business) and he never would accept a note. And he'd say, 'If your word's no good, your signature's no good.' "

About the 10th person who came in asking

if we were Santino's sons, I began to interrupt the story. "I know what he did," I'd say. "He lent you $500. He would also say, 'There's no note.' "

The person would give me a shocked look.

I inherited some traits from my father. Honesty, of course. And vision. And helping friends. Also, the belief that there's no country like the United States of America. We have our problems, of course. But ours is the greatest country on Earth, and we better defend it.

I own some personal property in Hidden Valley, apart from the Hidden Valley Properties corporation I've been a partner in since 1956. On this personal property I named a street Piazzo Circle, after my father.

In 1993, a man approached me to buy a lot on Piazzo Circle. He intended to build a nice home on it. There was one hitch: he wanted to change the street's name to something else, like Country Club Drive.

"Normally, I'm not this hospitable," I told the man, "but I'll give you three minutes of my time. I'm naming this street after my dad."

Then I proceeded to tell the man about Santino Piazzo coming to this country, and how he had helped so many people throughout the Truckee Meadows.

"Now," I said, "if you don't like the name of the street, I have a suggestion for you."

"What's that?" the man said.

"Get your ass in a car, drive around the Truckee Meadows. If you see a street sign you like, drive down the block, and if there's a for-sale sign on an empty lot, buy that!"

By God, he changed his mind about replacing the name of Piazzo Circle. He owns a nice house on it now.

3

Boyhood on Bell Street

When I started first grade at Mary S. Doten Elementary, I went through an adjustment typical of first-generation Italian-Americans. We spoke Italian at home, so I had to get up to speed in English in the classroom. It didn't take too long, though. Chet claims he had that problem for a couple of months. I don't think it took me that long. When a teacher came by with a ruler and wanted to beat my ears off, I understood that. It's an international language.

Olga, my older sister, was a brilliant student, and her success cast a shadow over Chet and me as we progressed through school. "Oh, are you Olga's brother?" we would be asked. The teachers would expect us to earn A-pluses, too. Neither of us were at Olga's level, but Chet was a good student, and I was above-average, about a B-plus.

Mary S. Doten was on the northeast corner of Fifth and Washington streets, a half-dozen blocks from my home. It was constructed in a Spanish mission-style, stucco on brick, which you can still see today in the preserved grade-school buildings of its era, McKinley Park (home to the city of Reno's recreation division) and Mount Rose (which still is a school). I thought it was a horrendous mistake when Washoe County decided to demolish Mary S. Doten. They could have converted it into a miniature Ghirardelli Square-type mall with exclusive

Chet (left), Melba and myself, about 1922.

shops. Sometimes these great eggheads charged with municipal planning make mistakes.

My teachers had a big impact on me. I remember each. My first-grade teacher was Miss Crawford. Second grade, it was Miss Quilici. Third grade, Miss Krump, fourth grade, Smith. All the schoolteachers were single women, school marms. They weren't allowed to marry and keep their jobs; they needed to focus on their profession.

Miss Crawford was a very kind person. We kids at Mary S. Doten grew up with switches and belts as the methods of discipline at home if we got out of line. Yet here was this adult figure of authority who was so very gentle. How — I thought to myself — can somebody be so nice? Krump, though, was a rough girl. She had a ruler about 18 inches long with a steel edge. If you didn't mind her, or kept talking during a lesson — which I did once — she'd come up behind and belt you on the back of the hand, knock the hide right off your knuckles. If a teacher did that today she'd be thrown right in jail. But I thanked mine later for doing it; it taught me discipline. It's entirely wrong that kids cannot be disciplined today in school. I'll tell that to anybody! Not long ago I visited with the principal of a local high school. We had a nice conversation. I said it's a shame teachers today cannot discipline the kids. She agreed with me.[2]

I didn't act up much in school. Before her children began school, our mother laid down three inviolable rules: "If I ever hear you that you had to stay after school; or if you get into a fight; or get in trouble with the law" — it would be grounds for punishment by the switch, which she kept on top of the stove. We understood.

I wasn't in love with school, but I didn't mind it. I was good at the basics — reading, writing and arithmetic. We got a great education — better than what students get nowadays. I'll argue that with anyone today. Here's a sad commentary on today's education: when I was running the store, I'd have college applicants come in who couldn't fill out a simple application form. Name, phone number, address, previous employment, recommendations. They'd sit and study it. When they finally got through, I would barely be able to read their writing, and their spelling was terrible. It shocked me. I'd get disturbed, watching one

labor over an application. I'd walk by and say, "C-A-T," and walk off.

Some years ago, a good friend of mine, Dick Trachok, who was athletic director at the University of Nevada, asked if I would meet with some deans on campus. "Certainly," I said. I told the deans, "It isn't your fault. Somewhere along the line, in grammar school or the secondary schools, they should have taught these kids how to read and write and spell and do arithmetic." And they agreed with me.

The schools I attended may seem old-fashioned today — with inkwells, even. (It was a sore temptation to secretly dip the hair of the girl in front of you into the inkwell, which would automatically earn you an "after-school.") But we really learned.

I especially loved the recesses and the sports. I was the athlete of my family. One of our games was called "Black Man." I don't know where the name came from. We'd divide the students equally on sides of the field, which was hard dirt, then we'd run at each other and tackle each other. You had to hit the person you tackled on the back three times to eliminate him. The side that got the most members through to the other side was the winner.

I was small for my age, and I was born in December, meaning I was the youngest in my class. But I was very scrappy. Having two older brothers toughened me up. But there was another factor involved in my fortitude. Ours was a tough neighborhood. I ended up having 100 or so fights as a child. These were not random spats, either. The neighborhood "godfather," as far as we kids were concerned, was Henry "Doddie" Zunino, who was about six years older than I.

---

[2] Years later, when I had children of my own and was living on Skyline Boulevard, a young mother in my neighborhood told me her 7-year-old daughter had been diagnosed as "hyperkinetic" — what today we call hyperactive. The daughter was taking medicine for her condition. I told the woman I, too, had been hyperkinetic as a kid, and my mom had the perfect medicine. The woman took out a pencil and said, "Give me the name, please." "Switch over the stove!" I said. She put her pencil away.

Doddie enforced unwritten rules. One was that you were not to pick on someone smaller than yourself. If you did, and Doddie heard about it, he would whip you. Another rule was that if a kid picked on a smaller kid, someone else had to stand in for the larger kid in a fight to settle it. The Irish kids and the Italian kids always were at odds, and there were plenty of disputes. Doddie always matched fights as evenly as he could. And he had rules of combat, too: never hit a guy when he was down; and never kick a guy.

Since I was so small, I continuously was pushed into the battle arena against small kids who'd been insulted. I'd be standing in line waiting to return to class after recess, and Doddie would come up behind and tap me on the shoulder and say, "You're fighting tonight."

I don't remember who I fought in my first fight. But I know that I won. The routine was the same. At 3:30 when school let out, you walked over behind Twaddle's Barn, about a half-block away. The barn was an old, empty livery stable, with cobweb-covered buggies you could see through the windows. (Twaddle's house, incidentally, is a preserved historic archive, on the northeast corner of Fifth and Ralston.) Doddie always was there as the matchmaker/referee. You'd show up and there'd be two or three other guys from the neighborhood, plus a similar number of opponents.

Many times I'd have to fight a guy I'd never met. When it was your turn, Doddie would bring the two of you together, and then you'd just go at it, boxing. My strategy always was the same: get the first punch in, then go as fast as I could for as long as I could. This meant going like mad for two or three minutes, the capacity before I was completely spent of energy. My target was the jaw, nose and eyes, never the body. The whole goal was to get the other guy to quit. Interestingly, I never cried during battle. I don't remember any of my opponents crying, either. And I always won. Well, almost. Throughout my neighborhood pugilistic career, I never lost, though I ended up having a couple of ties, when both of us were too exhausted to continue. But the regular pattern was the other guy turning away, knowing he'd had enough.

The biggest danger for me wasn't the fights, but the aftermath when I'd have to go home. I'd perhaps have a bloody nose, and my lips usually swelled up. The Orr Ditch runs under Washington Street. I'd follow the neighborhood postfight ritual and go down to the ditch and take out the cool rocks to apply to my mouth and relieve the swelling, so my mother wouldn't know I'd gotten into a fight. One time in grammar school, I beat up Junior Vietti, a kid in the neighborhood. Later, there was a knock on our door. There was Junior, with his mother. She told my mom I'd beaten up her son. My mom thanked her, closed the door, then whipped me with the switch.

Another time after a fight, I cleaned myself up very well at the Orr Ditch. My face shined, my hair was combed. At home, my mother said, "Something's wrong. You look too clean!" I didn't say a word. I just turned my head. She let it go.

Chet and I were very close. We slept in the same double bed. But we fought as brothers do. We argued to be arguing, including in bed, and our mother didn't tolerate that. She'd come into the room with a switch. One time, Chet got out of the blanket and used me as a shield, shoving me toward my mother. I absorbed the beating that time. Another time, he and I got into a fight in a vacant lot on Bell Street. Chet was beating the crap out of me. A man happened by and intervened. I turned on him and began punching the guy. *What the hell is this? This guy's hitting my brother.* Blood was thicker than water.

I guess I had a reputation as a tough guy. After you win eight, 10, 15 fights, the word gets around. That helped me, because it meant I had the fear factor working in my favor. I'd land a punch or two, and my opponent would be backing up, getting socked until he gave up. I'd fight three or four times a week, or once a month — just whenever I got the tap on the shoulder. In retrospect, fighting gave me mental toughness that applied to many areas of my life. I learned not to back away from a challenge, but to meet it head on. I believe the majority of people shy away from challenges. I feel sorry for them. I've heard so many people say, "Oh, God, this is tough!" My favorite saying is, "It can always be worse." So face the problem — and it's amazing how you can conquer the problem!

Sometimes I had to fight someone bigger and tougher, and I had doubts I could win. They included the two times I had ties. One was a guy named Sutton. He took all kinds of punishment from me. I hit him and beat him and hit him, and nothing happened. The other one's name was McVeigh. He was left-handed, which I wasn't used to, and getting his punches in pretty good. He quit and I quit; frankly, I think he was getting the best of me. Our fight seemed like eight weeks, though it likely lasted three or four minutes.

But the remarkable thing about fighting — in every case, without exception, a few days later you'd become good friends.

The Irish neighborhood was down the hill and to the west of our neighborhood. The Italians didn't hate the Irish, but the Irish hated us. I never did figure out why. Maybe it dates back to ancient history. Maybe it's just the stupid conflict that arises for no good reason. That's the way it has been throughout history.

My wife and I took a golf trip in 1985 to England, Scotland and Ireland. In Dublin, the van driver, a large Irishman named Jimmy, would take us golfers to the course, then drive the non-golfing wives to stores to shop, then return for the golfers. One time I was the first golfer back to the van. I said, "Jimmy, what the hell's going on up in Belfast?"

He shot me an indignant look. "Link," he said, "if you'll remember your history. In 1622 . . . "

I said, "Goddamnit, are you still fighting the battle of 1622, or what the hell ever it was?"

I don't know why people don't wake up to the fact they're living today, not 1,000 years ago!

One close friend of mine, an African-American, is just a great guy with a great personality. His name is Keith Terrance. He's a local fire fighter and goes by his initials, "K.T." I took K.T. aside one time at the YMCA and said, "I want to talk to you, just personally." I said, "Because you're black, you've had some problems. And because I'm Italian, when I was younger, I had some problems. It's very obvious that you've overcome that, and I want to congratulate you for that. You have a great personality."

He put his arm around me and said, "You have to overcome that, overlook that."

He's absolutely right. Isn't it a shame there aren't more people like K.T. in this world?

I was at an annual barbecue of my Rotary club. I was sitting with a very good friend, who is African-American. A guest of another member came by. He told my friend, "You know, you were walking around the market, and I didn't recognize you, but when I saw that watermelon under your arm, I knew who that was."

My friend started to get angry.

"Just sit down," I said. "Let that dummy walk out of here. Rise above that. I went through that when I was younger, too."

He thanked me later for quieting him down.

This is what you're confronted with in life. And you have to rise above it. If you can't rise above it, you have a very small brain.

That's what makes our country great. Diversity. Look around the world, different peoples constantly at each other's throat. In my ancestral country, Italy, the northern Italians just despise the Sicilians.

Here, in the United States, we intermingle everybody. Maybe there's hope for the world.

My parents, Santino and Emma, in the 1920s.

MY CHILDHOOD WAS AN orderly existence. My mother would be the first one up, to start the wood stove, the only place in the house there was heat in winter. She always made breakfast, and a big lunch for us when we came home at noon. She'd bake bread, and the house would fill with homey aromas. Mother labored all the time. We always had clean clothes and underwear. She washed by hand using a washboard and tub.

Life revolved around home, and school, and neighborhood games in the street, and chores, lots of chores. Even we small kids had to chop wood for the stove. We fed chickens and cleaned their coop, we fed rabbits and cleaned their hutch. Once in awhile Mom would say, "OK, go out and kill one of the rabbits." I'd grab a rabbit behind the back legs and conk it behind the head with a broom handle. Then we'd hang it by the back legs on two nails and skin it, cutting the hide around the back legs and pulling it down.

All the kids in the neighborhood did chores. It was part of everyday life. In fact, it was rare that anything real exciting or out of the ordinary happened in our neighborhood. But one afternoon in August 1924 was an unforgettable exception.

Olga was taking Chet and me down Ralston Hill to Humphrey's Meat Market. She had us by the hand. She was taking us along for company, but Chet and I always were eager to go to the meat market. The butcher had a soft spot for kids; he'd always give us a half a weenie or some similar treat.

. We'd just left the house. A buzzing drone came overhead — an airplane! This was an oddity in Reno. You'd see one, maybe, once a month, with the neighbors running out of their homes to gawk at the sky. I looked up, and there it was, a great big shadow passing over. It was coming in low, just over our heads, flying north. Instantly, it struck telephone lines across the street and crashed with an enormous boom into the McKinley house on the northwest corner of Ninth and Ralston.

It scared the living hell out of us. An instant later, I found myself in a dangerous predicament. Fallen telephone wires had tugged me to the ground, wrapping around me like black snakes. I was completely entangled.

"Don't touch them, don't touch them!" Olga yelled at me. I lay as immobile as I could, not handling the wires.

The entire neighborhood was out in the street now, at the crash scene. The gas tank had exploded in the McKinley house, and the structure was in flames. Firemen arrived within minutes. Two approached me wearing large white asbestos gloves. They disentangled me. I'd been coiled for 10 minutes.

Men, including my father, approached the crumpled plane and pulled out the pilot. His name was Billy Blanchfield. He was from Reno. Every year he'd fly over the cemetery. A buddy of his was buried in the cemetery, which was just east of our house, in the Knights of Pythias graveyard. Blanchfield would drop a wreath at his gravesite.

I watched his body as it was removed. It was cremated, charred, the flesh bubbling like bacon. No one shielded my eyes. Kids took care of themselves back then. And after all, I already was an old kid. I was 5.

Miraculously, no one had been home at

I join mortician Silas Ross and the Rev. James McGrath at Blanchfield's grave, March 1971.

the McKinley house. They were supposed to be home at that hour, but fate had intervened.

From then on, for years after, whenever Chet and I heard the drone of an airplane, we'd dart inside our house for cover. It seems strange, then, that after World War II broke out, I'd enlist in the Army Air Corps and he'd enlist in the Navy Air Corps.

I guess in life you just have to go on with things, and not be burdened by something that happened when you were 5. What should you do, go over in a corner and cower for the rest of your life?

Following the fatal crash, the airfield in Reno was renamed Blanchfield Fieid. Charles Lindbergh landed at the field in 1927, on a stop in Reno. I remember that like it was yesterday. Lindy's Spirit of St. Louis, a silver bird, flew over Reno and circled twice. We school-children took a field trip to Idlewild Park. A big platform was set up. It was a hot, hot day and we all were thirsty. I remember a great big pitcher of ice water and a glass on the platform.

Lindbergh finally showed up and mounted the platform. I don't remember a word of his speech, but I've always remembered him pouring himself a glass of that ice water.

The airfield, incidentally, is now the fifth fairway at the Washoe County Golf Course.

MY BEST FRIEND GROWING up was

Elmo Zunino, Doddie's kid brother. Elmo was a couple years older than I. He was kind of like a general, an organizer.

"Now look, we're going to go fishing," he'd say, then outline the preparation steps. "You do this . . ." Elmo was a terrific fisherman. I'd be fishing in the Truckee River and he'd say, "What the hell you fishing there for? Just little fish there. There's a sandbar — " And he'd toss his rod that way and catch a fish 6 inches long and say, "What'd I tell ya? Now move up here!"

Elmo was just a little taller than I, and reasonably dark. In later years, when he was out of school and working delivering groceries for Brunetti and Patrone's grocery store, he managed to fish three times a *day*. Before work, at the noon hour, and again in the evening. The funny thing was, Elmo never ate a fish. He'd give away those rainbows and browns to the neighbors, who'd sometimes hate to see him coming. We had iceboxes in those days. Elmo would walk into a house — everybody knew each other, we were informal — and he'd toss some fish into the icebox. "We hope he doesn't come again," some people would say. "We have too many fish!"

We'd make our own rods in those days. We'd come across bamboo and wrap our own guides on, and use salmon eggs or worms. We'd mostly fish the Truckee west of Reno. "There's a great big brown trout down there. Damn, I just can't get it to bite," Elmo said. But he ended up nailing it: a great big 10-pounder. He was just a heck of a fisherman.

Elmo had a cut-down old Chevrolet when he was older. We'd fish all the way out to Verdi. Finally, his mother moved in to curtail his obsessive angling. "You can't go out early in the morning to fish," she said. This forced him to devise a plan. He took a piece of chalk line. "Now look," he said to me. "I'm going to tie the chalk line around my toe, and I'm going to put it out the window. And you pull on the chalk line and wake me up at 5."

At 14, I was an early riser. I had a paper route and rose at 3 a.m. But Elmo was hard to wake up. I'd pull on the line and his leg would come out of the window, and he'd pull it back. And finally he'd wake up. He'd get in a couple hours fishing that way in the morning. Then, he'd crawl back through the window before his mother woke up.

My other really good friend was John "Babe" Marini. He was a kind, nice fellow, the opposite of me. He'd never scrap. I just loved the guy. (He died pretty young; I visit his plot every Memorial Day.)

Babe and I were classmates throughout school. He was a little heavyset. We walked to and from school together. His was a poor family. One of his brothers would race home from school for lunch, and by the time Babe got in there'd be nothing left to eat. This is no exaggeration.

His father worked for the Southern Pacific Railroad in Sparks, as a grease man greasing the bearings on the trains. His mother had passed away, leaving the father to raise three boys and three girls. John was the youngest.

We would swim together in Tule Pond. West of our homes was nothing but meadows and ditches. We'd play ball together. Sports was huge in the neighborhood. The girls would jump rope or play hopscotch, but we boys were into baseball, basketball, football. I was short, but very fast. Washington Street was paved when we were kids, and we thought that was terrific. No more worry about rocks or holes. We'd play tackle football in the street. Yes, we were tough. Get tackled on the blacktop and the hide would come off your elbows, knees, hands. We didn't know any different.

This is how we got a football for our games. One time, a bunch of us walked down to the old Mackay Field on the University of Nevada campus to watch the Wolf Pack practice. We sat near an end zone. There were balls all over the field. During the warm-up each player punted. One of the balls came our way. It stopped in front of us. No one came to retrieve it. I fell on it. Well, by golly, we decided, if they leave that ball here and nobody comes to pick it up, when it gets dark we'll take it home. Which we did.

Babe Marini slipped it under his shirt. What a treasure: a pigskin in good shape. I ended up the guardian of the football. We had a rule: no drop-kicking, for that would wear the ends out. The consequences of breaking it would mean 10 guys jumping on the offender. Everyone followed the rule.

Under the arc lights we'd play Black Man sometimes, but we didn't have too much time to play during the week. We always had so many chores. But if Chet and I got done with our chores, out in the street we'd go. There must have been 20 kids, easily, in our neighborhood.

Bedtime was 9 o'clock, and not a minute past. If we came in three minutes late, our mother would reach up for the switch on the stove and give us a couple whacks. If we came in at 5 after 9 we got whacked pretty good. We respected our curfew. She never had to come out and call us.

One time, I told my mother: "Mom, the Marinis have a 10 o'clock curfew." She looked me straight in the eye and said, "The Marinis are not living in this house." So our curfew was 9 o'clock.

We made our own basketball rims out of wine-barrel hoops. We made a backboard out of scrap lumber. We took a post, dug a hole, and attached the hoop with wire to the post. Behind the Marini house was a nice, level dirt yard for a court.

During spring and summer we played baseball out in the fields west of Washington Street, when we had extra time. One of Elmo's older brothers, Ernie, pitched for Chism Ice Cream in the amateur Twilight League, which played in the old Reneva Ballpark on the northeast corner of Wells Avenue and Stewart Street (all homes now). Ernie was a left-hander. His glove was worn out, and he had to get another one, so he gave Elmo the used glove. Oh boy! Now the neighborhood had a baseball glove — and so what if it was a left-hander's glove? It was the only glove in the neighborhood.

We decided to let the catcher use it. That was a thankless enough position. The catcher didn't even have a mask to wear. A black eye was taken in stride. If a guy tried to steal on him, the catcher would have to take the glove off his right hand to throw the runner out. Our baseballs were used balls with the covers knocked off, held together with black tape. They were very adequate. When I was 12 or 13, I was the batboy for the Chism team, and whenever a bat broke, that would be my pay. And so we'd have bats for our pickup games. I'd give the broken bat to Louie, an outfielder for Chism who also was the eldest of the Zunino boys. Louie was a blacksmith, and a kind, nice man who did favors for everybody. Louie would flute and glue and tape up the bat for me.

We thought nothing of our lack of good equipment. That beat-up, left-handed pitcher's glove seemed like a treasure to us. So did the bats, and the baseballs, and that wonderful football that we avoided drop-kicking.

Some of us were good athletes, especially Doddie, who, had he put his mind to it, might have made it in professional sports. He was a very determined guy, and was good at anything he tried. But none of us thought along the lines of making it as professional athletes. In those days, all we were trying to do was survive.

THERE WAS PLENTY TO do in our neighborhood, such as ice-skating on Shannon's Pond, northwest of Washington Street, wearing clamp-on skates. The winters when I was growing up were colder and had a lot more snow than now at the end of the century. Credit it to weather cycles. Every winter brought terrific snowfall, 2 feet. It was so cold, the milk would freeze and rise in the bottles on our doorsteps, and we'd cut the cream off the top with a knife.

One man in the neighborhood, Dave Gardella, a blacksmith, kept horses next to our neighborhood. He made a big plow out of planks. To get to Mary S. Doten we walked from 10th and Bell down Washington Street. We always prayed that Mr. Gardella hadn't plowed the street, which would mean it would be too high in snow and we wouldn't be able to go to school. But we'd be outside, looking up the block, and there he'd be with two horses drawing the plow down the middle of the street so we could go to school. We hated him because he was helping us.

No one had money, but that didn't deter us from trying to get into the Reno Theater, on the east side of Center Street where Harrah's is now. Sol Lockman owned the theater. He'd take the dimes at the door then go up and run the projector. We'd have one of us buy a ticket with the only dime we had, and the rest of us, six or so, would lie outside. The ticket-buyer would go

around to the side door on the alley and open it up. The briefly opened door would light up the theater with sunshine. We'd crawl in quickly on hands and knees.

Sol Lockman would shut the projector off, guess at the interlopers and kick about half of us out. The rest of us would stay and see the movie.

It's amazing what you do for fun when you don't have any money.

A barbed wire fence ran right through the middle of Shannon's Pond. The pond was a paradise for us. We had to avoid the barbed wire when we ice-skated. To swim we'd go to the old outdoor pool at Idlewild Park. It was full of moss, with algae growing a foot thick at the edges. The bottom was dirt. On the way home we'd walk across boulders on the Truckee River. When we got home, our bodies would be covered with ringworm. We'd be itching like hell.

There was one place that was off-limits, technically, but we couldn't stay away from. It was a reservoir in northwest Reno, owned by Sierra Pacific Power Co. A 10-foot wood fence topped by strands of barbed wire surrounded it. A man named Whiting was the reservoir's caretaker. He owned a Dodge touring car with a cloth roof. He lived about a half-mile up the street that sloped down to the reservoir. There was a long narrow wood raft in the reservoir, used by workers to clear away debris, and that was where we went to fish for the trout that came into the reservoir from Highland Ditch. The fishing was better there than on the Truckee.

A sentry was stationed at a big knothole in the fence facing west, to watch for Whiting. If he saw Whiting pull his car out, he'd yell and we'd jump the fence and run home. One time I was the sentry. I was goofing off, and all of a sudden I looked through the knothole and two eyes stared back. It wasn't

Whiting but his assistant, a rough-looking, burly guy. I yelled to the others, then clambered up the fence's horizontal 2 X 4s to jump over the fence. There he was, waiting for me. I jumped back down to the edge of the reservoir. The others already had taken off.

A concrete spillway divided the reservoir. I sprinted across it and jumped over the fence on the opposite side and hauled ass home.

In fall, when I was 13 or 14, Elmo and I would go duck-hunting at the reservoir. He'd "borrow" a double-barreled shotgun from his brother Louie and I'd sneak out the shells from my brother Louie, or vice versa. At the reservoir we'd stand outside the fence, aiming the barrels through a knothole at the ducks on the water. If I was doing the shooting, Elmo — the general — would tell me to wait. Then he'd bang on the fence. When the ducks flew up, 20 or 30 of them, he'd say, "Now!" I'd pull both triggers, and the kick would knock me on my fanny. Old Man Whiting would hear the blasts, of course. A minute later we'd see him get into his touring car to head down the hill.

We'd return after dark, climb the fence and pick up the ducks washed up against the bank. I wondered why he never figured out we were duck-hunting, and go in and pick up the mallards for himself. Instead, Elmo and I took home the bounty. My mother never questioned where I'd been hunting; had she, I'm sure I would have had to lie. Lying, though, was a cardinal sin, and you never wanted to be caught in a lie. My mother had no gray area. Right or wrong, and never lie — that was her mindset. Life is simple when you tell the truth, she said.

Every Sunday growing up we went to St. Thomas Aquinas. I went through catechism.

I remember two priests, Tubman and Moran. I didn't approve of either of them, even at my tender age. One Easter Sunday, one of the fathers said, "Now, all you women have Easter hats. You should be ashamed of yourselves, putting the money into those hats. That money should be put into the coffers of the church."

Even as a young kid, I thought: that is wrong!

Once a year both priests would both go to Ireland — using the money from the coffers of the church.

I guess I was a rebel at a young age. Still, I went to church, and said my prayers every night — mostly praying I wouldn't be caught for what I'd done that day.

I believed then, and always have, 100 percent in God.

I wouldn't substitute the childhood I had for any other. I was around kids all the time. I had a hell of a lot of fun. I also learned discipline from my mother and my schoolteachers, and adopted a black-and-white view of the world. I knew right from wrong. I learned to respect my elders, and to be thankful to people who guided us, like Doddie Zunino. I fought when called upon, and did my schoolwork (with Olga's tutoring), and did my household chores.

I had a rosy, optimistic view of life. I believed firmly that justice prevailed, and that good people were rewarded while bad people were punished. I went to sleep at night knowing that God was watching over me.

4

Life Isn't a Bowl of Cherries

I should have been killed about 30 times in my life. The first time — other than getting wrapped in wires after the plane crashed on our street when I was 6 — was when I was 10.

Angelo Pardini was an older fellow in our neighborhood. He owned a horse. North of 10th Street was all sagebrush, and people would toss refuse out there. Pardini had found an old buggy missing its tongue. He tied a rope to the flatbed buggy and put Chet and me on it.

He took off on his horse pulling the buggy through the sagebrush like a sonofagun. Then he stopped his horse. The buggy, missing the tongue, hit the horse in the rear. The horse shot away, throwing Pardini, and the buggy turned over. Chet was tossed free, but I got caught between the wheel and the body of the buggy. All I remember were the spokes hitting my head — *bang-bang-bang-bang*, with bright red flashes. It knocked me out.

The next thing I remember is waking up in the house of a rancher, Mr. Siri, who was a family friend, and people pouring water on me, cleaning off my head. I wondered how the hell I got there. Then I remembered: I'd been in that buggy. In those days you didn't call an ambulance, or a doctor, which was unaffordable except in real emergencies. Anyway, the people at the rancher's house straightened me out OK, and I ran on home. I'd lost a lot of skin on my head and face. My mother wondered what the hell had happened to me.

The kids in our neighborhood weren't sissies. I suppose any number of times our vigorous recreation could have killed us — whether drowning in the reservoir or whatnot. But we never thought about it. It was just our way of life.

DEATH DID TOUCH ME — my whole family, in fact — in a giant way when I was 9. It was July 30, 1928. My father was 49. He was driving a truckload of peaches back to Reno non-stop from Stockton. He worked such long, long hours — and tried to convince us we should, too — but on this trip he surpassed even his own prodigious capacity for work. Just west of Verdi, where the Lincoln Highway passed the California border and began a long slope down into a canyon to run alongside the Truckee River, Santino fell asleep at the wheel. The truck was in compound low gear and wasn't going fast, but it veered off the road, lumbered up the side embankment, tilted over and crushed him. His passenger, a man named Molinari who was a partner of my father's in one of his enterprises, survived the wreck. My father was killed instantly.

Sometime after midnight the lights came

on in our house. I heard my mother screaming. The news had been broken. No one came to inform us kids; we simply found out ourselves in a hurry.

I remember the funeral like it was yesterday, the casket in the church, and then in the hearse afterward, being driving to Mountain View Cemetery. My father had the longest funeral procession in the state's history at that time. The procession had arrived

Standing left to right — Frank Mortara, Frank Brunetti, Mom with Melba, Dad, Eva Brunetti, and Mary Brunetti. Front row, Pete Rissoni, Louie, Dede Brunetti, Olga, Link, Chet, Joe Brunetti. This was a 1925 family outing to the Little Truckee.

at the cemetery, a mile-and-a-half away, while attendees were still leaving St. Thomas Aquinas on Arlington and Second Street. My father had helped so many people — thousands of them — in his life. It was his mission, I'm sure. He didn't have much money, but he would lend part of what he had to friends, to help them buy a home or business or other things, and never asking for a note in return. And I don't believe he ever lost a dime. He was a humanitarian: he just liked to help people. Others

had helped him after he'd first arrived in America, speaking no English. He'd gotten hired at Verdi Lumber Co. As a result, he helped out as much as he could. I believe I inherited this trait.

My mother, God bless her, walked to Mountain View Cemetery and visited my father's grave every day, summer and winter, for several years. It was about one-and-a-half miles away. "I don't want him underground," she said.

Years later she had him exhumed and put to rest in the mausoleum on North Virginia Street, where his remains are to this day.

JUST LIKE THAT, MY mother was head of the household. She had no clue about our family's finances. My father had never discussed his business dealings, and they were so varied and complex they boggled the mind. I have mentioned the half-ownership of the restaurant in Lovelock, and the potato ranch in Beowawe, and the partnership in the potato grader, and the St. Francis Hotel — for which my father had taken a $25,000 loan. Many of his dealings he certainly had recorded solely in his head, not on paper.

When neighbors stopped in to express their condolences about my father, they would tell my mother, "Boy, if he would have lived, he would have been a wealthy man." I believe they were right. Santino had great energy, and great vision.

Slowly, my mother — with a large assist from my sister Olga — took stock of the business dealings. The Farettos, who had lent my father the money to build the hotel, told my mother not to worry about making payments. But she had other ideas. She was entirely repelled by owing money. In those days it was a sin to borrow money — something many would find hard to believe in today's America, where advertisements for credit cards and home-equity loans and debt-consolidation services and cash advances against paychecks are a regular staple of television and radio commercials and the daily mail. But my mother would not stand for owing money, and so, by early 1929, she had liquidated all the properties my father had accumulated except the hotel, and paid off all the debts — including the giant one on the hotel. How incredibly prudent of her!

In October, the stockmarket crashed, the banks closed and the Great Depression began. If not for my mother's wise moves following my father's death, we easily would have lost all our savings and whatever else we had, including what would become our family's source of income for many years: the St. Francis Hotel. My mother thanked the Lord many times for the way our financial situation turned out. My brother Louie owned the Model Fruit Market on the bottom floor of the hotel. Olga was the secre-

tary for the Washoe County district attorney, Melvin Jepson. But our mother had to support herself and the three of us youngest kids, including my sister, Melba. The hotel was the family's livelihood.

The St. Francis went through good times and bad times, but survived. The original managers, tenants named Brown and Burch, didn't do too well, and after the Crash of '29 Olga took over management. Other businesses were dying up and down Virginia

The St. Francis Hotel, 300 block of North Virginia Street, built by Santino Piazzo, 1925.

Street. The Tahoe Meat Market was on the ground floor of the hotel, beside the Model Fruit Market, and it eventually went broke, unable to meet the $60-a-month rent my mother charged. The hotel had a little lobby, no elevator, and served a middle-class clientele. There were no bellhops. Occasionally, Olga would run into Louie's store, where I was helping, and say, "Link, I need somebody to haul a bag." I'd perform the service, but I always refused a tip. Taking a gratuity was taboo for us Piazzo kids. We simply believed we were supposed to help out, period.

One time, I put a man's bags down and

he took money out of his pocket to pay me. I said, "No." He said, "Do you know who I am?" I shook my head. What did I know? I was just a kid.

"I'm Tex Rickard," he said. "I'm the manager of Jack Dempsey." It was true. He was the manager of the great heavyweight boxer, and he also had other investments. He was a wealthy man. But at that age I knew nothing of such worldly things.

"Well, that's nice," I said. "I don't know who you are, but I'm still not going to take any money." And I ran down the steps.

Later, Olga told me, "This guy's worth a lot of money, you should have taken a tip."

The hotel property still is in the family, although it no longer is a hotel and its upper two stories are closed. It sits across Virginia Street from the Eldorado Hotel & Casino. Pawnbrokers and a coin shop occupy the lower level. On the outer façade, on the third floor, is a marble plaque with "Santino Piazzo" inscribed on it.

MY MOTHER HAD TO rise to a different level of parenting now that my father was gone. Up to then, if we kids did something wrong, she'd follow the Italian custom of saying, "Wait'll your dad gets home." Well, my dad was not coming home now. So she kept the switch handier than ever on the top of the stove and began ruling the house with a heavy hand. She had to, or circumstances might have overwhelmed her.

We minded. Oh, did we mind. If we ever dared to talk back to her, before she'd get to us an older brother or sister would. We kept in line. And we kids thanked our mother later for the way she raised us: to respect our elders. It's too bad that the kids today, many of them, are not raised that way.

One time when my mother was out visiting one of our aunts, Chet and I ran into a band of turkeys on Washington Street. They must have gotten out of some farmer's yard. We herded them up the blocks, and put some in our basement. Others we put in lettuce crates outside. We were just kids; we didn't have better sense.

Mother got home and she heard, cluck-cluck. "What's that?" she said. She went down the stairs and found the turkeys.

She let the turkeys out of the house. Then out came the switch.

Easter Sunday was a very big holiday in the neighborhood. Olga made sure we younger kids had neat Easter outfits, including clean white dress shirts. We were getting ready to sit down for Easter lunch. My mother always cooked a huge meal for such occasions. There was a knock on the door. My mother answered it.

Doddie Zunino was standing there. "I want to talk to Link," he said.

I went to the door.

"There's a guy on Washington Street and you've got to fight," Doddie said.

And so there I went.

The guy was a good fighter, too. We fought for two-three blocks. I finally beat him up (and we later became friends).

I went home. My white shirt was bloody, my lips swollen. Mom really got mad. I didn't get whipped, but I should have.

Poor mother. I didn't want to let her down, but I was in a no-win situation. There was no way you couldn't listen to Doddie. If you turned down a fight he'd catch you later and beat you up.

SOMETHING OF MY FATHER surely rubbed off on me when it came to earning money. I discovered an entrepreneurial streak in myself at a young age. Of course, we poor kids in the neighborhood always were scrounging around for ways to make a little money.

Before Dad died, Chet and I pulled a nifty little scam. Dad often traded items; one time he came home with two donkeys from a farmer way out near Eureka. The larger of the donkeys was named Jack; the smaller one, Ass. They were inseparable. Chet and I sold Jack for 50 cents to someone on Washington Street. In the evening, he and Ass brayed for each other, and Jack came home dragging a piece of the fence he'd been tied to. We ended up selling him more than once; one time he made it back to our house dragging a farming disk. We'd accumulated several bucks by the end of the summer, or so Chet remembers.

The fields of sagebrush north of 10th Street weren't the only place people would dump refuse that contained salvageable treasures. There also was the regular dump up on Evans Avenue. We kids would scavenge for scrap aluminum, zinc, copper and lead out of car batteries, and even rags. It often was hard to find anything, since during the Depression people were very frugal.

There was a man, O'Keefe, on East Fourth Street who bought scrap materials to recycle. When we boys had enough stuff accumulated, we'd take metal and milk bottles down and collect 25 or 50 cents. Then there was a guy who'd come down the alleys on a horse and wagon crying, "Rags! Sacks! Junk!" and we'd sell our rags to him. He had a scale to weigh the rags. We'd have a gunnysack full of rags. He'd pay us so much per weight. We figured, well, if he's going to weigh them, let's put some rocks in the sack. The next time we were paid twice as much as usual. The time after — which

shows you how smart we were — we tried it again. This time he had a needle about 3 feet long. He ran it through the sack and hit the rocks.

I never splurged on anything, period, with the coins I'd amass. Every now and then my Aunt Mary — Lalla Mary — would hand Chet and me a dime. We'd run down to Wiggs' Grocery Store on the southwest corner of Washington and Seventh streets, and spend it on candy. Mr. Wiggs — a short, gray-haired Englishman — was the most patient man in the world. We'd look at the big showcase of candy — which then was six for a penny. We'd order 2 cents of this or that, then change our minds. It would take 20 minutes to spend a nickel. My favorite candies were red-hot dollars, red taffy that really wasn't hot.

I did lots of odd jobs while going to school.[3] I'd earn 25 cents for mowing a lawn. Most of the kids in the neighborhood were lazy, so I capitalized on opportunities. A cousin lived on Jones Street next to the river, about a mile from us. I'd walk down to his house and cut his lawn, too. There were other jobs in the neighborhood — pulling weeds in vegetable gardens or on truck farms. If you dug weeds all day on a Saturday or Sunday, you earned $1. And before school, at 7 a.m., I'd sweep out Louie's store, then head off to class at Northside Junior High.

I didn't enjoy working. But I enjoyed the money. My parents always told me, "If you make money, always put a certain percentage of that in the bank." By the time I was nearly 11 I had $220 in the Reno National Bank. That was a ton of money in 1929 for a young kid.

---

[3] Jack Threlkel, owner of Reno Garage, sponsored a semipro baseball team, and I would earn 25 cents a game, plus a bag of peanuts, sitting outside the ballpark fences, retrieving balls. Later, he had me work the scoreboard, posting numbers, for 50 cents a game — but no peanuts. The man who worked the concession stand slipped me a bag of peanuts anyway. Many years later, I told Jack. He grumbled that he suspected something funny was going on.

The bank was on the northeast corner of Second and Virginia streets, and owned by the legendary George Wingfield Sr., the Nevada business tycoon and political powerbroker. Right after the stockmarket crash, people with accounts rushed down to the banks, only to find the doors chained shut. That was one of the saddest days of my life. I heard people saying, "The banks are closed, the stockmarket's crashed." I didn't know anything about the stockmarket, but my money was in the bank. I didn't have a bicycle, so I walked from 10th and Bell to Second and Virginia. I grabbed the door handle of the Reno National Bank. It was locked tight.

All my money was gone, I thought. I was crushed.

The mood in society changed to one of sheer survival. In our neighborhood, people began burying their money in tin cans. People made do the best they could. I can remember times coming home to find the whole neighborhood ecstatic, because so-and-so had found himself a job, period. Most of the jobs were at the Southern Pacific's roundhouse in Sparks, where pay was $100 to $200 a month. I can't think of one able-bodied man in our neighborhood who sat idle. Maybe they dug ditches, with pick and shovel, for the Sierra Pacific Power Co. The Italian immigrants were not afraid to work. That's why they came to America.

Still, good, honest people found themselves in humiliating positions. In those days, it was customary for the farmers and ranchers to pay their bills once a year, after their harvest or livestock were sold. After the banks closed, my older brother, Louie, took me along in his car one time as he went to try to collect on an account from his store. The customer, Steve Landa, was a very reputable Basque, the largest sheepman in the state.

The rancher began to cry. "Louie," he said, "I don't have any money, either." *What an impression that left on a little kid!* He picked up a lamb to hand to my brother as payment, but Louie didn't take it.

As the years went by, the rancher paid off every dime. As for me, I was fortunate that Wingfield owned the bank my money was in. He slowly paid off everyone. I had a little passbook, and I'd intermittently receive a check in the mail for 50 or 75 cents, until I was paid off. It took more than a year.

And so I started over again to build up my savings. Dick Kirman, who would become governor in 1934, had the only local bank that remained solvent: Farmers & Merchants National Bank. It was on the northeast corner of First and Virginia streets. Years later, I heard a story from a friend, Clarence Thornton, about how customers had rushed down to that bank to withdraw their money. With the bank full of people, Kirman had come out of his office and addressed the throng. "I want you to know that your money is safe," he said. "We are solvent. And if any of you take your money out of my bank, I'll never accept you as a customer." The entire mass walked out of the bank.

As soon as I heard Farmers & Merchants was solvent, I headed down and began depositing my checks from Reno National Bank.

I later became very good friends with Kirman. He was just a tremendous, tremendous man. He also owned Bradley's Wholesale Hardware Store a half-block down from the Sportsman. He popped in one time and said, "Link, I want you to do me a favor."

"Oh yes, governor," I'd say. Even though he was out of office, we still called him governor.

"There's a young kid in the shipping room

who wants a pistol in the worse way. He's very reputable. I want to buy a pistol and you take it over there and give it to him. But don't tell him who bought it." That's the kind of guy he was.

Incidentally, in the years ahead I also became good friends with Wingfield. He is a legendary figure in state history, a man who initially made his fortune in the turn-of-the-century mining boom in central Nevada, and later was a political kingpin controlling both major parties. He had a vast and varied business empire, as well, and it's funny, for the longest time I never tied him into the Reno National Bank. Wingfield occasionally came into our store, so we knew each other. He had an office on the fourth floor of the building that housed Reno National Bank, on the northeast corner of Second and Virginia streets. I'd visit him in his office, and he got to liking me. He raised thoroughbred Labrador retrievers — the top strain at the time, Shed of Arden. If he liked you, he'd say, in a casual way, "Would you like a Labrador pup?"

Holy cow, I was flattered. I hunted a lot. He said, "I'm going to give you the pick of the litter." He told me to see a guy by the name of Dalton, who managed his ranch at Spanish Springs. I chose a pup. Boy, it turned out to be a great hunting dog. Dalton wouldn't take anything for his help, so I finally forced him to take a pocket knife. Wingfield came into the Sportsman after that, and wanted a compensator tube worth $3. I said, "No charge, Mr. Wingfield."

He backed up and said, "You take the money or I'll never come back in this store."

I said, "You gave me the best dog in the world and I can't give you a Cutts compensator tube?" and he said, "That's right."

So I took his $3.

Had I known he'd owned Reno National Bank, I'd have thanked him.

Many people lost all their savings when the banks closed. Wingfield paid everyone

Proud graduating sixth-graders from Mary S. Doten. I'm in the third row, far right.

off, though it took a long time. He was an honorable man.

From time to time you'll read a derogatory newspaper or magazine article about Wingfield. Why don't the writers mention how he donated that marvelous property downtown for the park that now bears his name?

IN SCHOOL, MY TEACHERS in first through fourth grades had painted a very rosy picture of the world. But by age 10 I had seen some of the darker colors of life up close.

My father was dead. The Depression had hit.

After I entered air combat during World War II I saw enough death and destruction to last me several more lifetimes. I'd even witnessed, from my cockpit, the netherworldly devastation of the most fearsome weapon imaginable: the atomic bomb.

When I was in my 30s, I got the notion of looking up my old schoolteachers. They still were teaching. I took Crawford, Quilici, Krump and Smith out to lunch at a restaurant on South Virginia Street. The five of us sat around the table. Even after all those years, I still admired them. They were great, dedicated teachers.

"You know," I said, "when I went to school you didn't teach us properly."

Their jaws dropped.

"You taught us that life was a bowl of cherries, and 'Run Spot, run,' and the flowers in the meadows and birds in the trees.

"You should also teach us that life can have tragedy, sickness and death," I continued.

"I think maybe you should tell them early in life that if you have any kind of a family you're going to have sickness, death, tragedy, and you might as well prepare for it."

They didn't disagree with that.

When my dad was killed when I was 9, it was a shock. Fortunately, my mother was a very strong-willed woman, and her resilience and intolerance for self-pity left an indelible impression on me.

Whenever her kids were wracked by self-doubt or had hit a stumbling block, she'd say, "What do you want to do, go over in a corner and die?"

It was a great saying. My mother taught us never to give up, but to keep going and make the most of it.

And so I learned an invaluable lesson early in life:

It can always be worse.

Appreciate what you have, and make the most of your existence.

If people had that attitude, it would make life a lot better for them.

5

Che Ti Dice La Patria?[4]

(Do What the Country Tells You?)

I graduated sixth grade at Mary S. Doten and went on to Northside Junior High on Fourth Street, between Center and Lake streets, where the National Bowling Stadium is now.

My father had wanted Chet and me to go into the trades. Chet and I were good with our hands. Journeymen made $10 a day. Huge money for then. He'd encouraged me to become a carpenter. And that became my aspiration.

Getting to journeyman meant working four years as an apprentice. Apprentices earned 62 1/2 cents an hour — or $5 a day. That, too, was good money. The best news was that you could accumulate experience that counted as an apprenticeship by taking trade courses, such as cabinet-making, and building and construction, in high school.

If you took these classes all through high school, you'd served your apprenticeship and could step right into a good occupation. I didn't wait until high school, however, to start taking shop classes. The first classes I signed up for in junior high were shop classes.

Darrell Swope, who later became the school's principal (and for whom the middle school is named today), taught shop, and was a very good teacher. He was a nice man, but also a disciplinarian. When he told you to do something, that's what you did. If you got out of line and he had a piece of wood in his hands he'd whack you across the shoulder or fanny. We were tough kids, of course; we could take it. But we also appreciated the way in which he got our attention.

We'd have to "square a board," using a plane and making the edge absolutely straight. Some students never could get it, but I could. I was used to working with my hands, doing chores at home, including building chicken coops and rabbit pens. My family had all the necessary hand tools. I'd wonder why the kid next to me couldn't square a board. I took the mandatory courses — algebra, English, history. I was fairly good at them. B-pluses. But shop classes were my passion. I was preparing for my future.

Times remained tight. Across the street from the junior high school was a hamburger joint with a soda fountain. A big sign advertised six hamburgers for a quarter. The burgers were smaller than at Harvey's Q Ne Q on South Virginia and Ryland Avenue, where burgers were a dime, but still — can you imagine, six for a quarter? Too bad no

---

[4] The Italian phrase "Che ti dice la patria" — "Do what the country tells you" — was popular during Mussolini's reign. Hemingway wrote a short story that captured the inhumanity of fascism and used that phrase as the story's title, adding a question mark to it.

one had a quarter to spend.

We'd organize to raise the money. "Mike, you got a nickel?" "Yes." "Jim, you got a nickel?" "No." It could take three or four days to collect five nickels. We'd write the five guys' names down and put the pieces of paper in a hat. The kid whose name was drawn got the extra burger in addition to the one he'd paid for.

We learned not to throw money away — to appreciate the value of money — during the Depression.

Northside was more than a mile from our home. Chet and I would run home, winter and summer, the whole way for lunch, and think nothing of it. Mom always had a big hot lunch waiting for us. She knew her kids' individual favorite dishes and would have them waiting. Mom made the most beautiful breaded veal cutlets, my favorite. There'd be a nice big salad and loaf of home-baked French bread. We'd eat, then run back to school, and still have time for handball before recess was over.

Today, kids mope around, waiting at a bus stop a few blocks from their school! I cannot accept that.

Sometimes, we kids would grab onto the back of a Model T Ford going up Ralston Hill to make our climb easier, letting it tug us as we walked. Often, however, too many kids would be hanging on and the engine would die. The driver never got mad; people were good sports back then.

We kids made good use of our time. At home there were chores, and we squeezed homework into our free hours. We got it done. One activity I was greatly interested in was the school basketball team. It was the only sports team at the school. I stayed after school for practice. Mother didn't mind. I wasn't tall, but I was very athletic. I captained the 85-pound team — the small-

est of three squads. I played forward. We competed against Billinghurst, the only other junior high in the area. We had some terrific games.

Not everyone went on to high school. Some kids graduated junior high and went to work. I could've done the same, starting as an apprentice carpenter. But my mother was adamant that her children go to high school. She wanted us to have a diploma. Louie and Olga had graduated. In later years, my mother even apologized to Chet and me for not having the money to send us to college. She didn't know that we wouldn't have gone even if she could have afforded it. We had been ready out of high school to go to work and make a living.

At Reno High, I started right off working to complete my apprenticeship. I wasn't interested in girls. My interests were working, and athletics. I kept on earning money in my spare time. I needed a bicycle to get a newspaper route. Buying one was out of the question. Too expensive. We didn't think about buying bikes, anyway. What I did was scavenge for parts. I searched fields and dumps. Mr. Caton, who owned the Reno Press Brick Company on West Fourth Street, excavated pits for clay; afterward, the abandoned pit would serve as an unofficial dump for the community. I spent many hours searching these pits for parts. I found a frame, back and front wheels, and a seat. It took a long time. Finally, I had all the parts except for the front forks. One day, I looked into one of the pits left by Caton, and there was a pair of forks. I jumped right down.

The forks didn't quite fit into the bike's cone, but they were adequate. And so I had my bicycle. I got a *Nevada State Journal* route.

The *Journal* was the morning newspaper. My route was in the northwest: 28 papers. Seven days a week, I'd rise at 3 a.m. from the alarm clock and pedal down to the *Journal's* offices on Center Street, between First and Second streets. I'd roll my 28 papers and stuff my canvas sack. The papers were small then — each was about the diameter of an index finger after I rolled it tight and bent it. We couldn't afford rubber bands. My pay was $14 a month.

Mr. Loftus was the circulation manager. Periodically, he'd call a paperboy in and say, "Mrs. So-and-So complained she didn't get her paper." "Oh, I delivered that paper," the boy would say. "A dog must have taken it. There's a couple of dogs in the neighborhood." A few days later he'd call another boy in. We found out later that such stories were ruses, scare tactics to ensure we kept on the ball.

I was a pretty good paperboy. But one time I screwed up. One of the houses was up by the reservoir at the end of Washington Street. In winter my bicycle would freeze up. It would be tough going in the snow at 3:30 in the morning with no car tracks to ease the way. I'd leave the bike where it was and walk the route.

There I was on Elm Street, freezing my butt off. And there was that big house on Washington Street a half-mile away from the rest of my route. One morning I trudged up toward the house and tossed the paper hard toward the front porch. It smacked a window and shattered it. An awful sound!

Back home, I told my mother. I knew what she'd say. "You go up and talk to that lady," she said. I was in a quandary. Replacing the woman's window would be very costly.

My shop teacher was Mr. Grey. I told him what I'd done. "That's OK," he said. "Take the school truck, and go to Commercial Hardware, and buy a pane of glass and glaze it." Since I was taking shop, he'd even give me school credit for the project.

I paid the woman a visit and told her I'd replace her window. She was very nice, a pleasant woman in her 40s. "Oh, you were accurate," she said. "It went through the window and landed on my stomach in my bedroom."

I measured the opening of the window, then I went down to the store and paid 50 cents for a pane. It was an easy job replacing the glass. I took a putty knife and removed the old putty, pulled the new pane into place and replaced the putty.

It was a good lesson.

RENO HIGH SCHOOL WAS on West Street between Fourth and Fifth streets, where the Sundowner Hotel & Casino is now. It was the only high school in Reno.

I wouldn't join a high school fraternity. The members did too much drinking, and I despised drinking. Growing up, we had wine at the table, but I never drank it. I didn't like wine.

I wasn't into the social life in high school. I was, however, interested in basketball. There were A, B and C squads. My mother, though, thought such an extracurricular activity was a waste of time. Just recreation, and not important. And so I didn't go out for the teams. Herb Foster coached football, basketball and track. I was short but I was fast, and he wanted me to go out for football and track. I'd watch the football team practice sometimes on the dirt field at Mary S. Doten.

Foster took me aside one time and asked me to go out for Reno High's teams; I said I couldn't. But I did run a lot on my own, for fun. I'd run around the reservoir a couple times by myself. I grew quite strong in high school: I had a 28-inch waist and a 42-inch chest. I eventually stood 5-foot-9 and weighed 158 pounds. I was in terrific shape. (Later, when I entered the service, I was an unusual athlete, a good sprinter *and* a good distance runner, from all my training. I even won two marathons.)

My senior year, I went out for the basketball team, hiding this from my mother. My fellow students had convinced me to give it a shot. I'd come home late. Mom probably knew what I was up to, but didn't say anything. Louie, Olga and Chet knew.

I ended up making the A squad, but as the 11th man. I played forward. For the zone tournament, Coach Foster cut the squad to 10. Al Conton, a good friend of mine, also was on the A squad. He broke his wrist in practice, and so coach added me to the varsity.

Basketball then had different rules than today's game. For example, there was a jump ball at center court after every basket. Thus, games were low-scoring. Reno High always had a competitive team, but we weren't the top team in the state that year, 1937. We surprised ourselves, however, by reaching the finals of the state tournament, at the old gym at the University of Nevada. We were up against Carson High — the top team. We were 1 point ahead — 18-17 — with a few seconds remaining.

I was on the court. I looked up at the clock. One second remained! My friend, Paul Seaborn, had the ball. All he had to do was hold onto it and victory was ours. But he didn't realize how little time was left.

He attempted to pass to me. Gino Lencioni from Carson intercepted the ball. Seaborn must have lost his senses. He lunged and tackled Lencioni.

The buzzer sounded. Too late — the referees whistled a flagrant foul on Seaborn.

That meant two foul shots for Carson, and a chance not only to tie but to win.

The bleachers were packed, the noise in the gym deafening. Lencioni put the ball down on the floor at the foul line and lay down himself, using the ball as a pillow, until the place quieted. It took a number of minutes.

Lencioni carefully aimed, underhanded, and made his first shot. The score was tied. Again, he lay down until there was quiet.

A good 20 minutes after Seaborn's foul, Lencioni prepared to shoot his second penalty shot. Again, he made it. Carson won by 1 point.

Seaborn was a very nice boy. He was round-faced, heavy-set, likable. He cried all night long over his boneheaded plays. He shouldn't have. It was just a game. But the experience ended up affecting him deeply. The rest of the school year, he kept bringing up how he'd lost the state championship. He was crushed.

I believe it affected him the rest of his life. He later moved to Washington state, and has since passed on.

Those kinds of matters you just have to shake off. I remember a state championship softball game, in Fallon, against a team from Las Vegas. I wasn't even in the starting lineup (I'd broken two fingers in my right hand the previous game, after Harry Paille slid into me), and was responsible for losing it. The game was close: we were a run behind.

One of our players singled, and the coach put me in as a pinch-runner. The next batter, Buster Ichanti, hit a home run. There was no fence at the field. The ball went out into the trees. I rounded second, missing the bag, rounded third and scored. The umpire called me out. We ended up losing by one run.

What the hell. You remember those things

for the rest of your life. But it's like my mother used to say, you can't go over in the corner and die. You've got to keep going.

MOTHER ALWAYS WATCHED HER money, and never splurged. But she saved, nevertheless, to take her children to Italy to meet our relatives. Her father was still alive. So in 1935 she took Chet, me and Melba on a three-month trip to the old country. Until then my biggest trip had been a few miles west of Reno, to Verdi. I was very excited. I wanted to see more of the world. I'd miss the first weeks of my junior year of high school, but would make it up. Chet had just finished high school, and Melba was still in junior high.

It was late summer when we took the train cross-country to New York, and boarded the Rex steamship across the Atlantic and Mediterranean — a seven-day trip to Genoa. Chet and I were seasick most of the way. The only remedy we had was vomiting.

We had no preconceptions about Italy. We just waited to be surprised. We just took life as it came. My Italian turned out to be just as good as my grandfather's. All we spoke at home was Italian — our Genovese dialect. The village, Levi, was a little insular Italian hamlet in the Apennine Mountains. The reception was just amazing. The family opened the best wine bottles, threw terrific meals, just catered to us. My older cousin, Eva Mortara (Lalla Mary's daughter), and her husband, Frank, had come along with us on the trip. Frank had a brother in Italy who was in the chauffeuring business. He took us all around Italy in a big touring car, a perfect guide. We drove to Bologna, Venice, Milan, Turin, Pisa, and all the way down to Pompeii in the boot of the country (but we didn't cross by boat to Sicily). We went to Rome and the Vatican. We walked into the Sisteen Chapel, and we were the only visitors. (In 1963, when I visited the chapel, it was wall-to-wall tourists.) We visited the Colosseum, all the great Roman sites.

It just was a great trip. The northern Italians are very honest, honorable people. I swelled with ethnic pride. As Americans, we were a novelty to the natives. Many of them expressed a desire to immigrate to America, but couldn't afford it, of course. My grandfather said, "You know, there's a man in another village who speaks English. We want you to meet him." The excitement built for several weeks. Finally the Sunday arrived for our visit

There must have been 20 or 30 of the old man's villagers at his house when we showed up. My grandfather said, "OK, speak English to him."

"Yesterday morning, Sunday," the man said to us.

"Yes," Chet and I said, "yesterday morning really wasn't Sunday, but it's nice to speak English. Is that all you know?"

"Yesterday morning, Sunday," he answered.

He repeated this approximately 10 times during our "conversation." Thank God, we didn't divulge to the rest that the man had a very limited vocabulary. He was a real big shot in the room for his linguistic prowess. Villagers shook his hand. They were very simple people.

They were good folk who simply were ignorant of the ways of the world. Remember how my ancient ancestor — furious about the usurious practices of the greedy marquese who ruled the village — stormed the castle in Piazzo and killed the nobleman? Levi had a priest who would take the season's first draw of wine and virgin olive oil, telling the villagers he was making his annual procession to Rome to give the goods as a gift to the church. He loaded up the goods onto two big horse-drawn wagons.

I watched with disgust. I told my grandfather, "He's not going to Rome, he's ripping you off." My grandfather, a very religious man, clasped his hands in prayer, looked skyward and said, "Lord, forgive him, he doesn't know what he's saying."

"While you're talking to the Lord," I said, "he knows that I'm telling the truth. This guy is not going to Rome. He's going to Genoa. Genoa is not far from here. Rome is a long ways off. He's ripping you people off."

But the people in my grandfather's village didn't even know where Genoa was.

The years went by. Grandfather died. I returned to Levi. By now, the residents — able to travel a bit in this day and age — had learned of the person whom the priest had sold the goods to in Genoa. The priest was very wealthy. Not much had changed since the Middle Ages.

Many years later, in 1963, on my third visit to Italy, I returned once more to my mother's father's village. I visited the little cemetery where my ancestors were buried next to the church. I was standing with my cousin and his wife on the steps of the church, and in a little voice my cousin's wife said, "You know, Link? The priest that we have now is kind of a mean person, too."

I said, "I'd like to talk to the guy!"

"Oh, be quiet, be quiet!" she said.

So I spoke real loud, in Italian. I said, "I'd like to talk to the priest! Well he please come out, I want to talk to him!"

He, of course, didn't come out. I'm sure he heard me. I would have given him a piece of my mind.

I'm Catholic. But I must say that religion, of all faiths, has caused more wars, more strife, more deaths and more problems than anything in the world. We have more strife in the world than we've ever had and it's all caused by religion. And that's a shame, isn't it?

The village of Piazzo, Italy.

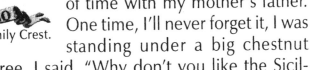

The Piazzo Family Crest.

People who are not very educated don't know what's going on in the outside world and believe everything that religion tells them. And that is wrong.

History always repeats itself.

I ENDED UP SPENDING a lot of time with my mother's father. One time, I'll never forget it, I was standing under a big chestnut tree. I said, "Why don't you like the Sicilians?"

Grandfather turned around and looked at me with a big stare. He said, "Because they live by the knife."

Nowadays, the Italians get along a lot better with each other, I believe. But in those days, if a Sicilian came north, they'd run him off; they didn't want any part of him.

Italy was in a very dramatic period when we visited in 1935. Benito Mussolini, the Fascist dictator, had led the nation to becoming an industrial power. He'd built the autostradas, put people to work, made the trains run on time, and banned the teaching of separate Italian dialects in school. This was a good thing; even in adjacent villages — separated only by a hill — the people would have a tough time understanding each other. "Il Duce" chose one dialect, Sienna, to be the standard, so all Italians could communicate. But his ambitions had now veered to the Napoleonic. Like all dictators, he was a fathead, drunk with power. He wanted to forge an Italian empire that would recall the glory of Rome.

We happened to be in Rome the day that Il Duce was to give a speech in the Piazza Venetzia. Thousands of supporters packed the huge square, chanting, "Il Duce! Il Duce! Il Duce!" The frenzy continued to whip up for a half-hour.

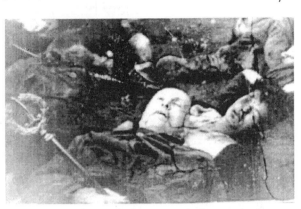

Above: Mussolini and Clara Petacci after muder by partisans at the end of the war, May 1945. Below: Mussolini, et al hanging in Milano Square.

"What the hell is this?" Chet and I asked our guide, our cousin's brother-in-law.

"Well, Mussolini's going to speak,"

Finally, Il Duce, a man with a big bald head, wearing a military uniform, strode out onto the balcony of his palace overlooking the square. He raised his big chin.

He announced that Italy was going to take over Ethiopia.

Chet and I were unimpressed. Big deal. We knew Ethiopia was a poor African nation. Haile Selassie had a couple airplanes; his troops carried spears.

"Will you look at that fathead! He doesn't know what he's talking about!" we said to

each other, in English.

Our guide looked at us in fear and told us to shut up. Someone may have overheard us.

Chet and I knew there was no free speech or a free press in Italy. Most of the countrymen knew only what their dictator told them. He had them brainwashed. Even at 16 I understood this very clearly.

His speech about invading Ethiopia went on 10 or 15 minutes. The masses loved it. Chet and I thought they were crazy.

Our relatives saw through Mussolini. I used to watch my grandfather play solo, a card game, in the evenings with the neighbors. I kept hearing them mention a name, "Sam" or "Jim" or the like. Grandpa and I walked home afterward. I asked him who this "Sam" or "Jim" was.

"Shh," he said. "Be quiet. That's Mussolini. If we mention his name, we disappear."

They'd been criticizing Il Duce, but not using his name.

Ever since, I've believed the best education for our graduating high school seniors is to take a trip around the world and experience other political systems. That way they'll understand how great this country is.

My mother passionately embraced democracy. Twice, she had broken hips, 10 years apart. Though in a wheelchair, each time she made us take her to the voting precinct so she could cast her ballots. That's how strongly she believed in our system.

We returned home on the Count of Savoy. This trip to Italy had taught me a great deal about personal freedoms. It had been quite a shock to be in a place they were absent.

I WAS ON TARGET to graduate from Reno High in 1936, but I wanted to hang around a little longer for another basketball season. So I took all my required credits except one.

That last year I landed my first carpenter's job, with Otto Curnow, a distributor for Overhead garage doors. Curnow had contacted Mr. Grey, the shop teacher, and he had recommended me. I was the top student in shop.

The trade classes were great. We even built houses. Mr. Grey taught us everything from laying the foundation to putting on the roof. I really learned a lot about carpentering.

Curnow employed me on weekends. He paid me $2.50 per door, which cost $50 installed. Curnow would deliver the door in sections, with the hardware in a sack, and the tracks. These were the days before automatic garage doors. I would fit the bottom panel to the concrete — "cut the horns off," they termed it — put the hardware on, install the track, the springs, the chain and lock. By getting around on my bike, I was able to install two doors in one day. I'd return to each job later, after they were painted, to adjust the springs for the added weight. It was simple.

If there were enough jobs, I'd hang four doors a weekend — $10. I still drive around town and see the doors I hung back in 1937, more than 60 years ago. I must have hung 100 of them.

I kept right on banking my money.

In June 1937 I graduated high school and immediately landed a job with a local building contractor, Gene Belli. In 1935, Belli had built a house for my mother on Bell Street, next to the family house. He'd used me for some labor on that project, so I already knew him. Then he hired me right out of high school.

In high school I'd accumulated more than three years toward my apprenticeship as a carpenter. A few months later I was qualified to be a journeyman. A man named Smalley certified me, verifying I'd done my four years of apprenticeship. I had to join a union — something I've always been opposed to — but I got my membership in the AFL-CIO chapter.

Belli was one of the nicest people I've ever known. His brother owned the Belli Ranch near Verdi. Belli worked 12 months a year, building homes. In the winters, the construction trade fell off and only the best hands were kept on while the others were laid off. I guess I was one of the better hands because Belli kept me on, and even asked me to be his partner. That was quite an offer, but I would turn it down.

We were building the Baroli homes on Lakeside Drive, south of Reno. The winter of 1937 was especially cold and harsh. These days, workers have large portable heaters; back then we had nothing. We couldn't even wear gloves, since we had to use our fingers. Hour after hour I pounded nails or sawed boards, and thought about what better ways there were to earn a living.

Chet was a tile-setter. He, too, was working that bitter winter. When he soaked tile in a basin, the water would freeze solid. He was fed up. It didn't take much to convince him and me to get into another line of work.

I don't remember if it was his or my idea, but we hit upon the notion of opening a sporting goods store. It made sense. I was the athlete of the family — I would head up the athletic equipment half of the enterprise. Chet hunted and fished, and tanned hides and performed taxidermy — that would be his bailiwick.

As brothers, we argued a lot. But blood is thicker than water. We figured we could make a go of it.

Our family thought we were crazy. Chet was 20, I was 19. It was the Depression. And there already was the Reno Sporting Goods store on Virginia Street, owned by a Mr. German. It was very successful.

"I think it's a bad idea," our mother said. But she never was one to say too much. That's all she said. She consulted with our uncles. They, too, said we were crazy. That influenced her.

But there was a vacancy on our hotel's ground floor. The Tahoe Meat Market had gone under. The meat market had been paying $60 a month rent. We figured we could cover that. Chet and I were still living at home, so we wouldn't have to worry about paying much for a living situation.

Each of us had savings built up. We each had about $800 in the bank.

We were so green, we didn't even know we needed a business license. (Indeed, we were open for many months before a city official came in and asked to see our business license. "What the hell's that?" we said. So we bought a license.)

Yes, we were naive. But we were game to go.

By the following June we would be in business.

In Business

Chet and I knew nothing about developing a business plan. Mother lent us $5,000, which we pledged to pay back as quickly as possible.

I went to Home Lumber, a yard in Reno, and picked up all the knotty pine we needed to finish the store inside. Price: $60; and I picked out the wood myself (impossible today). The space was 70 X 20 feet. I built the facing, counters, stairs and railing and the upstairs office. Chet and friends helped. We finished up in a couple weeks.

Next, we located a wholesale outfit in Sacramento — Thompson Diggs Co. The head of the sporting goods department was one Dom Civitello.

Civitello came up to Reno and looked over our situation. He taught us a lot of things. "The first thing I want you to know," he said, "is you're not going to have ready-made customers. You're going to have to take them from somebody else."

But he made up an order for us. I'll never forget — I thought it was too much. I canceled the order for a gun, the most expensive item on the invoice. Anyway, we had our fishing and hunting items on the way.

Our next trip was to San Francisco to order athletic goods. We visited Wilson Sporting Goods. The manager — a Mr. Meany — looked us over. I must have looked 14 to

An advertisement for the opening of the Sportsman, June 1938.

him. "You guys are nuts," he said. "We just lost several million dollars through the Depression."

He was nice, but firm. "I want you to get the hell out of my office," he said. "Don't you get into the sporting goods business."

Chet and I walked out onto Mission Street. We got our spirit back up and said, "Oh,

Christ, were not going to give up."

Wilson had a subsidiary line — Reach, Wright and Ditson. It was popular, but not as popular as Wilson. We took on this subsidiary line and stocked the store with baseball, softball, football and basketball equipment.

In those days, Wilson was, for lack of a better word, a crooked outfit. As time went on, a representative came in and said, "Now we're going to make you a Wilson dealer."

I was so happy! Finally, I could stock Wilson goods. So I went up to my old coach at Reno High School, Herb Foster, to try to sell him something. He said, "Oh, the Wilson salesman was in, and I bought some stuff from him."

The shyster had opened us up as a dealer, then gone up to Reno High and sold Coach Foster at our cost. I called the Wilson rep on the phone. I'll never forget his explanation: "Oh, that's a house account. That's too big an account for you guys."

A "house" account.

Something like that sticks in your craw for the rest of your life.

Years later, I got an exclusive local dealership for Worth baseballs. I already had two baseball equipment accounts. One was Jack Threlkel at Reno Garage — Threlkel sponsored the first semipro baseball team in the state — and the other was the state prison. I told the Worth representative, a man named Chuck Perish, my accounts. After I inked our deal, I got into my car and went to see Threlkel. He said, "The man was here from Worth and sold me." I went to the

prison, and it was the same situation.

About 30 years later I was in Chicago attending the National Sporting Goods Association's annual convention and show. I was in the Worth room. I said, "Chuck Perish was one of the most crooked bastards I ever met in my life in sporting goods." The kid I was talking to said, "That was my dad!" It didn't embarrass me. And you know what the kid said after that? "Y'know, I hate to tell you this, but he did that to a lot of accounts."

The first letterhead for the Sportsman, drawn by our sister, Olga.

Anyway, I had the pleasure of telling Perish's son what a lousy bastard he was.

Those were the things a small business had to contend with in those days.

CHET AND I OPENED the Sportsman Sporting Goods Store in June 1938. It would be a full retail store, plus handle school and team accounts. Everyone told us the rule of thumb was to survive for three years; after that, we'd be home free. So we set our goals on at least breaking even for three years.

The day we opened, Mr. German, owner of Reno Sporting Goods, stopped in. He was a kindly man in his 50s or 60s. He wished us well; he was a fine gentleman and I'm sure his words were sincere. He probably figured we wouldn't last long, though.

Slowly, clientele built. Leo DeLucchi was one of our first customers. One of our first sales was an alarm clock! Imagine that — at a sporting goods store. Our cash register was a secondhand contraption we'd bought from a service station. I don't think we paid $10 for it.

We settled into the rhythms and cycles of being downtown business-owners. Across

The Sportsman basketball team, Reno city league's A division champions, 1940. Top row — Myself (coach), Harry Paille, Bill Cassinelli, Fran Cassinelli, Jack Roberts, Harry Bell (statistician). Front row — Willie Curran, John Du Pratt, Earl Avansino, Jim Shepley.

the street, on the southwest corner of Fourth and Virginia, was Nay's market. Across the street were two bakeries: Baldini's Purity French Bakery and Siri's Sanitary French Bakery. On the other side was a restaurant owned by two Greek fellows my father had helped get into business. We mostly ate at home; we couldn't afford to buy our lunch.

Our workday routine was simple: we opened early and stayed late. We started work at 7 a.m. and stayed at the store until 8 p.m. — or later, if we had to. We sold sleeping bags, and sometimes we opened one up and slept in the store if it had been a long day and we had lots of work — in-

ventory, or cleaning, and so on.

Burnout? We knew no such word. Anyway, you never get burned out if you've had the right bringing up. (I get so disgusted with kids nowadays. A couple 12-year-olds came by the store one hot summer day, looking to earn a little money picking up garbage in the shrubbery. One of them came in after awhile and said, "Y'know, I've got to quit, it's too hot." I almost slapped him in the face! We never got too hot or too tired working when we were kids. We just got the job done. I feel sorry for kids who wilt under the task. Throughout their lives it's going to be that way. It'll always be "too hot" or "too cold." Always excuses. I took the 12-year-old aside and gave him a little lecture. If it's too hot, I said, go into the shade for awhile, wipe your brow, then go back to work. I paid him, anyway, and let him go home.)

Chet's and my first big goal was to pay our mother back her $5,000 loan. It didn't take more than a year or two. We set our minds to succeed in business, knowing it would be a great achievement. Neither of us took money out of the business. We paid ourselves each a $5-a-week salary, and gave Mom $1 a week each for room and board. Chet did taxidermy in the store, as well. And we slowly established ourselves.

Our customers were gold to us. We treated them like they were the most important

This is a gathering of participants in the Sportsman's Ducks Unlimited fund-raising shoot, in 1941. We raised $500.

people on the face of the Earth. Two of our earliest ones, Swede Mathiessen and Roger Teglia, are in their 90s now. Swede still has some of the items he bought — guns and a pair of binoculars. He tells me now and then, "Y'know, one of the screws is a little bit loose. Is there a warranty on those binoculars? Just kidding."

Jake Lawlor (for whom Lawlor Event Center is named) ended up being a tremendous customer. He started out buying equipment when he played semi-pro baseball for Jack Threlkel. Later, Lawlor became basketball coach at the University of Nevada, and finally the athletic director. We became the Wolf Pack's regular supplier of uniforms and equipment.

I should mention that it didn't take long for Chet and me to get rid of our relationship with Wilson. We went to MacGregor, whose people were very honorable.

From the beginning, I had plenty of contacts with softball teams since I competed. I knocked on a lot of doors. I traveled to Carson City, Gardnerville, Dayton, and out to Susanville and Westwood, Calif., since there were teams and schools there, and hustled to sell uniforms, equipment, bases — everything a sports team needed. Westwood — a town with a box factory —

was interesting. There was one guy who did the buying for all the teams. He was the only one I had to sell. It became a big, big account for us.

I'd get some big hits here and there. The walk-in business helped, too. Somehow, we stayed afloat.

I was no natural salesman. It was necessity that drove me out the door and on the road. Tricks I picked up? There should be *no* tricks about selling. The customer is the most important person on the face of the Earth for a salesman. And the salesman must be 100 percent honest — no tricks. The customer finds this out in a big hurry. The salesman must back up and guarantee everything he sells.

One time, early on, a Portuguese customer, Frank Fontes, sent a worker down to buy two boxes of .22 shells. He gave enough money for the young guy to buy two boxes of .22 specials, which are bigger than the .22 long rifle shells. The kid bought the .22 long rifle shells and spent the leftover money on drinks at the Little Waldorf downtown. Fontes called up later, sore as hell. Chet and I ended up walking all the way up to Fontes' slaughterhouse on West Seventh Street, with two boxes of .22 specials, no extra charge, for Fontes. It was a long walk and it was a

cold winter day, but our reputation was at stake.

We had few problems with customers, but one time —years later — the University of Nevada football team ordered jerseys for its opening game. The jerseys hadn't come in. One of the men in our store had signed for a certain number of cartons shipped from MacGregor. One of the cartons hadn't arrived: the ones with the football jerseys. I approached our employee and reprimanded him for signing for an absent carton of jerseys. I called up MacGregor and they made up another set for us. It cost us extra money to have the carton flow in. A year later we discovered that the missing carton was sitting on a dock in Denver. At least we had safeguarded our reputation.

In the early days, I'd deliver shipped merchandise myself. Chet and I didn't even know what a vacation was. About my only recreation was playing softball evenings in a league. It was not only fun: it kept me with contacts for selling equipment and uniforms. We competed at Idlewild Park. It was fast-pitch; there was no such thing as slow-pitch back then. In 1941 the Patterson's clothing store team won the state championship. I played second base and shortstop. It was a very competitive league, and I have the souvenirs to prove it. I broke my middle and ring fingers on my right hand — leaving them with oversize knuckles to this day. It was in a game against Reno Laundry. Harry Paille, a good friend of mine whom I played basketball with at Reno High, took off to steal second. I covered the bag while our catcher, Ben Ferrari, made an absolutely perfect throw. All I had to do was catch it and tag Paille out. I turned my hand with the ball in the glove. Paille slid in and smashed my hand — breaking my fingers and popping the ball loose. *Safe.*

I finished the game, of course. For several days after, I could put my fingers up to my ear and hear the crunching inside as I moved them. And they hurt. Finally, I went to see Dr. Lombardi. He was out of town. His partner, Dr. Lowline, put each finger in a splint. They didn't heal straight. I saw Dr. Lombardi at the Elks Club one day.

"Who fixed that?" he said, examining the fingers.

"Your doctor," I said.

"Oh," he said, "he made a mistake, come over and see me."

I was never able to bend my middle finger completely after that. But I've gotten along fine with it.

It can always be worse.

For years I'd kid Paille about it. I'd hold up my middle finger and say, "You're the one who broke that finger."

Softball really was a lot of fun. In 1941 I won the state batting championship with a .506 average.[5] I guess I could see the ball pretty well, but I developed my own approach that worked great. For years the Sportsman has had batting cages, and I hear coaches tell their kids the darnedest things about keeping

SOFTBALL CHAMPS SEPTEMBER, 26, 1941

STANDING: GERWIN BULLIS, BEN FERRARI, MIKEY DOYLE, JIM DOYLE, DAN CANAK, LINK PIAZZO, LYLE ROUSH BILL PATERSON, SR

KNEELING: BILL DEPOALI, PAUL ELCANO, PERRY CARLSON SHORTY CAPRIOTTI, BOB PECOLI, JOHN ARDEN J. SAVAGE (BAT BOY)

This photo shows our state championship softball team in 1941, sponsored by Patterson's clothing store. Standing (from left): Gerwin Bullis, Ben Ferrari, Mikey Doyle, Jim Doyle, Dan Canak, myself, Lyle Roush, Bill Patterson Sr. Kneeling (from left): Bill Depaoli, Paul Elcano, Perry Carlson, Shorty Capriotti, Bob Pecoli, John Arden, and L.J. Savage, our bat boy.

their elbows up and their feet planted, and so on. What I would do is look at the pitcher and say to myself, "I'm better than he is." This worked until Harolds Club brought in a pitcher named Hanie to compete for their team. Hanie was from Hanford, Calif., and the best softball pitcher in the United States. He'd pitched the national team to the world championship three years running. In that time, a grand total of three runs were scored off him, if memory serves.

The first thing he'd do with every batter is throw a pitch that would come straight at the plate and then rise on you. You'd see the ball clearly. The second pitch would come low and outside, the next low and inside. And finally, if needed, a straight fastball, and you'd be out of there. He had some stuff.

Softball may have been an amateur deal in Reno, but it was taken very seriously. People would fill the bleachers behind home plate or sit in cars lining the baselines. Lights eventually were installed. I built the

first scoreboard, in 1939, as an advertising coup. I bought tongue-and-groove flooring and big posts. I built a middle platform. I had two teams — 20 guys — help dig the holes. Then we lifted the scoreboard up and sunk it in the holes. It rose 25 feet. We poured concrete into the holes. The platform was for a guy to stand on to change the numbers for the score. And, of course, we had our store's name on the scoreboard.

I always was looking for ways to promote the Sportsman. The scoreboard served the field for years and years.

Another big promotion we began was the Sportsman's Softball Tournament, and it's still going every summer — the longest consecutively running softball tournament in the United States. It's run since 1939, even during World War II, when Reno Army Air Base won the trophy. Every team with at least a .500 record in Reno could enter.

The big team trophy in the store lists every winner by year.

---

[5]   One time, a guy, Petri, who'd gone to Reno High with me, came into the store. "I read in the paper that you are a pretty good hitter," he said. "I'm coming to see your game tonight." He seldom came to the games, but I saw him in the stands that night, in the first row, directly behind our dugout. Between innings I sat with him, in my satin-lettered uniform, instead of in the dugout. My first time up, I hit a single — not too impressive. The next

I made it into one of Lew Hymers' cartoons for the *Reno Evening Gazette*, with other faces "Seen About Town."

SOFTBALL PROVED SIGNIFICANT TO me for another reason.

I was 19. The Sportsman had just opened. I was playing softball in the evening league. A friend of mine, Ora Bevalacqua, had brought along another girlfriend, Helen Galbraith, to watch the ballgame. Afterward, another of my friends, a guy named Dot DePaoli, introduced me.

Helen was about my age. She was a Reno native but had attended Tamalpais High School in California, where her aunt and uncle lived. Her parents lived on Mill Street; her father was the refrigeration expert for Chism Ice Cream Company. Helen was a clerk at J.C. Penney downtown. She had long brown hair and a nice figure. I have no idea why she was attracted to me, or vice versa. It was just one of those things.

I had never dated. This was a whole new ballgame for me. My mother didn't object to the fact Helen wasn't Italian. She always said,

time up, I hit a double; he was a little impressed. The third time up I hit a triple: now he's impressed. The fourth time up — yes — I smacked a home run. Petri couldn't believe it. Neither could I. I'd batted 1,000 that night, hitting for the cycle. It was written up in the local newspaper. I never saw Petri at a game after that.

"You make your nest and you live in it." I knew darn well she'd have liked Chet and me to marry Italians and Catholics, but neither of us did. Nevertheless, mother was very nice to both our wives.

Helen was part Scottish, part French, and a Christian Scientist. I strongly believe in 90 percent of her church's teachings. Her family accepted me fine.

Our relationship wasn't smooth or storybook. We'd go together for awhile, then break up for awhile. This went on for about five years — all the way up until we tied the knot during the war. Helen had a good personality, didn't say much. After 54 years of marriage, both of us can be called hot-headed and strong-willed. Looking back, I know that marrying her was one of the best things I did in my life.

But back then we were just kids. And neither of us were ready to get married.

It took a war to push us into that.

Pilot or Bust

It was early December, 1941. Chet and I were skiing on Mount Rose on slopes known as the Sand Dunes. A businessman, Warren Hart, had a portable rope tow there. Forget chair lifts — there weren't even standard rope tows at that time. Hart had a Ford Model A engine that ran his rope tow.

Someone walked over to us and said, "Just heard over the radio: the Japanese bombed Pearl Harbor!"

This did not impress anyone.

"Where the hell's Pearl Harbor?" someone said.

"Well, so what?" someone else said.

Chet thought Pearl Harbor was a woman.

Little did we know that shortly after we'd be in uniform fighting the Japanese.

When we finally pieced together that Pearl Harbor was in Hawaii and the Japanese had sunk our Navy fleet based there, I thought, well, it's about time we go fight those guys.

I had no inkling war had been rapidly approaching in the Pacific between the United States and the empire of Japan. There had been some mention of it in the newspapers. Those already in our armed forces had been expecting an attack for some time, but the general public had remained oblivious. After the attack, an emotional President Franklin Roosevelt declared Dec. 7 "a day that will live in infamy."

Two years later, I would be flying a lengthy series of hot missions against Japanese targets in a North American B-25 medium bomber, a model that the Army Air Corps had named "the Mitchell." In that fact lies an ironic footnote. The plane was named for the late Army Brig. Gen. "Billy" Mitchell. During the waning weeks of World War I, he had commanded 1,500 French and U.S. aircraft — the largest concentration of air power assembled at that time. It turned out that he not only was a distinguished air commander, but a stunning visionary.

After the war, Mitchell had lobbied long and hard for the U.S. military to form a separate branch of the service — an air force. He claimed that the airplane would eclipse the battleship as a premier weapon in the next war. He also predicted this subsequent war would be fought against Japan, and that it would involve strategic bombing.

Such was his apparent clairvoyance that in 1925 — a full 17 years before the surprise attack on Pearl Harbor — Mitchell had predicted that the Japanese would employ deck transports carrying 50 airplanes each, and attack Ford Island and Clark Field on Oahu in the Hawaiian Islands at 7:30 in the morning. In fact, the attack on Pearl Harbor began at 7:55 a.m.

Mitchell's outspoken ideas annoyed traditional military strategists, and his bitter criticism of authorities led to his court-martial and conviction for insubordination. He was stripped of his rank and duties for five years. Mitchell resigned from the Army and kept on writing and speaking out on behalf of his views. He died in 1936, not living to see many of his prophecies fulfilled.

They never should have court-martialed that man. It was fitting the Army Air Corps named the B-25 in his honor. In my personal files I keep an old article about Mitchell. It's titled: "The Man Who Predicted it All."

On April 18, 1942 — a little more than four months after the Japanese sneak attack on Pearl Harbor — Navy Lt. Col. James Doolittle led a daring and risky raid of the Japanese mainland. Sixteen Mitchells took off from an aircraft carrier, the Hornet, 700 miles from Japan and bombed Tokyo and three other cities. They caused little damage — and all the planes were lost — but the raid provided an immense morale boost to American forces at a time when the tide of the war was tilted heavily in the enemy's favor.

Approximately three years and four months later, I would bear personal witness to the final result of the U.S. bombing campaign against Japan begun by Doolittle's raiders in Mitchells.

The images — among the grimmest in the annals of human history — haunt me to this day.

FOUR DAYS AFTER THE attack on Pearl Harbor, I turned 23. The Sportsman had passed the "three-year rule"; we'd survived

this critical period that everyone had said we needed to endure, after which we would be a going enterprise.

Indeed, it had worked out that way. We were making a profit. Not a big one — but we were paying all our bills, and had a little left over. We had paid back our mother her $5,000 loan. We had shown we weren't

Mom and her two uniformed sons — Chet, left, and myself, 1943.

young fools and dreamers; we had proved the nay-sayers wrong.

But now we knew it was our duty to leave the Sportsman and enlist in the military. Six-and-a-half years before, we'd been in Europe, impressionable teen-agers, and seen the face of fascism right in front of our eyes. Despite the problems in our own country, we knew it was the best on the planet and its ideals were worth defending. The least

Chet and I, as able-bodied young men, could do was to enlist. Of course, if we didn't enlist, we'd be drafted anyway. In early 1942, we enlisted.

Each of us aimed to join the Air Force, waging war in the skies. No matter our phobia with flight stemming from that day in 1924 when the pilot, Billy Blanchfield, had crashed into the McKinleys' house in our neighborhood. I guess the only real reason I wanted to get into the Army Air Corps (which came to be the predecessor of the Air Force) was that I thought it was the best branch, by far. I didn't want to be in the Navy and I didn't want to be a foot soldier.

Chet ended up as a gunnery officer in the Naval air force. Maybe that was destiny. He and I had started a skeet field off Airport Road (now Gentry Way), and Chet had put together an interesting contraption. He had fixed a post and a shotgun on an old tractor seat, and practiced shooting. Now he would be shooting at live targets.

As for me, I set my sights high: I would become an Army Air Corps pilot.

The technical training to get into the Air Corps was lofty, indeed. Most cadets were college graduates. I hadn't attended a day of college. I hadn't even been in a classroom in five years. Fortunately, the Air Corps allowed in candidates who could pass a refresher course.

Classes ran over several weeks. Then there was a test. I studied hard. I barely passed the test — by one or two points.

The next hurdle was the physical examination, which was in Sacramento. I passed this, too, but had to sign a waiver that the military wasn't responsible for my crooked fingers that had been broken. That turned out to be the least of my worries. I rued taking the eye examination.

I already knew my left eye had 20-30 vision — although my right eye was 20-20. I knew I needed to have 20-20 in both eyes to be admitted to the Army Air Corps. I had gone to see Jim Gasho, an optometrist in Reno, and asked, "Dr. Gasho, can you tell me the best optometrist in the United States?"

He said, "Well, they're right in San Francisco, the Barkan brothers, Stanford Lane Hospital.

I drove down and met Dr. Barkan. I said, "Doctor, I'm here for one reason. I know my eyes are 20-30 and 20-20. I want to know from you if my eyes see well enough to fly an airplane."

Dr. Barkan was an older fellow with a white mustache. He examined me. Then I sat outside the office awaiting the results. He came out and said, "Your depth perception is good, your eyes are good. Yes, they're good enough to fly an airplane."

He charged me $25. I thought that was a very high price. (I didn't have much money back then.) But I was satisfied I was pilot material.

Now, at my examination in Sacramento, I had a plan. I had gone down to the physical with a friend from Reno, Vic Hall. "Vic," I said before the eye test, "when you get in there, take this pad and pencil with you, and write down the 20-20 line." He managed to do this for me, recording the sequence of letters. When it was my turn, I asked the sergeant, "Can I take my eye exam tomorrow?"

"Oh, sure," he said.

I went back to my room at the Clooney Hotel in Sacramento, and memorized the 20-20 line forward and backward.

The next day, I passed the eye exam. The sergeant covered my right eye and tested my left eye. I read the line perfectly, forward and backward.

I was in.

Lying and cheating? Those are two bad words. I don't believe my method of passing the eye exam qualified as either. I already had determined via Dr. Barkan that I was capable of flying in the Air Corps. Sometimes, a person is justified in finessing his way past unreasonable barriers, if the end result hurts no one and allows the person to perform a benefit for his country.

So I had passed the refresher course exam, and my physical, each by the skin of my teeth. But I had passed, and that's all that counted.

BACK HOME IN RENO, Chet and I arranged for our sisters, Olga and Melba, to run the Sportsman in our absence. Olga would be paid $150 a month, which she would take out of the business. She probably should have been paid more, but she was family, and so we got away with it. We knew she and Melba would run the business honestly.

Just two of the draft-age males in our neighborhood ended up finding ways to dodge the war. The rest of us were on our way overseas. We were proud. My good friend Elmo Zunino enlisted in the Army infantry. I remember coming home on leave before being shipped out to the Pacific. I was in my officer's uniform, and Elmo was in his private's uniform. We walked down the street together. He was so proud of the salutes I received. One soldier didn't salute me. Elmo was offended.

"That guy didn't salute you!" he said.

"We don't go much for salutes in the Air Corps," I replied. It was true: we didn't.

Elmo ended up being killed fighting in Belgium. Another guy from the neighborhood, Reno Robustellini, who lived on Washington Street a half-block from us, and who'd set traps at our skeet field for 50 cents a day, also was killed in the war. I'm sure others from our neighborhood were killed, though I can't recall their names after all these years.

For whatever reasons inherent in bureaucracy, my orders to report kept getting delayed. It was summer now and I was playing in the local softball league, and an announcement would come over the loudspeakers: "Link Piazzo, enlisted in the Army Air Corps. He'll be leaving . . . " This would be greeted with a big round of applause from the bleachers. But whatever date was announced would pass as my orders from the Air Corps inevitably would be delayed. I'd be playing another softball game, and another announcement would come over the loudspeakers, and there'd be applause. And the next week, there I'd be on the field, *again*. People got to wondering what the hell's this guy doing.

It got to be embarrassing for me to continue playing softball. After the fourth announcement, I refused to take the field. I was one of the best players on the team, Patterson's, which would go on to win the state championship that year. "You've got to play," my teammates told me. "No way," I said, "I'm going to go out there and they're going to wonder, 'Why the hell's he still here?'"

I thanked God when I finally was summoned to report for good, to Santa Ana (Calif.) Army Air Base.

I DROVE MY 1939 Buick to San Francisco and reported on Monday, Aug. 3, 1942, to a Lt. Oates at 444 Market St., at 8 a.m. I finally signed in to the Army. I received special orders to travel to Santa Ana Army Air Base. It was against regulations to drive one's own automobile there, but I drove my car anyway, and stored it in a garage in Santa Ana.

There were 1,500 or so cadets at the base, most of us shooting to become pilots. Very few of us would be washed out during the 12 weeks of ground school, our basic training in this pre-flight phase. But we had aptitude tests to take, and then math and physics tests. I knew I was perhaps the only non-college boy in camp. Did this intimidate me? Not one bit! I decided that while they had been in school, reading books, I had been out in the world running a business. My mind was every bit as fit as theirs, and perhaps more mentally tough.

We were issued "flight suits," which looked like prisoners' coveralls. I already was feeling homesick. I was the only guy from Reno in camp. I was assigned to Tent 17. I found the other three tentmates lying on their cots. We had been assigned alphabetically.

"There's that Yankee bastard," one of them said, in a Southern accent, as I entered.

I looked at him. He didn't look too big. "I would like to have you stand up and say that again, you sonofabitch," I said.

The guy, whose name was Perdon, didn't stand up. The guy next to him, Plon, who was a big fellow, turned to Perdon and said, "I would advise you not to get up."

These three were from the Deep South: Alabama and Mississippi.

"You stupid jerks," I said, "this is World War II. You guys still fighting the Civil War? Why in the hell don't you dummies wake up?"

That was my introduction to my tentmates. I believe I gained a little respect from them. (We later became close friends.)

Although the tide of the war in the Pacific and Europe had not turned in the Allies'

favor, morale was high in camp. All we had to do was remember Pearl Harbor. It was either them or us. Period. We wanted to get overseas — whether in the Pacific or the European theater — and get our job done. We knew if we didn't finish it over there, the war would come to our shores. There was nowhere to hide from it.

(As a footnote, a retired schoolteacher who works out at the YMCA, as do I, said, "Link, I know you were in World War II. Did you ever feel badly about killing people?"

("Come over here, closely," I said. "War is very simple, you know. They either kill you, or you kill them. Period."

("Was that a dumb question?" he asked.

("No," I said, "that was a *stupid* question.")

My entire soul was committed now to becoming a pilot, the most prestigious post possible. Many worthy candidates would wash out somewhere along in the process — if not in pre-flight, then in the subsequent flight training — and many others would wind up for one reason or another classified as navigators or bombardiers instead of pilots. But in my heart I would settle for nothing less than becoming one of the elite, a pilot, actively ending the war.

I knew this would be a tall order for me to achieve. Not only were the vast majority of Air Corps cadets college graduates, but many had amassed hours upon hours of civilian flight time. CPTs, for "civilian pilot training," we called them. What an advantage they had over a working boy like me! Not only that, but I still had to contend with another eye exam.

Tents were set up, with cadets lined up for 100 feet. I sat down for my turn; it was the first time I had seen an eye exam with letters flashed on a film screen.

I already had memorized the three or four

different sequences of letters in 20-20 lines, which I had obtained from Dr. Gasho. But now, on the screen, all the letters in the lines were blocked out except for a solitary letter. It was impossible to figure out which letter in which line was being shown. All I could do was strain the best I could — and guess and pray.

"D, R, P . . ." I read out. I didn't recognize a single letter with my left eye. Fortunately, the sergeant performing the exam was busier than hell.

"OK, next," he said.

My relief was immense. Even today I marvel at how I was able to slip through. Perhaps the sergeant had figured that all we cadets had 20-20 vision and that this exam was a big waste of time.

The aptitude tests were no problem for me. Neither was the physical training. I always loved to run, on my own back home, lapping the reservoir near my house. I stood a shade under 5-10 and weighed 159 pounds. Most of the cadets were in damn good physical shape, but I was in great condition. And during pre-flight I not only finished strong in the required marathon, I finished first.

I handled the exhausting basic training — the marching (*Squads right. Squads left.*) and the rifle training. We rose at reveille at 0530 hours. All day long we trained, and at night we studied until the curfew at 2100 hours. It was during the book work that I saw my chances of clearing the hurdle of pre-flight begin to dim. I simply lacked the classes in physics and math the others had taken in college. Every night I'd pore over the pages of my books, cramming by flashlight under the covers after curfew hours.

We were more than halfway through pre-flight now, and I knew I was falling behind. I decided the only way to avoid being washed out — and likely become an Army infantryman — was to find a way to extricate myself from the training, and in effect get "washed back," buying myself time to catch up.

This I executed to perfection.

We had been issued used shoes — pairs previously worn by soldiers — and I had picked up a slight infection on one of my toes. It was probably athlete's foot, and didn't amount to much. But I decided one night the best thing I could do was to aggravate the infection. So after my tentmates were asleep, I stood on that foot, bearing down on it, for much of the night. It worked: it inflamed the infection.

The next morning I limped into the barracks, putting on an act, and told the C.O. — commanding officer — "Oh boy, I've got an infection in this foot; I can hardly walk."

"I hate to tell you this," he said, "but I'm going to have to assign you to the hospital."

That was exactly what I wanted!

"The hospital?" I said with a hurt look. "Oh my God."

"You've got to take care of it," he said.

In the hospital I studied my books rigorously, catching up to my classmates. Physics, math, theory of flight. Perdon came to visit me every day. We were friends now. "Now, you let me know when you guys are graduating," I said. I figured that would be the point for me to get out of the hospital and begin with the next class, ahead of the pack in training.

Perdon kept me abreast. After a couple weeks, the class graduated. When the doctor came to see me I said, "Oh boy, my foot's in great shape, I walked all over the place!" Of course, it never had been in that bad of shape.

I started all over again in pre-flight. This time, the book work was fathomable. I knew the system. I graduated.

IT WAS TIME TO receive our classifications. We cadets lined up in rows in front of a large platform. A major, a big, broad-shouldered man, addressed us: "I know most all of you want to be pilots. You're going to be classified tomorrow. And if anybody comes to me for a change of classification, you are automatically washed out."

He stepped off the platform.

The next morning we each received large envelopes with our names on it. Mine had a big stamp on it in red letters: "Bombardier."

I told my tentmates, "I'm going to go see the major."

They thought that was a terrible idea. "Did you hear what he said, they're going to wash you out!" one said.

I figured it was worth a shot. What the hell had I got to lose? I'd already come this far — getting through the physical with my broken fingers, and the vision exam with my bad left eye, and the refresher course, and book tests. I decided it was my lack of college education that had "weeded me down" now, out of the running to get my pilot's wings.

I walked over to the major's office, clutching my folder with "bombardier" stamped in it ignominiously in big red letters. Four or five secretaries were sitting in the outer office.

"I want to see Major _____," I said to one of them.

"What for?" she said.

"Change of classification."

"Oh my gosh!" she said, putting a hand on her forehead. I had been the only cadet foolish enough to buck the major's warning.

One of the other secretaries stood up from her desk in the back and approached. She was about 30, and wore glasses, and otherwise was nondescript. "I want to talk to you," she said.

We walked to the side. In a low tone, she said, "He's a nut on model airplanes. Tell the major that you build model airplanes."

Isn't it funny how a complete stranger can, with a few words, entirely change the course of your life?

I had one lucky card up my sleeve. One of my nephews, Olga's son, Sam Dibitonto (who later served a term as Reno mayor), was a model airplane aficionado. Sam was 11 years younger than I. I'd spent many hours helping him make his balsa wood models, which he hung from the ceiling using monofilament fishing line. I had absorbed all the foot-to-inch ratios of a model plane's scale to an actual plane: 30-to-1, 20-to-1, and so on, and I knew all the models. I was well versed.

I was ushered into the major's office and stood at attention. He looked up gruffly.

"What are you doing here?" he said.

"Well, sir," I began, "I think you made a mistake in my classification."

"Made a mistake?!"

"Yes sir, I have over 1,000 hours of stick time that's not logged." In actuality, I'd been up in a plane one solitary time — and hardly at the controls. My friend Don Dondero had told me about taking an excursion flight in Carson City for $1. I had subsequently taken such a flight out of Hubbard Field in Reno. I was probably 12 at the time.

"Gee, I'd like to be a pilot," I continued. "Also, I built model airplanes all my life."

"Model airplanes?!" he shot out, excited.

"Yeah."

"What models?"

Boy, I named them all. Stearman, and so on.

We kept talking, and talking. The secretary was right: he was an absolute fanatic about model airplanes.

The major grabbed the folder out of my hand and crossed out "bombardier" and took out a big stamp. *Thunk.*

"Pilot" now was stamped on my folder in big red letters.

He handed my folder back to me.

"You're dismissed," the major said. "And don't let me down."

I wish I had that secretary's name. And I wish I had the major's name. I would have written him after the war to say, "I didn't let you down. I was awarded 13 medals, including the Distinguished Flying Cross, and flew 67 combat missions."

Wouldn't that have been nice?

Once again, I had pushed ahead — in the face of sure failure — with my highly improbable dream of becoming a pilot.

Something was looking out for me from up above.

Just as with the eye exam and my foot "injury," I had bent the rules with my story to the major about my 1,000 hours of unlogged stick time. I believe the ends ultimately justified the means. If you can shorten a war, flying 67 combat missions, it was well worth it, even by bending the truth and cheating along the way to become a pilot and put yourself into position to help your country's cause.

THE NEXT PHASE WAS six weeks primary flight training — actually getting up in planes. If I passed, I'd go on to six weeks of basic training, then six weeks of advanced training. I was stationed with about 100 other cadets in Tulare, Calif.

The favorites to succeed in primary training were the "CPTs" — the cadets who had earned flight certificates in civilian pilot training. We were studying at Rankin Aeronautical Academy, a civilian-run airport. "Tex" Rankin, a stunt pilot, owned the academy. As a child I'd seen him perform a show at Hubbard Field in Reno, flying through the hangar upside-down. On his helmet was a streaming ribbon with a hook. As he shot through the hangar, he picked up a handkerchief from the ground with the hook.

Aviation officials, perhaps the Civil Air Patrol, eventually grounded Rankin. He was considered too dangerous in the air. During primary training, he addressed us cadets. "You know, every time I hear the 'Star-Spangled Banner,' " he said, "a chill runs down my spine." I feel that way, too.

Cadets weren't free to move about and talk to people. But I managed to get close to him before he left and said, "Mr. Rankin, I want you to know that I saw you fly in Reno upside-down. You picked up a handkerchief with your helmet."

He remembered the stunt, of course.

"You know, I'm grounded," he said. "You see that mountain over there?" He pointed. "I go over that mountain and I fly anyway." My kind of guy!

There was no way to keep a guy with that kind of nerve on the ground.

We trained on Stearman monoprops. My instructor was a gruff guy named R.J. Lehmann. The first day of flight training, he took three of us out. He rested his hand on a Stearman and said, "I want you to know, this airplane never hurt anybody. It never *will* hurt anybody. It's this goddamned ground that kills you! So for Chrissake keep the sonofabitch in the air!"

That's the way he was.

"You know, they give you that bulls— about flying an airplane, you know, 'coordination' and all that s—," Lehmann said. "If you have to stick your goddamned leg out or hand out to steer the airplane, do whatever it takes!"

I don't think he was a World War I vet, but Lehmann was a terrific pilot and one hell of a guy.

On my training flights, he sat in the front cockpit, I sat in the cockpit behind. We had World War I-style Gosport tubes attached to our flight helmets. He could talk through the tube to me, but most of the time he didn't talk at all. He was a rough, tough sonofagun. I respected him completely.

If I made a mistake he'd push his control stick right to left, which would bang my knees with my control stick. That was his favored method of communication. Another mode was sneaking out of his front cockpit while the plane was in flight, and pulling the tube out of the half-inch hole in my helmet. "You dumb sonofabitch!" he'd say. "I said 500 feet, not 520 feet!"

That's the way he was. But he was one hell of a teacher.

The rule was that if you amassed more than 10 hours of instruction but still hadn't soloed, you washed out. You only got to solo if your instructor deemed you ready.

The CPTs each soloed after one, two or three hours of training. Of course, this worried me. But one day, Lehmann and I landed in an auxiliary field and got out of the plane. We were alone. We sat on the ground.

"You think I'm too tough on you guys?" he asked me.

"Hell," I said, "I worked for a foreman, a carpenter, who was rougher and tougher than you are."

The foreman's name was Wright. I worked under him during my first job out of high school, employed by Gene Belli. If you made a mistake working on a house, Wright would throw a hammer across the floor and hit you in the leg. Most guys would quit af-

ter an incident like that. I was fortunate: he never threw the hammer at me. But I admired the hell out of Wright; he was a tremendous worker. Every Friday he'd give us our checks and say, "You know, we didn't get much done last week, but we got to give her hell next week!"

That's what I told Lehmann.

"I want you to know something else," he said. "I don't know what in the hell's keeping you going, but you keep improving."

I hadn't known I'd been improving.

"I want you to know something," he said. "If you ever solo, and you go to basic, you're going to be way ahead of these guys. Because they didn't learn to fly the right way, and a lot of them are going to be washed out."

I thought to myself, this guy's crazy!

After nine-plus hours, I still hadn't soloed. The writing was on the wall. Then, after landing after yet another training flight, Lehmann jumped out of the plane. "OK, take it off!" he said.

Holy s—! I took off. I immediately felt my instructor's absence. Without him in the plane with me, there was less weight and the plane rose much faster.

Normally, Lehmann would go into the Ready Room next to the field and have a cup of coffee while a student soloed. But not with me. I could see him on the airstrip, sitting on a parachute, arms folded, staring skyward, wondering if I was going to make it down alive.

I flew the Stearman around and made a good landing.

Once again I'd cleared a hurdle. And as always, by a hair's width.

Lehmann walked over to me. He was not smiling. He did not offer his hand in congratulations. That's not the kind of guy he was.

"Good job," he said, curtly.[6]

VERY FEW CADETS WASHED out in primary flight training. They all were CPT pilots. It was now February 1943. For basic training we were stationed at Lemoore Army Air Base in Lemoore, Calif.

Basic training involved different airplanes and instruments, and acrobatics — dogfight maneuvers, such as slow rolls, snap rolls, loops and Emelmans, which are going straight up, then turning upside-down, twisting around and coming back.

I was just amazed: Lehmann's prediction came true. About a third of the cadets washed out!

The rule of thumb was that no one washed out in basic; they did so in primary. But the reverse occurred. The CPTs had cruised through primary training, soloing very quickly into the course, but still — as Lehmann had averred — actually had not learned to fly properly. During basic, their weaknesses were exposed.

For me, basic was much easier than primary. I'd learned to fly from scratch during primary. Now I was refining and adding to my solid base of skills.

I was made a cadet officer, which surprised me. I was sitting in my barracks when a couple officers came in. I started to rise but they said, "No, no, sit down."

One said, "We've been looking over your records and we'd like to have you become a cadet officer group commander."

Geez, these guys are nuts, I thought to myself.

I found myself head of the whole damn group of 200 or more cadets. My job was lining up the cadets at the flight line. I got along very well with one of my roommates, Harold Petty; I made him my adjutant.

Harold and I had to march the group to and from the flight line, and then in front of the grandstand, and call everyone to attention. We'd stand sharply in our uniforms. One time, one of the cadets was standing in formation with his sleeves rolled up, against regulations. He was toward the back.

"Get that guy to put his sleeves down," I said to Petty.

Petty talked to him, then returned. "He won't put his sleeves down," he said.

Very weird. So I went over to the cadet. He was a good-looking kid.

"What do you want?" I asked, "an engraved invitation to put your sleeves down?"

Actually, I suspected he wanted to get washed out.

"If you don't get those sleeves down I'm going to knock your goddamned head off," I said. Everyone heard it.

He put his sleeves down. We marched off the flight line.

That afternoon, the captain called me into his office. "I hear you had a little discussion with a cadet this morning."

I feigned ignorance.

"You don't tell a guy you want to knock his goddamned head off. What you should have done is said, 'Fall out and go to your barracks,'" the captain said.

"I know you got him to put his sleeves down," he added.

"Oh, thank you sir, OK," I said.

If the cadet hadn't put his sleeves down, I believe I *would* have knocked him on his ass. Then *I* would have gotten into trouble.

This cadet was an exception to just about all the rest of us. Most couldn't wait to get overseas. I did, too, but I was a bit older than most of them, and I hardly glamorized

---

[6] Lehmann's training stuck with me during combat. Every time I got a new plane — after my B-25 got shot up — I'd take it up to altitude ceiling and run it through harsh maneuvers, all the time cursing it. I was showing it I was in control. "You control the plane. Don't let it control you," Lehmann said.

the eventuality. I saw no need to rush it. The others were gung ho: "Gee, I can't wait to get my wings and get overseas."

"You dumb bastards," I said, "they're killing each other over there. Did you know that?"

Still, I never sought a way to get myself washed out. I had committed myself to combat. This involves, in an odd way, holding two completely contradictory beliefs in one's mind.

Gregory Peck, in his role as a bomber group commander in the movie *Twelve O'clock High*, made a statement that perfectly summed up this mentality. I can't quote it verbatim, but it was to the effect that we know we are going to get killed, but at the same time we think we're going to make it back home.

In my mind I resolved that, hell yes, I was going to get killed. And so I told myself, "Why should I be nervous or frightened?"

And, indeed, I never, ever was frightened during combat.

Combat still was a ways away, though.

After basic came advanced flight training, in Stockton, Calif. There were fewer of us, now, about 75 cadets in our class. I corresponded regularly with Chet. He was doing fine. He was moving up the ladder in the Navy, and eventually would rise to lieutenant J.G. (junior grade). He and I had no college, but we were more mature than the college boys who'd been in school while we were running a business. We were focused.

Advanced training was in larger planes. I'll never forget training in the "war-wearies," British planes, Averill Ansons, that had been in combat. We called them "banana boats." They were orange, with fabric on the outside. The bailout procedure was to put your head down and run through the airplane,

busting through the outer fabric. When you landed you were supposed to spasmodically hit the brakes, which were disk brakes, so you wouldn't blow out a tire. If you blew out a tire, they had to junk the plane because they didn't have spare tires.

It was good experience, but not good flight training. The banana boats flew like balloons. After we landed, we'd put a web strap around the control wheel and secure it. We'd get in the final approach, get out the web strap, secure the control wheel, then sit back with our arms folded and let the plane land itself.

Very few, if any, of us washed out of advanced training. We were highly skilled. Then came time for our wings to be pinned on. My mother came down. The Army also had a set of wings for relatives. So Mom got her pair of wings, too.

I now officially was a pilot, a second lieutenant in the U.S. Army Air Corps. It was quite an accomplishment. We new officers really felt like we had it made, now.

One of my roommates was John Pratt, a little guy from Lewiston, Idaho. He'd always come to me for advice. He wanted to get into a fighter plane in the worst way. Instead, he was put into B-17 long-range bombers. He ended up being killed in Europe.

My aspiration was to get into a B-25 medium-range bomber. I liked a twin-engine airplane, instead of a single-engine fighter plane. You lose one engine, you can get home on the other one. (This did happen to me a few times.) I also liked having a co-pilot. I thought the B-25, the "Mitchell," was very well-designed. It carried a six-man crew: pilot, co-pilot, navigator, radio operator/gunner, engineer/turret gunner and tail-gunner. The pilot controlled the .50-caliber machine guns in the nose for strafing, opened up the bomb bay, released the bombs and, of course, piloted the plane.

Instead of getting assigned, I was sent through a series of transitions. I was ordered to someplace in Texas, but at the last minute the orders changed and I was sent to Mather Field in Sacramento, which was a transition school, to train on B-25s for six weeks of intensive training, after which our group would be sent overseas. At the end of those six weeks, the C.O. came in and said, "We need A-20 pilots in Europe."

We were assigned to Will Rogers Field in Oklahoma City to train on A-20s, which were twin-engine light bombers with four-person crews. I preferred B-25s; they were better planes. I remember going into town and the locals telling me, "Oh, you're from Reno, Nevada, the town that's open 24 hours a day?" Oklahoma was a "dry" state in those days, meaning that you couldn't buy alcohol. That is, over the counter. The citizens would buy their bad liquor from the bellhops, and pay a lot of money for it. About 10 p.m. about two-thirds of them would be drunk.

As the six-week mark approached for us to be sent overseas, orders came in again. The group was being sent to Florence, S.C., for more A-20 training. Who can explain the military? There seemed to be no logic to it.[7]

We did our training flights over the jungle-like terrain of South Carolina. Not long after we arrived, the C.O., a major came into the barracks. He asked me to be a co-pilot on his B-25. (How peculiar, for an A-20 outfit.) He said, "I don't want to get lost in these goddamned jungles." By now I knew the area pretty well. But there was no way you could get lost, anyway. You flew over great big water towers with the names of the towns written on them. I didn't tell him that, though.[8]

The six-week mark approached again. By this time I had accumulated more warplane training than anyone in the United States. The major, a very nice man, turned to me and said, "You like B-25s, don't you?"

"I sure do," I said.

"Would you go back to B-25s if I could arrange it?"

"Major," I said, "I don't think you have that kind of juice."

Two days later I went to the Ready Room. "Pack your bags," he said, "you're going to Greenville, South Carolina. B-25s."

Another transition!

This was the third time I was delayed from going overseas. Frankly, I was yearning to go. I'd been trained and prepped for combat. But in the service, you do what they tell you, period. I had accumulated so much experience I could fly lower than other pilots, and could bomb ground targets on the beach and strafe towed balloon air targets better than anyone. Like anything, the more practice you get, the better you get, until your reactions become almost automatic. Later, this extra training proved a blessing in combat.

(Much later, when I was based at Mindoro in the Philippines, I had a very good friend, Capt. "Moose" Johnson, who was C.O. of an A-20 outfit. He had been a captain be-

---

[7] After yet another delay in orders, my crew flew up to New York. In a Brooklyn bar near Ebbets Field, the home of the Dodgers, the bartender gave me and my co-pilot, Selby Dotters, a hard time. We had to order drinks by their correct name, he said. He added that he didn't like soldiers. Dotters, a tough guy who liked to fight, placed a $20 bill on the bar and told the bartender it was his if he'd go outside in the alley with him for five minutes. The bartender called the military police. MPs arrived. One of them whispered to Dotters that he should wait until the bartender got off his shift, then kick the s— out of him. I looked over at Dotters when the bartender's shift was up; Dotters was so drunk, he had to be helped back to his room.

[8] While stationed at Florence my group were administered eye exams again — my first since getting my wings. The doctor told me my left eye was "weakening" since the test showed its vision was 20-30. Of course, it had been 20-30 before I'd even entered the service. He prescribed me four pairs of glasses — one to keep with me, one for my flight outfit, one for my locker and one extra pair. I picked them up a few days later and threw them in a garbage can. Now that I had my wings I knew the Air Corps wasn't going to wash me out.

fore the war, and thus hadn't received all the intensive training I had, beginning as a cadet. He was not a good pilot, but he was my best buddy over there. I gave him the nickname "Moose" because he was a great moose-hunter where he came from, Alaska. In fact, I visited him several years later in Alaska and went on a fishing trip. All his neighbors were calling him "Moose." It had stuck.

(Moose used to kid me about the A-20 being faster than the B-25. One time I went to his intelligence officer and learned where his mission was. I learned exactly what time Moose would be coming back. I was leading a squadron of B-25s. I went up to about 10,000 feet and made circles, waiting for his squadron to return. I looked down; he was at about 2,000 feet. I dived down and called him on the radio. I told him I was way behind him. I dived down, going about 230 mph, and at the same altitude waved at him and zoomed right by him. He never figured out what I had done to reach such speed. From that day he was convinced the B-25 was faster.)

My extensive training experience also meant that the commanding officers would see my records and call me in for advice. Here I was a second lieutenant, being sought out by captains.

One day, in Greenville, a captain called me into his office. "Look, I need your help," he said.

"What's the problem?"

"Well, we've got this lieutenant who flies beautifully. But when he comes down he runs off the taxi strip. Will you fly with him?"

"Sure," I said.

I flew co-pilot with the lieutenant on a night flight. Sure enough, he performed each of my commands perfectly. He made a nice landing, then went down the taxi strip

and off of it.

We hit the brakes.

I turned to him, glaring.

"Who in the hell are you kidding?" I said. That's all I said.

The next morning I went to the captain. "I think I got this guy figured out," I said. "He's getting ready to go to combat. He wants to get washed out. Anybody can see that. Let me give you some advice."

"What's that?" the captain said.

"Call him in and say, 'Look, we're having trouble with your flying. I've got ahold of the Army, and they need foot soldiers in Europe. They're killing the s— out of them. And you're going to lose your rank and as a buck private, in two days, you're going to Europe."

The captain took my advice.

The next day he called me in and said, "Geez, it worked!"

The lieutenant was no longer running off the taxi strip.

HELEN AND I KEPT in touch by phone and letter. When I was in Florence, I asked if she wanted to get married. "Sure," she said.

She had enough money for a train ticket. We married in Florence. We were married by a Father Tobin at the Catholic church. Helen, though a Christian Scientist, didn't mind a Catholic wedding. The father got special dispensation to marry us. We had a nice ceremony. A roommate, Matzka, was my best man. There was a roadhouse in Florence, the only one there that served food and drinks. South Carolina was a "dry" state back then. Unbeknownst to us, a buddy of mine flew to Reading, Pq., picked up a bunch of liquor and brought it back. Boy, what a wedding reception it was that night!

The adjutant general told me two days

even plan on coming home.

Wedding day, Florence, S.C., March 27, 1944. Behind Helen and me stand Matzka, my roommate at the time, and his wife. They were part of our wedding party.

AFTER ALL THOSE CLOSE brushes with washing out of pilot training — everything from the two eye exams to the classification as bombardier to the last-ditch chance at soloing during primary training — I had surged ahead of the pack.

That's life, huh?

You just do the best you can with the tools you have, play the hand that the good Lord deals you, and things turn out as they should. If you sit on your ass and accept what they throw at you, you'll never get respect.

Millions, in every generation, never learn this message.

Gen. Douglas A. MacArthur said, as printed in *National Geographic*, March 1992, Page 81, "It's the orders that you disobey that make you famous." This, from a career military man, whose field is predicated on following orders.

You must seize your own destiny. If you can do some good by violating an order — well, then, do it. What the hell's an order?

Yes, I had finagled my way through to get to where I was, a highly trained Army Air Corps pilot. But no one was hurt, only helped, by this.

I had put myself in position, as a pilot, to help shorten the war.

later, "Boy, you destroyed the whole air base. They all got gassed up and had a good time."

Helen followed me to Greenville. I had my 1939 Buick with me — I'd driven it to each new assignment — and when the six weeks of B-25 training were up, and I finally received my overseas assignment, I drove with Helen all the way back to Reno. She came with me to San Francisco to see me off. I would be flying to New Guinea on a C-47 transport plane, out of Hamilton Field. I bought her a diamond wedding ring in San Francisco.

Chet, also, had married in the service, to Darlene Gilmer from Loyalton, Calif., shortly before I tied the knot. Neither of us thought ahead to settling down, though.

When you're going into combat, you don't

Here is my certificate for completing primary training, and a photo of my primary instructor, R.J. Lehmann — who was tough as nails and had to be the best instructor in all the Air Corps. He wrote across his chest on the photo: "Happy landings."

8

More Lives than a Cat

It was a relief to finally get orders to go overseas. We had been trained for combat. Our group training in Greenville, S.C., was assigned to a replacement center in Nadzab, New Guinea.

I was indifferent about going to the Pacific instead of Europe. In the service you better not set your mind to something, because somebody else tells you what to do.

Fifty or so of us second lieutenants in the B-25 group were flying to New Guinea, with a stop in Hawaii. We would be replacing pilots shot down in other outfits of the Fifth Air Force. Already, via the communication channel known as "latrine teletype," we knew there were some outfits we didn't want to be assigned to. It's akin to scuttlebutt, I guess, but it's ephemeral, and you always wonder how in the hell you got the information. We all knew we wanted to go to a medium-altitude outfit, but not to the "suicide squadron," the 17th. It had sustained

This Japanese statue was meant to commemorate Japan's air power and military victory over the United States. That's me on the right, giving my editorial comment following Japan's surrender.

heavy losses.

It was late 1944. We felt the Japanese still were getting the best of us, and we had a heck of a lot of work to do. For some reason, I wasn't getting pumped up with stress. My philosophy in life always has been, Why worry? What the hell good is it?

The base on Nadzab was typical: tents, dirt floors, cots. It was hot, tropical, humid, all the time. We slept under mosquito nets lest we be eaten alive. We took adabrin tablets to guard against malaria. It turned our skin and eyeballs yellow. We used to laugh about it. In briefings, we'd be told that when the sun's up you don't get malaria from a mosquito bite, only after sundown. We also were told that only the female enophales mosquito transmits the disease. Of course, how the hell could we distinguish a mosquito's gender? Typical of the service.

The natives were friendly. Short, dark, stocky people in weed skirts. They couldn't speak English, of course, but we would buy fruit from them. They chewed betel nut, which turned their teeth orange. We also met the Anzacs — Australian and New Zealand troops. They were very friendly toward us Americans. We had run the Japanese out of the Australian port of Darwin, preventing a full-scale invasion. The Anzacs were rough, tough soldiers; most of them were missing their upper two front teeth. I got to know some of them real well, and I said, "What the hell's the matter with you guys, you get into a fight and get your teeth knocked out?"

"No, no," they said, "it's the wa-tuh, it's the wa-tuh." They had real bad water in Australia, evidently, and they'd lose their teeth.

We had very little food in supply.[9] Our staples were biscuits and canned beef, which had earned the name "bully beef" during World War I, and tasted as if it dated back to that war. I said to the supply sergeant, "For Chrissake, is this all you can get?"

"Well," he said, "there's an Aussie major in charge of unloading down at Lae (where our LST ships came in with our supplies) and he steals all our good stuff and there's nothing we can do about it."

I and my navigator borrowed a Jeep and drove down to the port. The thief taking our supplies was an Aussie major named Mitchell, a good-sized Anzac with his hat turned up at the side. He had a beautiful shack, with a neatly shingled Neppa roof. Neppas are reeds that grow tall; the natives cut them and lace them with bamboo to make fantastic shingles that provide ventilation but also have leaves that expand with moisture, keeping rain out. Mitchell was hoarding goods. We didn't know if he was selling them on the black market.

I'm target-shooting with the Stanley Owens 9 mm automatic at Lae, New Guinea. Mitchell, the Australian major and deal-cutter, had traded me the gun for a .45 pistol and trench knives. I sent the gun home in a crate.

We couldn't fight him — what could two guys do? — so we decided to "join" him. That is, we decided to see if we could work with him.

He invited us to lunch. We had good food — meat, eggs, beer, all unheard of in that corner of the Earth.

"Anything we can do for you?" we said.

"Yeah," he said. "I could use some trench knives."

These knives were issued to us, but they weren't even sharp, and most of the guys threw them away. That's the military. We also were issued wool-lined suits for the South Pacific. At Hamilton Field back in San Francisco, troops returning from the Pacific Theater had told us, "All the winter stuff you got, throw it away and buy booze." It was good advice; over there, you could sell booze for $125 a bottle. I had taken what money I had and bought Three Feathers whiskey, the cheapest brand, and sure enough, was approached by guys as soon as we landed offering to buy booze for that

---

[9] We were supposed to share everything on base. One time, a group of us were lined up shaving in the morning. Someone smelled aftershave lotion. A couple of us walked down the line, sniffing, until we found the guy who had a bottle of Mennen. We made him give two drops to each of us.

astronomical price. I didn't sell any, right away, but once in awhile, if I went broke playing poker, I'd sell some.

Mitchell figured to use trench knives to barter with the natives. Back at camp I collected a half-dozen trench knives, drove back to Lae and traded with Mitchell. We had been issued .45 automatic pistols, notorious for their inaccuracy. I wanted a Stanley Owens submachine gun. It had a strap iron for a stock; press a button and the stock came off, press another button and the barrel came off. It could be stepped on in the mud of the jungle, and still fire. It was a fantastic gun. I traded my .45 and some trench knives for a Stanley.

Mitchell also said for a panel of parachute "silk" (nylon) he could get a bargeload of fruit from Salamaua, a native village down the coast. I went back and talked to a quartermaster I knew and asked if he had any parachute silk. "How good does it have to be?" the sergeant asked. "We just surveyed two tons of it. Moisture got into it."

"Surveyed" meant they had decided to get rid of it.

He agreed to give me all two tons for a quart of Australian beer.

My navigator, Bill Eakin, and I got a 2½-ton truck and hauled the nylon behind my tent. Eakin suggested we cart it down to Mitchell. "No," I said, "we don't want to flood the market. He can buy all of New Guinea with this. We just take two panels."

We had hundreds of panels, but brought down just two —and Mitchell was tickled with it; he could barter easily with it. It was a precious commodity in New Guinea. He traded us fruit.

In camp we got an order. It said there were items that we were prohibited from sending home as souvenirs. These included weapons and ammunition. Our packages would be X-rayed and the penalty for violating the order would be a court-martial. We pilots got together and said, "How dumb can these people be? Would we rather go to jail or go up in combat and get killed?"

We made big boxes out of three-quarter-inch lumber, and shipped our items home. We sent home everything that was restricted. I sent home my Stanley, and an M-1 rifle and two big bags of ammunition. I still had space in my box. I stuffed in GI blankets, and a drum I'd gotten from Mitchell that everyone wanted. It was a native drum cut out of a coconut tree, with crocodile hide over the top. I still had some space. I looked around, and found a great big can of pepper. What was that doing in our tent? I put that in there.

"Good," we said, "now they're going to court-martial us so we don't have to go to combat."

We thought it was a big joke, this threat of court-martial.

About four months later, I got a letter from Mom saying, "Thanks for the pepper. We can't buy any pepper. I gave a cup to all the neighbors." (The other items also arrived.)

We were in Nadzab two or three weeks. Eakin and I were only able to make a couple trips with the parachute panels to Mitchell before we were assigned to combat outfits. We flew over our tents and saw those two tons of parachute nylons lying behind our tent, worthless to us now.

THE OUTFIT I WAS assigned to was the "suicide squadron," the 17th squadron of B-25s, which had been wiped out three times. This is how I drew the assignment:

While I was stationed at Nadzab, I and other B-25 pilots were flown down on cargo planes to Townsville, Australia, three times to ferry B-25s back to New Guinea. The planes were assembled in Brisbane, Australia, then flown to Townsville. We would fly them to New Guinea. About the third time, there was a mix-up in orders, which happens in the military.

"What are you guys doing down here?" we were asked. "We don't have any B-25s.

TYPHOON, I E SHIMA

I stand at our base on Ie Shima after a typhoon. What was left of our medical dispensary is in the background.

Get back in that cargo airplane and go home."

I spotted an A-20. "What's that A-20 doing out there?" I asked.

"Well, we're waiting for somebody to ferry it," one of them told me.

"I'm an A-20 pilot," I said.

"How much time do you have in them?"

"Over 1,000 hours," I said. Actually, I had more like 40 hours.

"Well, there's something wrong with it," I was told. "Go talk to the crew chief."

The crew chief was sitting on the ground, leaning up against the landing gear.

"Sergeant, what's wrong with this airplane?"

"Why?"

"I want to fly it to New Guinea."

"Well, the cylinder head temperature goes up and the oil temperature goes down."

Our flagpole on Ie Shima after the typhoon. I'm standing at lower left.

"Sergeant, that's impossible."

He got mad at me. He stood. "What do you mean that's impossible?"

"They either both go up or they both go down, period."

Now we were mad at each other.

"I want to test-hop this thing," I said.

"OK," he said.

I took off over the Coral Sea. One of the gauge needles showed a rise in temperature, the other a drop. That was impossible, of course, because if an engine gets hot, no way part of it will get colder.

I couldn't get the cowling to open. The cowling consists of the little flaps around the engine that open to cool the engine, and close to keep it warm.

I landed.

"Do you know anything about cowling?" I asked the sergeant. "Your cowling is stuck. Can you get the goddamned cowling to work? And I've got news for you: both the oil temperature and the cylinder head temperature are going up. One instrument is not working, the one showing it going down."

The sergeant fixed the cowling. I test-hopped the plane again; the cowling worked. The temperature gauges worked, too.

I went over to a major and said, "The plane's working OK."

The major said I could ferry it back to New Guinea. The other pilots already had returned. The problem was there only were two parachutes: one for me and my navigator, but not for my engineer, Nelson Morrow. I couldn't strand him in Australia.

I set about borrowing another parachute. Of course, we usually flew as close to ground as possible, about 40 to 50 feet, which meant a parachute would be useless, anyway. An A-20 is supposed to only have two parachutes, so I was unable to get one from the supply sergeant. I saw a B-24 on the tarmac. It was empty. So I "borrowed" one from it.

I informed the major we now had three parachutes. He didn't ask me where I got the third one from. We were cleared to take off.

We got out over the Coral Sea, and there was smoke coming out of the cockpit. It smelled like an electrical fire: burning wires.

"What the hell's going on?" Eakin called from in back.

"Christ, it's full of smoke up here," I said.

"Well, what the hell," he said, calmly. "We might as well get killed here instead of going to combat. What the hell's the difference?"

All of a sudden the smoke died down. It was a seven-hour flight to New Guinea. I had to switch gas tanks. It was a new, different model from the type I'd trained on. I couldn't find the switch. I reached down and got the technical manual out. Thank God the plane had one.

Captain Piazzo.

I tore out the fuel system pages and handed one-half to Morrow, the engineer who was lying behind me, while I pored over my half.

"I found it, I found it!" Morrow called out. "There's a toggle switch under the dash, on the left side."

I reached under and found it. We were getting close to Port Moresby, at the tail end of New Guinea. I started smelling that burning-wire smell again. This plane really was a mess!

I landed at a remote American airstrip. We opened up the battery compartment over where the engineer had been lying. There were about 20 batteries, all bubbling. What made them bubble, we didn't know.

A man came out from the coconut trees. He was bearded, wearing a pair of shorts, very motley.

"Do you have a putt-putt here?" I asked. A "putt-putt" is an energizer for starting an airplane.

"Did you come to pick me up?" he said.

"Hell no, why?" I said.

"I'm here alone and they're supposed to pick me up and they haven't showed up yet."

"We're going to New Guinea," I said.

"No, no," he said, "they're supposed to pick me up and fly to Australia."

He didn't have a putt-putt, either.

We jumped back in the airplane. I figured it wouldn't start.

By golly, it did.

We took off.

We were over the ocean off Lae. Morrow, the engineer, behind my head said, "Let's try to fly 400 miles an hour." No

An interrogation in the Ready Room on Mindoro following a mission. I'm second from left in the foreground. Col. C.T. Thompson is to my left in the background; he had been my co-pilot that day.

one had flown that speed. It was a mythical goal.

"OK," I said.

I took the plane up to "ceiling" — past the 10,000 feet limit, above which we were supposed to have oxygen masks, and up to 16,500 feet.

Then I dove, turning the trim tabs forward. We headed straight for the ocean. How dumb can you be?

Morrow was reading the air-speed indicator. "Three-hundred," he said. "Three-twenty. Three-twenty-five."

The blue ocean was fast rising up.

"Three-ninety-five . . . "

The ocean, the ocean . . .

Finally, Morrow yelled, "Four-hundred!"

I started to pull back on the controls. But I was going so damn fast, it was like pulling on a wall.

Hell, we're going to crash in the ocean, I thought.

I pulled as hard as I could, using every ounce of strength.

So this was what it was like to die, crashing into the ocean, in a completely stupid

and senseless endeavor.

Finally, right above the ocean — perhaps 100 feet — the plane pulled out. But in doing so I ruptured the hydraulic system. The indicator showed the fluid level dropping. The bomb bay doors came open. It didn't hurt a damn thing, so I didn't give it another thought.

Unfortunately for me, the day of stupidity hadn't ended. We flew over Lae. I remembered Major Mitchell telling me that if we ever flew over, to please buzz his headquarters.

I looked down and saw his headquarters. I buzzed his shack. All those wonderful Neppa shingles blew right off the roof.

Oh God, I thought. Wait until Mitchell sees me.

(I visited him later and he thanked me, thinking the incident was hilarious.)

We flew to Nadzab. I felt like a big shot, the guy who didn't have to return from Australia in a cargo plane like the other pilots, but who had flown an A-20 back. What the hell, I buzzed my outfit two or three times.

I looked down: the men were racing from

tents and jumping into the slit trenches.

I thought, Oh Christ, what the hell are they doing that for?

I landed. The hydraulic fluid lasted enough for our landing gear to operate.

A military police sergeant was waiting for me on the taxi strip. I stopped.

"I got orders, lieutenant, to take you up to our commanding officer," he said.

"What the hell for?"

"You buzzed our outfit," he said.

"Get your ass off the taxi strip and let me check this airplane in," I said.

He did. Then Eakin and I walked over to the colonel's office. He was too busy to chew me out, so a major did instead.

He was madder than hell. "You know," he said, "the Japs, with an A-20 they captured, bombed and strafed our outfit yesterday."

And there I'd been, buzzing the base with an A-20 with its bomb bay doors open.

"Holy cow," I said.

"The colonel doesn't have time to talk to you," he said, "but you're grounded for two weeks and your flying pay is taken away from you for two weeks."

That didn't bother me. But during the two-week period I was grounded, the other pilots in base were assigned to the medium-altitude outfit that everyone wanted to go to.

The colonel called me in and said, "You're assigned to the suicide squadron."[10]

This squadron, the 17th squadron, 71st group, had been wiped out three times already, its crews replaced. They had gone in to bomb Japanese naval task forces, comprised of battleships, cruisers and destroyers. Indeed, such missions were suicidal. The ships' guns would blast the planes out of the sky.

Now my crew was assigned to the 17th, on the front lines, the first squadron to strike the enemy.

I wasn't even a little bit depressed, though. I never got down at all. Eakin and Morrow, well, they had gone along with me in the A-20. The co-pilot, Dotters, however, was very pissed off at us. He hadn't been with us, yet he was suffering the collective punishment. The radio gunner and tail-gunner, being enlisted men, not officers, didn't say a thing, of course.

We were issued a brand-new B-25 D Model and flew to Leyte, in the Philippines, our new base.

WE LANDED AT LEYTE. Boy, everything was shot up. We had arrived shortly after the Allies had invaded to retake the territory. The mud was thick on the ground, and the enemy was still out in the coconut groves. Sniper fire was a constant danger.

"Where's the 17th?" I asked a captain from another outfit, the Air Transport Command.

"The 17th?" he said. "The 17th was wiped out."

Usually, when an outfit was said to be "wiped out," it meant half the planes were shot down. But in this case, he meant all 27 planes in the squadron were destroyed.

Here I was, having landed with a brand-new D Model, and very little gas, and unable to locate my outfit.

Finally, another guy with Air Transport, a captain, said, "You know something? I think a few of them were left and they flew to Mindoro. I *think*."

A glimmer of hope. I looked at a map. I didn't have enough gas to get to Mindoro. It was several hundred miles north.

"I can give you enough gas to get there, and that's all," the captain said.

---

[10] Ironically, a guy I'd roomed with — Harold Petty — was assigned to a medium-altitude B-25 outfit in the South Pacific, and was killed. The 17th, incidentally, was the most decorated squadron in either theatre of World War II, and most of the medals were awarded posthumously.

I flew to Mindoro. All there was for a base were makeshift tower and coconut trees. I buzzed the tower, as per regulations, and received a red flash from a Veri pistol. That was a signal for "no landing."

I circled the beach and came back, and this time I received not one but two red flares. That was a signal for "absolutely no landing."

I was puzzled. I could have safely landed on the beach with my gear up, but it would have destroyed the plane. Or I could try the tower again. I didn't have enough gas to go anywhere else.

I circled and passed the tower again. I looked down at the landing strip. There were a bunch of craters from Japanese bombing. I figured that was the reason I was being warned away. I made another pass and saw where I could go diagonally and land, avoiding the craters.

This hill on Ie Shima was called "Nellie's Tit" but also "Million Dollar Hill" because it was estimated it cost that much for us to capture it from the Japs. Ernie Pyle, the famous war correspondent, was killed at the base of the hill.

And so I did. I put the engines back and hit the brakes. Nothing happened. We didn't slow. I kept skidding. I applied the brakes but it didn't help.

The reason the tower had signaled me not to land was because it had rained and the strip, made of coral, offered no traction. It was slicker than ice.

I ran off the end of the runway — half the plane was off it — but thank God I hadn't crumbled the nose wheel. Had the plane been damaged, there was no equipment there to fix it and it would have just been left there. My crew would have had to somehow work our way back to Leyte with the natives, and I sure as hell didn't want to do that.

I let the hatch down. My co-pilot climbed out. I looked down and saw him, lying on his back. He went right down the moment he hit the slick coral. Personnel came out. They didn't say a word at first.

"Geez, we didn't crumble the nose wheel," I said.

I climbed out of the cockpit.

They thought I'd made a spectacular landing. I didn't agree; hell, I'd gone halfway off the runway, into the sand.

We moved the plane back onto the air strip and I taxied it over to headquarters. The officers were just happy to see a new airplane to go back into combat.

Ours was the first plane of the rebuilding 17th squadron to show up. A few more planes were located at Leyte, and they began to arrive. Headquarters sent back to Nadzab for more planes as we pieced together a full squadron. In a matter of days the "suicide squadron" would be complete.

Tents were pitched as crews came in. There were four or five of us pilots in camp now. It was a beautiful clear, warm day. An LST ship — a huge barge — came from Leyte to Mindoro and approached to land at our beach. It was full of our supplies, the food, the 500-pound bombs, the equipment and so forth.

We pilots sat on the beach. Aircraft identification had been required in flying school, and you had to pass 100 percent — able to perfectly identify all military aircraft used in both theaters. "What the hell is that?" one of us said, pointing at a plane flying down the beach, about three miles away.

"I think that's an AT-6," another of us said. That was an advanced trainer. What would it be doing out here?

We were stumped.

All of a sudden we realized what it was: a kamikaze. It hit right in the middle of the LST ship.

The "My Buck" crew. Dotters took the photo, so isn't pictured.

Boom! — there it went. Right in front of our eyes. What the hell, that's war.

"Jesus, all our bombs," someone said. "We won't be able to fly any missions."

"Jesus," I said, "terrific. How sweet can it get? Now we don't have to fly any missions."

As for food, a quartermaster commandeered all the food on the island and stored it in a compound surrounded by barbed wire, and guarded by sentries. Our rations, it was announced, would consist of coffee and biscuits. Capt. "Moose" Johnson, my best buddy, had a plan. He knew the quartermaster was a captain. Moose had somehow obtained two major's leaves. He "raised" himself to a major, and did the same to me.

Now we "outranked" the quartmaster. Moose did all the talking — he was regular Army, and a captain before the war, and conversant in military talk. The two of us approached the quartermaster and Moose told him he was commanding officer of an A-20 squadron and that I was C.O. of a B-25 squadron. He demanded 28 boxes of 10-in-1 rations. The quartermaster questioned Moose — upon which the "major" chewed the captain's ass out. He said we were scheduling missions. We immediately received the rations.

The day after the LST ship was sunk, here comes a bunch of C-47s. They were full of 500-pound bombs for us to fly our missions.

Sometimes the military can be efficient, if it wants to get you killed quicker.

And so, just days after arriving, we were ready to fly our missions.[11]

An artist in the outfit painted a picture of Helen, in a bathing suit, on the side of the B-25, as well as the words "My Buck." I called all the B-25s I would fly in combat "My Buck." "Buck" was my wife's nickname.

We had three squadrons in our bomb group: B-24s, B-25s and P-51s.

My goal was flying 300 combat hours. After that I'd be sent home.

I DON'T RECALL MY first mission, except that I took my crew down beforehand to our airplane and said, "I don't want anybody screwing off, not even three seconds.

---

[11] While stationed on Mindoro, shortly after our troops ran the Japs out of Leyte, enemy night raids on Mindoro grew frequent. We dug slit trenches, about 3 feet deep, inside our tents next to our cots. When air raid sirens went off we were supposed to take cover in the trenches. The enlisted personnel always jumped in — but we airmen never did. It was a matter of honor.

Anti-aircraft guns were positioned next to our tents, with brass casings stacked high. I would visit the gunners — who never hit anything — and say, "Why the hell don't you get some of those farmers from the Midwest who can hit something?" They'd get pissed off. But, *boom-boom-boom*, they never hit anything but air with their guns.

Your life depends on him, his life depends on you, my life depends on you guys, your lives depend on me. If I catch somebody screwing off, I kick you off the crew, period."

I never had to request a crew member be transferred. We had a great crew. We each knew our jobs, and we had tremendous camaraderie.

I sure do remember the third mission.

Gregory Peck had been in a training film we had watched in our pre-flight training back home. In the film he was wearing "pinks," light-pink trousers, shirt, tie, tunic and garrison hat. "Gentleman," he had said, "this is a Ready Room. This is where you'll be briefed prior to your mission." Then he'd introduced the intelligence officer, the meteorologist and commanding officer. It was a film to orient us to what we would encounter overseas.

The next segment showed Peck entering the Ready Room. "This is the same Ready Room," he said, "and this is where you'll be interrogated following your mission."

The film made everything seem orderly and sane. Now, in the combat zone, I found out what Air Corps procedure really was like. "Interrogation" was an intelligence officer sitting at a table as my crew gathered around after returning to base, asking, "What the hell went on? What the hell did you see? What in the hell did you destroy?"

Before my third mission, it was raining at Mindoro. Our "Ready Room" was a big perimetal tent. In it was what we called a story pole, and a Coleman lantern flickering because water was hitting it. It was 3 or 4 in the morning, dark as hell, with four inches of mud on the floor.

We pilots sat on a bench, ankle-deep in mud, to be briefed on the mission. Here came our C.O. — Capt. Bert Sill.

Lars "Bull Moose" Johnson, commanding officer of an A-20 squad, was my closest friend in the Pacific.

"Gentleman," he said, "I would like to have known you better, but this morning we're all going to get killed."

He was leading the squadron, so he would get killed along with us.

I thought to myself, Now where in the hell is Gregory Peck? He sure showed us a different Ready Room in that training film.

We could barely see each other in the darkness by the flickering flame of the Coleman. "There's a task force off the coast," Capt. Sill said. That's how the 17th squadron had gotten wiped out three times before — attacking a task force.

In a task force there always is one battleship. There are maybe two cruisers, and four to six destroyers.

"Now," Capt. Sill said, "don't try to attack the battleship. There's no way you can even put a dent in it. And don't try to attack the

More Lives than a Cat

These photos depict the grim irony of the two twin co-pilots, Nat and Fred Hovious, who must have had an agreement for one to film the other in flight following a bombing mission. Instead of getting as close to the ground as possible and heading for the ocean after dropping their bombs, the twins' planes were at higher altitude. The result: one brother filmed the other's death as his plane was shot down. Nat was my co-pilot on the "Mission from Hell."

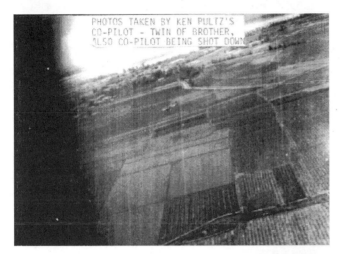

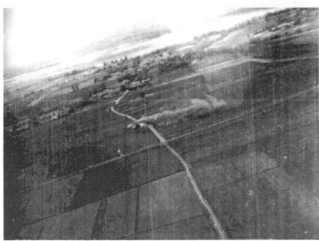

cruisers."

The destroyers are supposed to protect the battleship and cruisers. They're smaller, but still have plenty of firepower.

"Let's try to knock out some destroyers before they knock us down," he said. "And we are going to get killed."

We knew how it was supposed to be done. We were to come in about 40 feet off the water, fire our .50 caliber machine

A low-level strafing and bombing mission on Formosa.

guns at the water line, softening up the ship's side, then dump a 1,000-pound bomb in, hitting the ship horizontally, and blow the destroyer up.

Our squadron took off in the dark and rain. The lead naviga-tor, in Sill's plane, must have been half-smart. He went in the wrong direction. We couldn't find the task force. Had we, I

Doing my laundry on Mindoro.

would not be sitting here writing this narra-tive.

And so the 17th squadron survived that morning instead of being wiped out for a fourth time.

I felt great. We didn't get killed. We'd get killed, instead, tomorrow. Or the next day.

FIGHTER PLANES WERE SUPPOSED to provide us bombers cover every mission. But if the fighter pilots knew it was going to be a real hot mission, with Zeros coming at us, they'd somehow fail to find us at the designated rendezvous time. We'd fly our mission without them.

They knew exactly the coordinates, but they'd claim, afterward, back at the base, that they simply couldn't find us.

We had a P-51 fighter squadron in our bomb group. As the days passed, I became the B-25 squadron leader, because I was the best pilot (thanks in part to all my extensive train-ing back home). As squadron leader, I could request what fighter cover we'd have. I always re-quested the old P-40s, which weren't in our group, but maneuvered better than P-51s. In fact, P-40 pilots would hope the Zeros would come at them, because they could outmaneuver the Zeros and shoot them down. They were the best airplane for fighter cover that we could get in the South Pacific.

On New Guinea everyone had wanted to avoid getting in the Suicide Squadron. To be sure, the squad-ron had been wiped out three times — but going against naval task forces. Otherwise, it turned out, the 17th was a great outfit to be in.

When we went against land targets, we'd take our B-25s as low as we could get them, maybe 40 or 50 feet off the ground. Flying low was the best protection we had.

Our squadron flew every day, but the crews alternated and we flew every other day. One day on, one day off. It was a rhythm. Before we went to bed, we'd check the chalkboard, which would list what crews would fly the next day. If we were on it, we'd get up at 3 the next morning, shave, get breakfast, and find out in the Ready Room what the target or targets for the day were.

The squadron leader or, occasionally, the group commander, would give us the briefing. A map of the Philippines would be hanging up. We knew the islands well. The target would be pointed out, then the navigators would make damn sure they knew where they were going.

Our crew stayed together the entire 66 missions we flew (I also flew one with another crew). The co-pilot, Selby Dotters, one time got the bright idea that we didn't need our navigator, Bill Eakin. Eakin was a good enough navigator. He only got us lost a couple times. But long missions meant we had to thin our engines out — moving the mixture control to save fuel. "Eakin's nothing but excess baggage," Dotters said to me. Then he went to Eakin with his opinion: "Goddamnit, we don't need you; you stay on the ground!"

A day or two later, we were returning to Mindoro. "Well," Eakin said over the plane's intercom to Dotters and me, "if you think you don't need me, why don't you put that hood over you and I'll give you the headings, then I'll tell you when to take the hood off and you find out yourself if you think you don't need me."

A hood was green canvas a pilot pulled down to be able to fly by instruments in case of inclement weather.

We agreed to his dare, like damn fools.

I knew we were now south of our airfield at Mindoro. I took off my hood. We recognized all the islands north of Mindoro, but the islands below us were foreign to me. The navigator gave me several conflicting headings over the intercom. Now I had to decide whether we were east or west of Mindoro. I made a 180-degree turn and

flew up the coast. I stayed on course, and found our airstrip — just by sheer luck.

We got out of the plane. "See," our co-pilot said, "what'd I tell you? We don't need you." (He, of course, continued to fly with us.)

In addition to myself, Dotters and Eakin, our crew had radio-gunner Harry Hall, whose job was to run the radio, of course. His liaison set supposedly could reach 1,000 miles, but never worked. And we never found one that worked at any time. The tail-gunner, John Griffin, had a terrible job, bouncing around at the back of the plane, but he'd blast the hell out of a target with his two .50-caliber machine guns, after our plane passed over and bombed it. He also was supposed to protect us against Zeros, but the Zeros, we found out later, never attacked us because we flew at low altitude and our turret guns could knock them out of the sky — or so they thought.

In combat, our engineer, Nelson Morrow, manned our turret guns, which were atop the plane in a section behind the pilot, but I'm sure no one could hit the broadside of a barn with them; yet, we found out after the war that the Zeros were afraid of us. They were under orders not to attack any plane that had a turret. The Japanese were running out of airplanes. One time we flew a mission, returning at low altitude to Luzon, and encountered five Zeros above us. I alerted Morrow, our engineer, and the tail-gunner and waist-gunner, figuring we were going to get attacked. We weren't attacked.

The first thing I'd do on a bombing mission was open the bomb bay doors. I had a button to release the bombs, and a button for the guns. The B-25 was meant for strafing and skip-bombing at low altitude. With a target a mile away, I'd bring the plane down, and send a burst from the row of .50

calibers in the nose and know right where I was to hone in on the target. I'd keep strafing, hitting the target, and right as I reached the target I'd drop the bombs.

The ground officers would tell us to press the gun buttons two seconds, then release them for two sec-

The crew of "My Buck," which completed 66 missions together.

onds, so as not to burn out the gun barrels. The hell with that, I decided. I'd keep those buttons pressed down the whole time.

A bombing run lasted a matter of seconds, and I was supposed to lift my fingers off the buttons for a second or more? Forget it!

When I burned a barrel I'd know it. The guns would shoot a tracer every six bullets — a red flash. A burst from a .50 caliber created one streak of light. A flame would twirl when a barrel's rifling burned out, meaning it was useless, for it wouldn't fire a bullet straight. But I would keep pressing.

Out of 10, or 12, or 14 guns — depending on the model of B-25 we were in at the time — I'd burn out, perhaps, six or eight guns. But I'd be strafing the hell out of the target. It was how I chalked up my 90 percent average kill rate.

I burned so many barrels that the major in charge of armament had sent the word down that I had to knock it off. "The major says you're burning too many barrels," a sergeant told me.

"Tell the major to go to hell," I responded.

A few days later, the major called me down to the flight line. "We're out of .50 caliber barrels, primarily because of *you*," he said. "You've burned out more barrels than any-

body."

"We're out of barrels, major?"

"Yeah."

"What do we do, stop the war now, major? If you open up your goddamned eyes, we've got other outfits out here that all have .50 caliber machine guns: B-24s, P-51s, P-40s. Can't you get off your ass and go borrow some barrels until you can get some more?"

He did, of course.

He was one of two officers who outranked me whose asses I ended up chewing.

Well, there were three, come to think of it.

GEN. MACARTHUR ISSUED A direct theater order to our squadron. Such an order meant we had to scramble and get into our planes. MacArthur had great respect for our squadron, knowing we were front line and the ones he called on first.

The order was to hit Japanese rolling stock — trains, trucks, cars, wagons, horses. The target was north of Clark Field on the island of Luzon. The Japanese were retreating north as our forces slowly retook the Philippines.

I had a grid map, about 6 inches square, and my mission was to knock out all the rolling stock in that grid.

Four of us airplanes had different grid maps. We were supposed to break off over Bataan, then rendezvous at a certain hour.

Master Sgt. Barlow was the line chief in charge of all the crew chiefs. He was a man with a gray handlebar mustache. I was in my airplane. I saw my bomb bay gas tank was empty. That could prove fatal if we were hit by enemy fire. A bullet could hit the empty tank and explode the fumes. This I knew.

Barlow approached the flight line in his Jeep. From my plane, I said, "Barlow, fill the bomb bay tank."

"No way, that will delay the mission," he said. "This is a direct theater order."

"Sergeant, fill the bomb bay tank. That's an order!" I said. I already was a captain.

He looked at me, cussing, and filled the tank. We didn't need the gas; I just didn't want an empty tank.

We broke off over Bataan. I cleaned my area out real good. All railroads, highways and roads run through villages. The theater order had included a line at the bottom: "Do not strafe the villages — Gen. Douglas A. MacArthur." We were only to hit rolling stock. But I knew the Japanese weren't stupid. They didn't have their guns out there in the middle of the ground in daytime. They had their emplacements camouflaged in the villages.

I passed over a village and got all shot up. This happened in a matter of seconds, though I couldn't hear it with my headset on. I lost my right engine, and my Plexiglas canopy was blown out. I got a call from Harry Hall, my radioman-gunner, over the intercom. "Gas all over the place," he said.

"Harry, you're not smoking, are ya?" I asked.

No answer.

"Harry, you're not smoking, are ya?" I repeated.

In a meek voice, he responded: "I was."

The enemy fire had knocked the end off the bomb bay tank and spewed gas out, extinguishing his cigarette. Had the gas come out another part, it could have created fumes that would have been sparked by his cigarette and blown us up.

I had one good engine left, and needed to rendezvous over Bataan to return home. I had plenty of fuel, except the gauges were going down in a hurry. The tanks were supposed to be bullet-proof. Ha.

No other planes were at the rendezvous point, and I didn't wait around. I was losing gas fast. I headed back to Mindoro.

We made it. I landed. I asked our crew chief to drain our tanks to find out what was left. There were about six gallons remaining in the whole airplane. We'd barely made it.

The other three planes — 18 crewmen — on the direct order mission had been shot down. We should have been shot down, too. Instead, the mission turned out to be the first of two that would eventually yield me the Distinguished Flying Cross. Had I not asked Barlow to fill the bomb bay tank, I wouldn't be here today. Period.

I saw Col. C.T. Thompson, our group commander, at interrogation. "You know," I said, "MacArthur, on this direct theater order mission, says, 'Do not strafe the villages.' You tell MacArthur that I said to go f— himself if he thinks *I'm* going to send any more airplanes out on these suicide missions. It's ridiculous. You go over a village and they just shoot the hell out of you."

"Captain," Col. Thompson said in an even voice, "would you like to call the general and tell him that?"

That was the end of that conversation.

After interrogation, I returned to our tent. My co-pilot, Dotters, grabbed me by the collar. He was out of his mind.

"You keep bringing us back, goddamnit!" he said. "When are we going to get killed and get it over with?"

His face was white. His hands were shaking.

"Get your hands off of me!" I said. "I might accommodate you the next time we go out. Be patient."

He went over to his cot and sat down, brooding, head in hands. He always brooded after a mission. I, on the other hand, never worried. I was fatalistic: I figured if I wasn't killed this day, I would be the next, and what the hell good would it be to worry about it?

I could have reported Dotters to the flight surgeon, but I didn't. He might have been psychoanalyzed and grounded, ruining his military career.

I'm glad I never reported Dotters. I knew the next day he would be all right. He was a good co-pilot. In flight he never bugged out, or acted nervous. He performed everything I told him to do. He only fell to pieces on the ground.

Maybe the difference between us was that, as a co-pilot, all he could do was sit passively during a mission. As the pilot I had control of the plane, the guns, the bombs. I kept active, absorbed in my tasks. He, on the other hand, had a front-row seat to terror, with nothing else to occupy his mind.

There is an after-note to this particular mission.

The crew chief came to our tent, after Dotters had gone through his tantrum. "Link," he said, "I'd like to have you come back to the plane, to flight line." It was maybe a half-mile away, on a dirt road.

"What the hell for?"

"I want you to see something in the airplane."

"Piss on that airplane, and junk it."

That's what they did with shot-up planes, junked them. They removed two items: the thermos jug and the pair of binoculars. Then the plane would be carted to the "bone yard" to be cannibalized for parts.

"I want to show you something," the crew chief said.

I went back with him to the plane. There was the engine shot out, and the Plexiglas canopy shot out, and holes riddling the body. I didn't give it much attention. The mentality was: tomorrow's going to be much worse.

"Sit in your cockpit," the crew chief said.

So I climbed in and sat down.

"Look up to your right," he said.

I did. A metal-piercing bullet — .25 caliber, solid steel — was lodged in the aluminum right next to my head. Inches away. Had its progress not been spent by the time it had reached that point, it would have continued and torn a hole right through my head.

Again, I thought, so what? It was my mindset. If I hadn't been killed this day, I would be the next, or the one after that.

The crew chief, however, carefully dug the bullet out and put it on a chain for me.

That wasn't all. The B-25 D model had a crawl space to the nose, under where the pilot sat, and that's where the navigator sat in the Plexiglas nose manning two .50 caliber machine guns.

"Look down that crawl space," the crew chief said.

The aluminum floor was bent up, like it had mushroomed.

"Now let's go back and take a look at that seat," he said. We dug the parachute out from under my pilot's seat, and the 1 1/2-inch armor plate of steel was bent up like a horseshoe right under where my ass had been. A .20-millimeter shell had hit the plane.

I wish like hell I'd saved that armor plate. That .25 caliber bullet on a chain became an important souvenir for me. Back home after the war I wore it around my neck. Every time I thought something was a little rough in business or some other aspect of civilian life, I'd take that little bullet into my hands, look at it, and say, "Things aren't so tough."

It can always be worse.

I DIDN'T EXPERIENCE ANY special exhilaration from combat. I looked at it as a job. I had been a carpenter, and then I'd sold sporting goods. Now I was in the Air Corps, and the job was either they killed you or you killed them.

After a few weeks at Mindoro we were transferred to Luzon and began flying hot missions to Formosa — the heavily fortified island off the Chinese coast. We'd target airstrips and alcohol plants; alcohol was used in explosives. Formosa (which now is Taiwan) had 1,600 gun emplacements. The Japanese had been pushed out of the Philippines and now were backed up to that small island, giving it all they got. The missions were murderous.

My best buddy in the war, Lars "Moose" Johnson, landed this A-20 but forgot to put the landing gear down. He chalked it up to combat fatigue.

The Japanese didn't put the guns out in the fields where we could see them. They hid them in villages. And on every mission over Formosa, our group got shot at and hit, and we lost airplanes and crews.

I told my pilots in our squadron: "Going to and from a mission, if you run into a village, strafe it." Two other flight leaders came to me and one of them said, "Gee, isn't that being a little mercenary?"

"There're Japs in there," I said, "and they're killing us. And if you try to turn away from a village, you give them a beautiful target."

(Remember the comment I'd made to our group commander, Col. Thompson, after the Luzon mission that had got our plane all shot up? The comment about what MacArthur could do with himself, since he'd issued the order not to strafe villages? As a colonel, Thompson was not about to say to me, a captain, "Gee Link, you know, you're right." But my point about the suicidal aspect of not strafing villages must have registered with him, and I believe he decided to work my opinion through command. A suggestion was probably made to Gen. MacArthur that we had better strafe villages, given our squadron had lost three of four airplanes over them, and the fourth should have been shot down. Two days later, on the next theater order we got, it said, "Strafe the villages.")

I greatly admired Col. Thompson. Before hot missions he'd sometimes erase the co-pilot's name in the lead aircraft from the chalkboard and write in its place, "C.T. Thompson." He'd end up flying with me, though, as group commander, his job was running the group and he didn't have to fly. I never asked him why he'd take the risk. I guess he was just setting a great example.

Thompson had put his name down to fly with me on a hot mission over Formosa. The two other flight leaders came up to me and one said, "Now, we'll see if you strafe a village with Thompson flying as co-pilot."

Bill Eakin, my navigator, and I with two natives on Mindoro who were guiding us on a wild boar hunt. They were much quicker than us, and we soon got lost behind them. We saw no wild boars.

We hit our target, and did a good job destroying it. Coming out, there was a village. I didn't hesitate. I strafed the hell out of it. A bunch of ducks, geese and chickens flurried up.

After we landed and got out of the airplane, Thompson said, "Piazzo, there sure was a lot of fowl in that village."

"Yeah," I said, "you notice, colonel, they were all white."

That was our entire conversation. If you've been in combat, you'll understand our reticence. It was the way you are after finishing a combat mission.[12]

A few times during the war, I did have thoughts of, well, maybe there weren't Japs in those villages, and maybe I was destroying innocent villages. But I also knew Japs were all over, and they were our enemy, and they were in villages, and they were shooting at us, and I had been fired on by them. Their guns were camouflaged behind nets in the villages.

I devised a plan for attacking targets on Formosa when I'd lead the squadron. I knew

that low altitude was the best place to be on an attack; it would take the artillery crews on the ground time to reposition their guns. I'd fly up the west coast of Formosa at 5,000 feet, letting their radar pick us up. Then I'd drop the squadron down to sea level, turn around and come back, throwing the enemy off our trail. I knew Formosa like the back of my hands. There were many dry riverbeds outside of monsoon season. I'd fly us down these riverbeds. I knew all the headings, and had my navigator, Eakin, squeeze my right or my left shoulder to keep me on course to the target. He'd time the minutes and seconds per heading, then hit my shoulder.

About a week after the first such maneuver, the Japanese strung big steel cables over the riverbeds. I encountered the first one, and pulled up. It would have cleaved us in two. That was the end of our riverbed navigating.

Only once did I see an actual human killed by our attack. We had hit a target, and I looked over to the left, and I saw a man carrying cargo — wheat or whatever — on his head. Our tail-gunner got him.

A lot of our targets were villages, the houses made of bamboo. We seldom dropped 1,000-pound bombs, since we couldn't fit many into our bomb bays. We mostly dropped 500-pound demolition bombs; but we used "frag" bombs with parachutes, which were anti-personnel fragmentation bombs that blew shrapnel sideways when they hit the ground. The frag bombs would kill people as they ran out of bombed factories. We also dropped napalm (incendiary) bombs.

My second mission over Formosa gained

---

[12] Here's another anecdote about Thompson. While stationed on Luzon, he called me in and asked if I had ever been buzzing. Then he laughed: buzzing was common in our squadron; after all, we flew low-level missions. Thompson then showed me a directive he'd received about my A-20 buzzing incident on Nadzab that had gotten me grounded for two weeks without flight pay. The directive said it was against regulations to take my pay away. Thompson handed me a check and laughed, again, about my buzzing.

me the second of the two required recommendations that eventually earned me a Distinguished Flying Cross. I was leading the second flight, the left flight, following the lead flight. The lead ship opened its bomb bay doors, and I opened up my bomb bay and my wing men opened up their bomb bays. Then I realized we were hitting the wrong target. So I closed my bomb bay. This was the only time this ever was done in combat, I was told. Normally, the planes follow the lead ship.

I looked up and saw the real target about three miles to the southeast. I pulled up and started making a sharp turn. I had a poor left wing man — his name was Thorn, and he was a terrible pilot. I knew he couldn't hold the turn. I gave him the signal

Our B-25 crew at a 1990 reunion in Reno with our wives. Left to right: John Griffin, tail-gunner; Harry Hall, radio-gunner; myself; Nels Morrow, engineer. Bill Eakin, our navigator, had passed away and co-pilot Dotters was unable to attend.

that I was making a steep turn. I lost Thorn, he slid under, and I lost my right wing man, too. Now I leveled off and saw my target. I strafed and bombed it. It was an alcohol plant. The Japs always had alcohol plants next to airstrips, and in gullies. Formosa has a long range of uninhabitable, steep mountains along the east coast. The Japs knew we could only hit them from the north or south; from the west, we'd run into the damn mountain. The island only was 225 miles long, and 90 miles or so wide. Thirty miles were taken up by those mountains.

And here I was, coming in from the west.

I was engrossed on hitting the target — I knocked out airplanes and buildings and destroyed the airstrip, but I did not see the alcohol plant. I had forgotten about the mountain range, which was shrouded in clouds. I pulled up as fast as I could and started to make a 180-degree turn on instruments. I thought, Christ, we're going to crash any second now.

I broke out of the clouds. We always were told in training never to hit a target twice. You surprise them the first time, then they go to their guns and nail you the second time. But as I passed over the target, I spotted the alcohol plant. I was out of bombs. I blew it up with my guns. I'd destroyed the whole damn target — just absolute luck, by the grace of God.

In interrogation, the squadron leader said, "You're not going to believe this, we hit the wrong target."

"Maybe you did, but I didn't," I said. He hadn't even known I'd broken off.

I couldn't convince him.

"Wait'll you see my can," I said, referring to the film.

The intelligence officers showed the footage from his flight. "See, what'd I tell ya?" he said, sitting next to me.

"Well, you haven't seen my can yet," I

said.

When I saw the footage, I couldn't believe myself what I'd done. I'd destroyed the whole damn target. One airplane.

My crew was just tickled to death. The rule was that if you hit the wrong target, you didn't get a day off but had to go up the very next day. This happened often. And boy, the enemy would be ready for you then.

We were happy as hell we'd hit the right target.

ONLY ONE OF MY 67 missions did I fly without my regular crew.

A brand-new crew arrived. I wasn't supposed to fly that day, but the new crew's pilot got sick and they needed a replacement. I went down to meet them. They'd never been in combat. The

The officers club on Luzon, which I and my houseboy, Jackson, built with lots of help from local Filipinos.

co-pilot happened to be the identical twin brother of a co-pilot of one of the crews already in our group.

The co-pilot and navigator told me their radioman was a hell of a radioman because he'd been an instructor in the States. It was late in the afternoon, and kind of foggy. Our target — of all things — was a task force. Thank God it only was part of a task force. Nevertheless, it would be a dangerous mission.

"Come over here, navigator," I said. "Do your own navigating, because we're liable to get caught in the fog, we're liable to get caught in the night, and we're liable to have to break off from the formation. And I want you to know where in the hell we are."

Most navigators relied on the lead plane to reach a target and get home.

"Y-yes, s-sir," the navigator said.

He stuttered! That was unusual. How in the hell did he get to be a navigator? His stuttering gave me the impression he was nervous.

We flew toward the target. Sure as hell, we got socked in by fog, and it got dark. Sure as hell, we had to break off. One moment we were flying in formation, and I was trying to follow the exhaust from the plane ahead, and the next, all of a sudden, I had nobody to fly with. We were on our own.

As a pilot you develop a sixth sense for where you are. I was now flying on instruments. We were off of Mindoro. First thing, I gained altitude, then I let the co-pilot fly. I called up the navigator on the intercom.

"Where are we going to break out on the Philippines?" I asked.

"Manila Bay," was his response.

"Manila Bay?!" I said. "You dumbs—, for Chrissake, we won't get three feet in there. It's occupied by the Japanese. Change your heading for Chrissake!"

In the meantime I looked at the instruments. The co-pilot had the plane in a spin. He couldn't even fly co-pilot.

I took us out of the spin. "Did you know you had us in a spin, for Chrissake?" I asked.

He hadn't even realized it.

Now I had to fly the airplane, plus figure out where in the hell we were. I remembered some great advice at that moment. It had come from a pilot who had been in combat. He had told me it when I was still stateside.

"If your navigator ever gets lost, take the maps away from the dumbs—, because he'll really screw you up. He's lost, then he tries everything and he gets you all screwed up, then you got to find your own way."

I called the navigator over. "Give me the maps!"

He looked at me like I was crazy.

He rolled them up and put them on my lap. I didn't realize that he'd kept one, which he shouldn't have.

I decided that if he figured we were coming out of Manila Bay, we had to be north of Mindoro. That, at least, was a start: a tiny glimmer of hope that we could find our way. It was night, I was flying on instruments, the navigator was useless, the co-pilot couldn't co-pilot. And to top it all we were running a little low on fuel.

I called my radioman — who was supposed to be this great radioman. "Get on the liaison set and see if you can get ahold of August Crystal, see if they can get a beam on us and tell us where the hell we are," I said. August Crystal was our secret code name for a directional-finding station. It sent out a sound beam.

The radioman didn't respond.

I called the radioman again on the intercom. No response.

I looked back. The airplane was on fire!

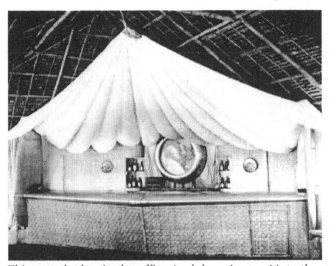

This was the bar in the officer's club on Luzon. Note the B-25 tail section as the bar top, and the cowling at the back of the bar and the parachute above. Jackson wove the bamboo latticework of the bar.

The liaison set had blown up.

We were fast running out of options. There was the radio altimeter, but these things never worked on our planes. They were as worthless as the liaison sets. I turned it on anyway.

The damn thing was working!

When a plane is over water, the needle stays constant, on 0; when the plane is over land, the needle comes up and gives an altitude reading. *If the altimeter is working.*

We were over water, which was a relief. I knew we were on the west side of the Philippines, and I knew the general heading of the islands. I was starting to feel better, but only a little bit. We were running out of fuel.

Normal Air Corps procedure called for a pilot to tell the crew what he was doing. I got on the intercom.

"Here's the deal, now," I began. "We're lost as hell. And I think that we're north of Mindoro and I'm trying to find our way home. If you guys have any ideas, let me know."

This was a brand-new crew. These guys didn't know what the hell to do.

The tail-gunner got on the intercom. "Help me find each other! Are we lost?! Are we going to die?!" He was hysterical. This was not the sort of input I was seeking.

"Sergeant," I said, calmly but firmly, "Listen closely. Don't use the intercom again. I don't want to hear from you, period. Do you hear me?"

Lt. Kluthe flew this mission over Formosa, and it would have given him his 300 combat hours so he could return stateside with no further combat. But he didn't return. His wrecked plane is in the lower right of the frame.

"Yes I do," he said.

That took care of him.

The co-pilot, navigator and radioman would be no help; the tail-gunner had proved himself a liability; and all that left was myself and the engineer, the latter whose role was nil in flight, anyway.

The needle on the radio altimeter rose. I took the plane up higher than the altitude of the highest peak in the Philippines, about 5,000 feet. I prayed that we really were north of Mindoro. Basing our survival on this assumption, I took a general heading of the Philippines, toward Mindoro. I turned right over the ocean, then headed toward what I prayed was Mindoro.

Meanwhile, the navigator announced he knew where we were now: over Mindinao. Three-hundred miles south of Mindoro, and 100 percent Jap-infested! He was totally lost.

"Get on the radio," I told my co-pilot, "and call August Crystal."

"What's August Crystal?" the co-pilot asked.

This truly was the flight from hell.

"Never mind!" I said. "Just call August Crystal, and say, '5-9-0 (whatever our number was), come in August Crystal.' And keep doing that."

We both had our headsets on, listening for a voice to respond to us.

About 10 minutes passed.

"I got August Crystal!" the co-pilot said, suddenly.

I was shocked and pleased as hell.

I called August Crystal myself. But I got no response.

I figured the co-pilot's headset was stronger than mine. I switched headsets.

I called August Crystal and connected. "August Crystal, this is 5-9-0 . . ." I said.

"We're lost, pick up a heading on us, will you please?"

"Yes, OK," the voice said.

"Hurry it up 'cause I'm running out of gas," I said.

"Gotcha zeroed in. You're 120 miles out," the voice from the control tower said. He gave us a heading. August Crystal always directed a plane in a different direction, then had it come in by a roundabout route.

"I don't have gas to go 120 miles," I said. "Can you turn on your spotlights?"

"Can't do it," he said. "Bandits hit us tonight." ("Bandits" meant Japanese planes.)

I was desperate. "Call Col. Thompson," I said. "Tell him the situation. I'm going to head in toward Mindoro. You alert the PT boats, have them come at a reciprocal course and I'll try to ditch this thing at night, and maybe they can find us."

It would be like finding a grain of sand in a dark puddle. We were going to die in the frigid sea.

It wasn't more than a minute later when here came the blessed bright beam. Col. Thompson had said, "Turn on the spotlight!"

What a near-disaster! The man in the control tower running August Crystal had completely miscalculated our distance. We were so close to the base at Mindoro that I'd overshot the field.

If it hadn't been for Col. Thompson's intervention and the spotlight being turned on, I'd have flown far beyond Mindoro.

I made a sharp turn. I later was told by the guy manning the control tower that he'd never seen a turn that tight by a B-25. "I thought you were going to land on the tip of your wing," he said.

We landed. Just like after the mission to Luzon on the direct theater order, I had the crew drain the fuel tanks to see what we had left. And just like the Luzon mission, there were six or eight gallons left in the entire plane.

You talk about God.

Thus ended the flight from hell. We piled out of the plane.

The radioman disappeared. This crew was just in from the States, and it turned out they had brought booze with them. The rest of us didn't have any.[13]

The radioman returned with a bottle of Hague and Hague Pinch Bottle: the most expensive scotch. It was then I saw his hands had been burned trying to put out the liaison set that had caught fire. But he hardly seemed to care. He and the rest of that rookie crew were thankful to be alive. They thought I was the greatest pilot who ever lived.

We celebrated for a time. Then I found out that the tail-gunner had pissed and soiled his pants. That snapped the situation back to reality.

"Don't thank me," I said. "Thank the good Lord."

Each of them wrote home about the incident.

There is a postscript to this tale, and it isn't a pleasant one.

On a later mission, the two twin co-pilots were flying in planes in formation on a mission from Luzon over Formosa. The target had been hit and the squadron was returning. Standard procedure after hitting a target was to get down as close to the ground as possible — tree-top level — and hit the

---

[13] Beer was rationed once a month. Between missions, to unwind, I'd take the crew up to altitude ceiling — 16,500 feet — and each of the guys (not me, since I was piloting) would drink a bottle of beer. In the thin air they'd each get drunk on a single bottle. But back on the ground, they'd sober up fast.

One time on Luzon, Eakin heard about a Filipino who had a still. He said the guy was asking for $200 plus an Army Jeep in exchange for a bottle. I told Eakin to give him $220 and the Jeep, but also to tell the MPs to check out the guy for a missing Jeep, so we wouldn't be out a Jeep for the liquor. The trade went down just as I planned. Eakin thought I was a brilliant businessman.

/7IRG(5M47-2-6)(1-0-17)(2-16-0830-1110)(24 · 100÷800')(CORREGIDOR INVASION)(438X1-36)

Our troops invade Corregidor as we re-occupy it from the retreating Japanese. Bataan, three miles north of Corregidor, is in the background.

throttles forward and go for the ocean.

The rookie's brother wanted to take a picture of his twin. I don't know how they coordinated this foolhardiness, but the planes got up to about 4,000 feet. The brother got his picture, all right — of his twin's plane getting shot down. He got a whole series of photos, as the plane crashed on the ground in the middle of Formosa. In fact, I have the pictures in my den at home.

That was the end of the crew I had saved on its first-ever mission.

Years later, the surviving twin and his mother visited me. They were from Jackson, Miss. I took them out to dinner. That night, the mother said, "I want to thank you so much for bringing my son home the night you got lost."

Hell, he got killed later! I thought, what the hell's the matter with her?

People can be strange. She still had a warm place in her heart for me because her son had written home about me after that flight from hell.

OH, HOW I ADMIRED Col. C.T. Thompson.

Our squadron was the lead combat flying outfit in our group. We were the first ones in against enemy targets and bore the brunt of their firepower. Much later, what we called a "fat-cat" outfit of B-25s would hit the targets in mop-up missions. We'd have gotten shot up and shot down, but they'd return to base without a scratch.

If that wasn't enough, they flew European-style: 25 combat missions, and they could go home. We were locked into flying 300 hours of combat. How do you account for such a discrepancy in policies? Easy. That's the military for you.

The military would take typists and make them mess officers. This actually happened in our outfit. The military is all screwed up.

The enlisted men in our squadron, enraged about the fat-cat outfit, got together and decided to go on strike.

Col. Thompson called me in. "I hear there's some unrest in your outfit," he said.

I always played these things down. Let the men grumble. It never amounted to much in the scheme of things.

"There's a little talk about combat hours," I said.

"Well you assemble everybody, all officers, all enlisted men, at 1400."

Two of our bombers on a mission somewhere. My B-25 is on the left.

I got everybody together at 1400 in front of the platform. The colonel got up in front of us. He was in his 30s, a bit shorter than I was, but a leader every inch of him.

"I hear there's some unrest from you people," he said. "I'm not sure if you're aware of this, but we're at war with Japan . . . "

We looked at each other like he was crazy.

". . . and you're unhappy about flying 300 combat hours, and you're all flying every other day. Until you get a little happier, you're now all flying EVERY day. Dismissed!"

He walked off the platform and returned to his office.

The enlisted men gathered together. Gee, they said, maybe we better get happier.

A half-hour later, the men came to me and said they thought they'd better shut up.

I went to see Thompson.

"Colonel," I said, "you got the job done."[14]

ANOTHER TIME, COL. THOMPSON called me in. He knew I had A-20 flight time.

"There's a new airplane down at Mindoro," he said. "There's a factory man with it. I want you to go down and check it out and give me a report on it." I was to recommend whether the military should buy the plane.

To me, going to Mindoro was like getting a vacation in Hawaii, right in the middle of combat. I couldn't believe my great good fortune.

I took my engineer, Morrow, and navigator, Eakin, with me to go check out this new plane, this A-26 that the brass was eager to take on. It was supposed to be a little faster than our other planes, and maneuver a little better.

We flew to Mindoro to check out the plane. The next day I was in for another surprise: a Major Harris, a group adjutant, flew down to Mindoro with a pair of captain's tracks for me. "Congratulations, Piazzo, you're now a captain," he said. The tracks were accompanied by a little note from our group commander, Col. Thompson.

---

14 Col. Thompson did overrule me on one occasion. After we set up base in Luzon, we officers sat at a big dinner with the mayor of the town and other dignitaries. I was next to the mayor; he told me the U.S. military owed the town $40 to pay for coconut trees we'd cut down. I was incensed: coconuts grew on the island the way sagebrush does in Nevada. I asked him what the Japs had paid for destroyed coconut trees. Nothing, he admitted. I told him we'd pay exactly what the Japs had paid. The next morning, Col. Thompson ordered me to fill out a voucher for $40. That's politics.

After six weeks in combat I had been promoted from second lieutenant to captain. But I didn't like it; I didn't want to have a higher rank than my buddies. What's more, I didn't give a damn about rank.

So I refused it.

"You're crazy," Major Harris said.

"No I'm not, I don't want to be captain, period," I said.

Unbeknownst to me, he put my promotion through, anyway. The next day he came up to me and said, "I'm sorry, it's too late. You're going to be a captain."

All my training stateside had made me the best pilot in the outfit. Thus, I had the best kill ratio.[15] Sixteen-millimeter cameras were strapped to the guns and bomb bays on our planes, and after a mission, intelligence officers developed the "cans" (cassettes) of film right away. The intelligence officers would judge how much of a target was destroyed. My 90 percent kill-rate average was uncommonly high.

At Mindoro, I ran into a buddy, "Bull Moose" Johnson, who was a captain, and would remain so for the duration of the war. He saw my captain's bars and figured I'd put them on as a joke, just to fool him. I never did convince him until later on, after the war, when I visited him up in Alaska.

Anyway, back to the A-26.

Eakin and I checked in with the major there, and he introduced me to the man from the airplane factory, an old, bald guy whose task was to sell me on the airplane.

The major was a real miserable bastard. "Geez," I said to him, "I'd love to take this airplane up to my outfit and check them out, show it to them."

"Under no circumstances!" he said.

The factory salesman ultimately failed to sell me on the A-26 because — against his urging — I insisted that I fly the plane in formation. That's when I discovered that the cockpit was too low and you couldn't see the lead plane in formation, and vice versa.

Returning to Mindoro after a test flight, the airfield was socked in with fog. We couldn't land. I told Eakin to make sure he got the name of the man in the control tower and the precise time, to the second, that we radioed him. We continued on to Clark Field in Luzon. It, too, was socked in. Again, my navigator recorded the exact time and the name of the guy in the control tower. I ended up flying back to my outfit at Lenguyen Gulf. They all came out to check out the new airplane. We were big shots.

The next day, I took the A-26 back to Mindoro. The miserable major really chewed me out. I explained how we had been socked in at the other airfields and couldn't land. He didn't listen to that. He got mad — so I got mad, too.

"Major," I said, "if you ever have guts enough to come up there where they're fighting the war, you might have to borrow an airplane from me, you chickens— so-and-so."

Back on Luzon, I reported to Col. Thompson. I hadn't made up my report on the A-26 yet.

"Well, make it up, in duplicate," he said.

I put all the information in it. Maneuverability. Fuel consumption.

My last two paragraphs were forthright in expressing my opinions. "From a pilot's standpoint, due to maneuverability and speed, I find it to be an excellent ship. However, I feel that its limited visibility for formation flying and limited stations

---

[15] Yes, all that extra training had honed my skills. Before takeoff, the right wing man would taxi to the end of the airstrip, then the lead ship (mine) would taxi up, followed by the left wing man. A B-25 has a 67-foot wing span. I would taxi out, facing the left wing of the right wing man, lock my left brake and hit my right engine. I had a $5 standing bet that my wing tip would not be more than one foot from the other plane's wing tip. I never lost.

for photographic work greatly hinder the tactical value of the A-26 for the type of work that this squadron has done in the past."

In my last paragraph, I wrote: "Under no circumstance should we take this airplane on."

Col. Thompson called me in. He was angry. "Captain," he said, "you do not make that decision. Take that paragraph out of the letter."

I went back to my tent and reworded the paragraph: "It is understood that the above report is my personal opinion of

MANILA 6-7-'45

Manila on June 7, 1945, after we stopped bombing the city.

the A-26 type airplane, and does not necessarily express the opinion of any other member of the 17th squadron."

The colonel called me back in. He still was clearly upset.

"Colonel," I said, "I want to promise you something."

"What's that, captain?"

"I promise you, if you take on the A-26, we'll lose half of our crews going to and from the target and not from getting shot at. You can't fly formation in this thing."

He never said a word. Senior officers never give you that satisfaction.

But the Air Force never took on the A-26. Several months later, the A-26 was modified, with the cockpit moved three

feet higher.

As for my confrontation with the major in Mindoro: I found out he had written a report on how insubordinate I had been, and how I'd gone against all regulations. The report had gone all the way up the chain of command to Gen. MacArthur's office, then down the chain to our base. I read the last sentence. It said, "reprimand mandatory." It was signed by MacArthur's office, and by everyone else on the way down: the wing commander, and so on. It looked like a scroll.

There was a court-martial hearing. Thank God I had told Eakin to take down the time, the second, we radioed each airfield, and the name of the man in the tower. Eakin had a tendency to be lazy.

Here are two of our enlisted men hauling supplies with the help of a Filipino boy sitting astride a water buffalo.

The court-martial board had researched the entire incident in detail. The members deliberated.

Finally, a bird colonel came back into the room and said, "I've reviewed the case. The man is correct. Dismissed."

YES, EVEN AFTER ALL my combat hours, I had come very close to being court-martialed. They would have done it, too, had I not been scrupulous about recording my flight log. I'm sure many men who valiantly risked their lives in the war ended up disgraced by court-martials for outlandish reasons. That's the service for you.

I remember on Mindoro, the mess hall always was dusty and dirty. We could hear the mess sergeant chopping big gallon cans with a cleaver. He'd hit them three times and they'd open up. The contents were dehydrated: mashed potatoes, everything. He'd put the food on a bench without even removing it from the cans and yell out, "Soup's on!"

We'd come in with our mess kits. The wind would blow the dust on the food in the cans. "Jesus," some of the guys would say.

"That's not dust," I'd say, "that's pepper!" I'd just be kidding them.

We had to eat this crap to live. But I got mad about the way our food was being handled, so I went to see the C.O.

"What the hell's the matter with you guys?" I said. "You got a goddamned mess sergeant, all he does is open up cans."

"Well you got any suggestions?" Col. Thompson asked.

"Yeah, let's go through the MOs and find a guy who was a waiter or a cook. Bump him up in rank if you have to."

Searching our files, we found a guy who had been a fry cook in Brooklyn. We called him in and made him our mess sergeant.

It worked out well. The guy was smart. He laid a rope around our compound and said that anything that came over the rope belonged to us.

A pig strayed across. That night, we had a roast pig.

Another time, a calf came over the rope. We ate like kings.

Getting the ex-fry cook to be our mess sergeant was a rare victory in the ranks. An outcome of logic. What I call a "forced reversal."[16]

THE MILITARY THREW ALL personality types together. Some guys I'll never forget — just terrific people. Others I'll never forget for other reasons.

Between flights we did what we could to unwind. Poker was one diversion. We didn't get paid much — about $250 a month — but what difference did it make on poker

---

[16] When we were bombing Manila at night, I told the pilots I was leading to avoid hitting the San Miguel Brewery. It was a large and established entity in Manila, and after we drove the Japs out we wanted it working. Well, only one bomb hit it. When we left Mindoro and were stationed at Luzon, I visited the brewery. Its managers were grateful we spared it. They gave me a free case of beer. Today, the brewery is very prominent in the beer industry, with many subsidiary businesses in the Philippines.

stakes, when we were probably going to be killed, anyway?

We'd make big bets, and that meant sometimes you incurred a big gambling loss. No one had $300 handy to pay up with, so records were kept. It made things a little more interesting. If you really needed money badly to pay a guy off, you could get an advance, what they called "partial pay." You'd go to the Partial Pay window, and next to you, at the Partial Post window, was the guy who beat you, sending his winnings back home.

I won more often than not. If you lost enough you ended up improving and becoming a good poker player. One thing I learned was that you can never beat a drunk. It's an old saying. At Nadzab, before I entered combat, I was playing poker in my tent one night. It was late; my co-pilot already was asleep on his cot. In walked one of our buddies, all gassed up. "C'mon," he slurred, "I wanna play. Are you playing stud . . .?"

He got in the game and beat us all. He couldn't be bluffed. He was aggressive and reckless, and ended up leaving the tent with all our money.

We played quite a bit of poker, on an extra cot or a makeshift table. We wore out whatever deck we used. I remember one deck was so bad the numbers were worn off and we had to count the pips to know what a card was. If a guy was half-smart, he could tell by the backs of the cards what they were, from whatever marks were worn into them from overuse. But nobody was that dishonest.

All of a sudden, one of the young guys received a set of plastic cards from his mother. He became the most popular guy in the whole squadron. The house rule was that nobody could bend those cards. They

were magnificent, we actually could read the numbers on them.

When I first went into combat, based on Mindoro, we had a mission to the island of Biak rained out. Sheets of rain made it too difficult to fly, so we stayed in our tent and played poker all night. I got beat and didn't have any money left. A fellow from Reno came into the tent. He was on his way home after finishing his combat tour. We shook hands; his name was Franklin Davis.

"You got any money?" I said. "I'm broke and I want to play poker tomorrow night."

"No problem," he said, without hesitation, "how much do you want?"

Here I am with Jackson, my Filipino houseboy, as we harvest bamboo for construction of the officers club on Mindoro. A bamboo bush is behind us.

He gave me $300, a small fortune.

I tore a scrap of paper off and wrote a note on it to my older sister, who was running the store for Chet and me. "Dear Olga," I wrote, "Franklin Davis lent me $300. Give him $300." And I signed it.

The next night, though, I won all my money back, and paid him.

About 20 years later I ran into Davis at the Chinese Pagoda restaurant in Sparks. He was there with his wife and son. I told them the story of how Franklin had made me the generous loan; then I bought them all dinner.

On the other end of the personality spectrum was a communications officer who won big at poker one night. All of us at the table were pilots except for him; his job was on the base, taking care of the radios and intercoms in the planes. A ground officer. At the game's conclusion, we started recording who owed what to whom, in the common fashion. "OK, Mike, I owe you $200." "OK, Link, you owe me $150." And so forth. The communications officer stood. "Wait a minute, fellas," he said. "I happen to know that tomorrow morning you guys are flying a hot mission. I want my money tonight." We wanted to kill the bastard on the spot. I went to Col. Thompson. "If you don't transfer him, we're going to kill the sonofabitch!" The colonel, as usual, didn't give me the satisfaction of a firm response. "Thanks for the information," he said.

But two days later, the communications officer was gone from our outfit. The colonel never said much, but he was full of action.

ANOTHER TIME-KILLING PASTIME on Mindoro involved bets on pack rats.

Our outfit had been billeted by the local dump, and we were inundated by the pack rats, dark-gray, furtive creatures 10 inches long. They stole in at night and ate whatever sustenance they found. True to their name, they'd leave something in its place, such as a shoe, dragged back to the spot. I had size 9 shoes. I'd get up in the morning and find, perhaps, two left shoes — one a size 10, one a size 8. Soon we had written our names on our shoes, and developed the ritual of assembling at the flagpole each morning. We'd call out the names on the shoes we'd found, and return them to their owners.

Some great brain in the military had issued us birdshot for our .45 automatic pistols, to take care of the pack-rat problem. That's like trying to eliminate all the sand in the ocean, one grain at a time. We learned to live with them, since we had no choice. The pack rats didn't attack people, except in rare circumstances. I'd given a pair of shoes to my Filipino houseboy, whom I'd nicknamed Jackson.[17] Jackson was 15 or 16, and a great kid. A few days after I'd nicknamed him, he said, "Sir, I want to thank you very much. I am honored. You have nicknamed me after one of your great presidents!" I didn't tell him that my nickname was meant to be just, plain "Jackson."

Jackson went to put his foot in a shoe, and a pack rat hiding inside bit him in the heel, tearing a chunk out.

We used to build makeshift shelves out of wood — I made most of them — and put them in our tents to hold our incidentals. On the top of our shelves we'd put the rock-hard biscuits wrapped in heavy oil paper, and write our names on them. At night we'd hear the pack rats crunching on those biscuits. It sounded just like a horse chomping. In the morning we'd check which biscuit had been eaten the most. The pot could have $50 in it. The guy with his name on the most-eaten biscuit would win the entire pot.

The pack rats liked anything salty. As newcomers to Mindoro, we got up that first morning and discovered there were no tongues in our shoes. The rats had chewed them all up, attracted by the dried sweat in the leather. None of us ended up with tongues in our shoes. We had canvas "B-4"

---

[17] I'd brought Jackson with me when our outfit had moved to Luzon from Mindoro. At that time we were flying the B-25 D model with the Plexiglas nose where the navigator manned two .50-caliber machine guns. That's where I asked Jackson to sit on the flight. When we landed at Lenguyen Gulf in Luzon, hundreds of Filipinos were standing at the edge of the landing strip, waving at us. They saw Jackson in the bomber's nose and he immediately was a bigshot Filipino. He couldn't understand the natives' dialect, but he learned it quickly.

Later, when we moved to Ie Shima, Col. Thompson said it would be best not to take Jackson for there were no "natives" on the island. Jackson had a brother on Luzon who was a guerilla soldier helping us, and so he remained on Luzon.

bags to hold our clothes. The bags were lined with leather trim. Your first morning in Mindoro, you'd pick the bag up and it would fall apart.

Once in awhile a rat would walk across the bamboo poles next to your cot, lose its balance and fall into the mosquito net draped over you. Immediately, you'd have to belt it off; the rat would get excited, trying to scramble off the net, and pee all over you. If you were a heavy sleeper, you'd wake up covered in piss in the morning.

The rats ended up proving useful to us as elements in a very gruesome game. To those who will find it inhumane, I only can say that we soldiers in combat lived in such a state of tension — alternately terrified or bored — that any relief was welcome.[18]

One night, my navigator, Eakin, woke me up with a flashlight. "I got a box full of rats," he said.

We received big boxes of "10-in-1 rations." Very little stuff in it was good eating, other than the bacon and cheese. There must have been 50 rats in the box Eakin indicated, attracted inside by crumbs.

"I'll hold the flashlight," Eakin said. "You stab. You only get one stab."

I took out my trench knife. I plunged it into the box.

I held the flashlight for Eakin, and he took a stab.

The co-pilot, Dotters, woke up. He directed his flashlight over at us. There we were, covered in blood, knives in our hands.

ABOVE: This is one of the two white "Betty" bombers, Japanese planes, that bore the surrender delegation to the American-held island of Ie Shima on Aug. 19, 1945. The Japanese envoys were transferred to an American C-54 transport plane en route to Manila, where they met with representatives of Gen. Douglas MacArthur, the Allied Supreme Commander, to make plans for the final capitulation by the Japanese empire and its occupation by Allied forces. BELOW: The Japanese surrender delegation awaits transport on Ie Shima.

He jumped out of his cot.

"What the hell's the matter with you guys!" he said. "What are you stabbing each other for?"

---

[18] Speaking of morale — "Tokyo Rose" became famous during the war in the Pacific for psychological warfare against us. Nearly every evening we could tune into the Japanese signal broadcasting the sultry female voice to us. The signal would play popular American music — songs geared to make us homesick as hell — and that sultry voice would come on to taunt us.

The remarkable thing was that shortly after our missions, the voice we dubbed "Tokyo Rose" would report on who the Japs had shot down — including the planes' numbers, and sometimes, even, the pilots' names. Tokyo Rose was amazingly accurate. When we did a lousy job on a target she would mention that.

A friend painted this picture for me.

"We're not stabbing each other, we're killing these rats."

"Oh," he said.

He quickly joined in our game.

That was the way we were. Absolutely "shack-happy."

WARFARE CAN WARP a person. It also can reveal extraordinary qualities.

There was a major named Henley in the Seventh Army. He was called a liaison man. His job meant living close to the Japanese troops. He had two or three enlisted men with him. All of them were tremendous woodsman. They lived in caves. Henley had a Piper Cub airplane and a Jeep, which he camouflaged.

Henley would drive his Jeep into our base bringing maps, and tell us where to bomb and strafe. Sometimes he'd signal us with smoke bombs. His directions were precise.

I became very good friends with him.

One day, he came into base and said, "Boy, I'll tell ya. The Japs are coming in like crazy." The area cited was off the beach a little ways north on Luzon. He gave us the coordinates.

We had nine airplanes ready in the squadron that day. We flew three flights of three each. We did not see any Japs or equipment on the ground. All we saw were coconut trees. But we strafed the hell out of the area and dropped the bombs.

Henley drove down a week later and said, "You guys killed 750 Japs and destroyed the whole outfit."

Another day he drove into our base and said, "Geez, I'd give anything to be able to catch some fish. We don't have any fishing tackle."

I went into our life rafts and found tackle for him.

A week or so later he came back to make his regular report. "That fishing tackle isn't worth a goddamn," he said. "We can't catch any fish."

I came up with a plan to get him some fish. Talk about violating regulations! We had a mission to Formosa. I told the flight leaders to tell their pilots: "Reserve one bomb." I said there was a Japanese submarine off shore, and added that it was a "secret mission" to bomb it.

We returned from the bombing mission over Formosa, each of our six planes in the squadron retaining one 500-pound bomb. Henley had told me exactly where he was camped. I had briefed him that on a particular day, at a particular time, I'd get some fish for him.

The bombs usually were set for a one-tenth second delay, to allow us to get away before the explosion. I had instructed the armament personnel to put a three-second delay on these last bombs for our "secret mission."

As we reached the spot off shore from Henley's hidden camp, I gave the order for the bombs to be dropped. We dropped them, then made a circle. Below, thousands of fish lay belly up at the surface. One, probably a whale, was 50 feet long, white-bellied and dead in the water. One of the pilots thought it was the Jap submarine.

Henley came down to base a couple days later. "Holy Christ," he said. "We've been eating fish. We smoked a ton of them. Oh, what a wonderful thing!"

It was a successful fishing trip. If Col. Thompson had caught me doing that, I don't know what he would have done.

HERE ARE A COUPLE other crazy things we did while stationed on Luzon.

Our squadron was set up next to a cemetery. Our officers' mess hall was directly across the street from the cemetery and we witnessed several funerals as we sat eating.

Several times, returning from a mission, I would buzz the cemetery — just hot-dogging — and fly very close to the tombstones. One day a sergeant informed me that Lt. Enzenbacker was going to fly lower over the tombstones than I did. Enzenbacker was a good pilot and a good friend. I often selected him to fly as one of my wing men.

The day he decided to fly his low stunt, I was looking out the windows of our mess hall. He did a pretty good job of flying low, perhaps as low as I did, but not lower. His only problem was that he forgot to pull up in time. He ran into the top of a coconut grove at the end of the cemetery. Tons of coconuts rattled to the ground.

I jumped in my Jeep and drove to the flight line. Enzenbacker had torn off his right wing tip and destroyed his right landing light. The lieutenant in charge was making out a report, which would be placed in Enzenbacker's record.

I instructed the lieutenant to tear up the report, and to go to the bone yard, get a wing tip and landing light, and replace them on the plane without recording the incident. He reluctantly did so, and Enzenbacker was very appreciative.

Here's another bit of hijinks. On occasion, when the bay at Lenguyen was calm, a few of us would each put up $5 and a can of beer (which was more precious than money) as a prize to whoever flew lowest over the water. Four or five pilots would participate.

We would fly over the water — and feel the vibration of the propellers cutting through the water (it's a wonder we weren't sucked under). To those on shore we must have looked like boats. We would land and measure the depth of the salt on the props;

Hiroshima shortly after the atomic bomb was dropped on Aug. 6, 1945. I had
these photos taken by my crew on my secret, unauthorized mission.

Nagasaki, shortly after the atomic bomb was dropped on Aug. 9, 1945.

Nagasaki 1945

the plane with the longest run of salt, from the tip of the prop down, won.

I participated in this contest three times and won each time — thanks, once more, to my far greater amount of flying time.

THE NUMBER OF BOMBS, each representing a mission, painted on the side of my crew's B-25 added up. We accumulated more than any other crew.

We never felt like the tide of war had changed so greatly in our favor that we were home free. The danger always was there.

When I sat with Col. Thompson, giving him my report on the A-26, I said, "Colonel, I think we're winning this goddamn war. We came all the way from Australia. We're now on Ie Shima."

Ie Shima is the closest island to the Japanese main islands. We were preparing for the final invasion. We knew our casualties would be enormous. We expected the Japanese to fight to the last man. It was not a pretty picture.

I, however, had reason to relax. I had completed all my required 300 combat hours. My combat flying was done.

And then — out of the blue — the news came that we had dropped a "big bomb." That's what we called it. It had wiped out the Japanese city of Hiroshima. Three days later, another "big bomb" destroyed the city of Nagasaki. We didn't even know they were atom bombs — or what atom bombs even were. We knew nothing about radioactivity.

The two "big bombs" had destroyed "the two big bomb towns," Hiroshima and Nagasaki, on Aug. 6 and 9, respectively. We were elated that the war appeared to have been won. What relief!

But we were mystified about the "big bombs." It turned out that even some of the

My photos of Hiroshima and Nagasaki are in the George S. Patton Museum, near Indio in southern California.

PHOTOS TAKEN BY CAPTAIN LINK PIAZZO. B-25 PILOT. 5th AIR FORCE. 17th SQUADRON IN AUGUST 1945, SHORTLY AFTER THE BOMBS WERE DROPPED.

crewmen on the Enola Gay, which had dropped the bomb on Hiroshima, were clueless about the nature of the weapon they were disgorging.

Col. Thompson called me in. "I don't want any of your airplanes going over the big bomb towns," he said. "They're highly restricted."

Here we'd been dropping bombs that we thought were big — 1,000-pound bombs. How could one bomb wipe out an entire town? I was hungry to check it out.

That evening, I prepared a personal mission. I had access to any of our airplanes.

Here were two towns, completely wiped out. My curiosity overwhelmed me.

I went up to our photo lab technician. "I want you to get the best cameras you got, two cameramen, we're going on a secret mission," I said.

I recruited my radioman, Harry Hall. "Harry," I said, "you call in on the radio different coordinates from where we are."

My co-pilot, Dotters, and navigator, Eakin, and the three photographers rounded out my surreptitious crew. I told them we were conducting a secret reconnaissance mission to Sakashima Island.

The big, heavy K-17 cameras were loaded on board my B-25. We weren't carrying any guns or ammo.

We took off at 4 a.m. I flew to Hiroshima and Nagasaki. It was Aug. 11.

I came in low, 20 feet off the ground. Hiroshima was charred black. Buildings were completely gutted, the concrete standing. Silhouettes of people were burned into the walls as shadows.

I've had the question asked 1,000 times over the ensuing decades. "What was your impression?"

My answer, "Eerie. Absolute eerie."

We'd been dropping 500- and 1,000-pound bombs for three-and-a-half years. And to see what one bomb did gives you nothing less than an eerie feeling.

I flew down one of the main streets. Ten or so people were in the street. They turned around and waved to our plane.

"Geez, that was really funny, they waved at us like we were friends," Harry Hall said.

To this day, I have absolutely no idea what accounted for their waving.

I flew over Nagasaki. There were no people in the streets.

This trip impressed on me how omnipotent my country was at that moment in history.

It's claimed now, a half-century hence, that there are bombs of mass destruction that make the A-bombs that we dropped on Japan look like firecrackers. There is no doubt in my mind that one of these days, maybe after my lifetime, one of these crazy bastards with these bombs of mass destruction is going to say, "We've got the power, let's press the button."

One of these days, a country like China or Russia is going to decide to take on the rest of the world. Read history. Look what's happening in tiny Iraq; the world can't control its dictator.

I was 26 that day I flew over Hiroshima and Nagasaki. It wasn't until years later that I realized I had caught an up-close glimpse of what Armageddon will be like.

IMMEDIATELY AFTER RETURNING TO base, I had the photo lab technician develop our film of 36 exposures. I had him make up a set for everybody in the crew, plus four other sets for close friends of mine.

It was a day or so after our secret private mission. We were sitting at the outdoor theater on base. The projector shut off. Over the public address system came an announcement: "We have word that one of our planes went over the big bomb towns. Anybody with information about this, report to headquarters immediately."

The announcement was repeated.

"Very serious consequences" were promised for non-compliance.

It's amazing how news travels in the military.

No one rose from a seat.

Most of my crewmen panicked and burned their photos. They were sure they would have been court-martialed.

Harry Hall, the radioman, destroyed all but six of his exposures. He cut each in half and smuggled them home in his stationery. Four decades later, he wrote a detailed account of the secret mission for *Soldier of Fortune* magazine.

I kept all 36 of my prints. I ended up smuggling them home under my shirt.

Many years later, when I was a member of the Indian Wells country club in Palm

Desert, Calif., I made a few sets of prints for friends. Another of my friends visited the George S. Patton Museum, near Indio in southern California. The museum has memorabilia from both the European and Pacific theaters. My friend told the curator about my photographs.

The curator called me at Indian Wells. He introduced himself over the phone.

"A friend of yours says you have low-level pictures of Hiroshima and Nagasaki."

"Why do you ask?" I said.

"I'd consider hanging them in the museum," he said.

Helen and I drove down and showed him the pictures.

He selected four. They are exhibited on a wall under a flood light, along with a plaque with my name on it and statistics on the atomic bombings.

Peter Mausolite (bottom left, in uniform), myself and Al Solari in Tokyo, with Japanese residents, 1945.

THREE DAYS AFTER THE bombing of Nagasaki, Japanese emissaries from Tokyo landed on Ie Shima in a white Betty bomber with a big cross on it. They had come to surrender. We transported them in our airplanes to Manila, where they met with Gen. MacArthur. They later gathered on the battleship Missouri. They signed the surrender document.

The war was over.

A few days later, Col. Thompson called me into his office. "We'd like you to go to Japan and open up our outfit," he said. The group was moving base to Japan for the occupation. There was an area with a bunch of huts, and he wanted me to get it prepared, check out the air strip, and so on.[19]

"Is this an order, sir?" I said.

"No."

"Well, thank you, but no thank you," I said.

The colonel, however, was insistent. I would be stuck overseas another few months before being shipped home, he said.

"I promise you this," Col. Thompson said. "If you go to Japan, you will get home as fast as these people who are getting ready to leave from here," he said.

I questioned it.

Thompson also said this: "I'm going to make you a major."

I didn't like that idea, either. I knew taking the commission would mean still more time being stuck overseas. Like everyone else, I was aching to get home as fast as I could.

"I think there's a regulation where a guy has to stay in the rank that he's raised three months," I said.

"That's correct," he said, "but I think it'll take three months before we leave here."

---

[19] When we were moving to Ie Shima from Luzon, Col. Thompson had told me to find lumber to build the latrines. Ie Shima was a small island with no timber. So I tore up the floors of the nice officer's club I'd built on Luzon and had the wood loaded into the bomb bays of several B-25s.

A ground sergeant came up to me and said the enlisted men were not going to fly on the bombers to Ie Shima if we were going to carry lumber. It seems that before I joined the squadron, the outfit had transported lumber, stacking it above the bomb bays — where it had destroyed a plane's control cables, jammed the controls and caused the plane to crash, killing the crew.

I told the sergeant we were ferrying the lumber in the bomb bays and there was no danger, and that we were leaving at 5 the next morning. If he and the others weren't on the planes they could find their own way to Ie Shima, and after they arrived they'd be busted down to buck privates. The next morning they showed up at the bombers to travel to Ie Shima.

Later, I told Col. Thompson what had happened, and asked if he would have backed me up about demoting the enlisted men. In a typical response from him, he didn't say a word.

"No thanks," I said, refusing a major's commission.

I relented that evening about setting up the base on Japan. Peter Mausolite, an intelligence officer and friend of mine, told me, back at the tent, that he was looking forward to going to Japan. He picked up native languages wherever he was: New Guinea, the Philippines. He knew I'd choose him if I went to Japan. So I changed my mind. But I would never be a major.

Back when we were based on Luzon, the squadron commander of the P-51 fighter planes in our group was a guy named Bill Shomo. Major Shomo was a very good friend of mine. We'd help each other. If one of us needed a Jeep, he'd borrow it from the other. Coming back from flying fighter cover on one mission, Shomo encountered a Betty bomber, one of the Japanese heavy bombers. Fifteen Zeros were escorting it.

Shomo made a pass and knocked one of the Zeros down. He made another pass and knocked another down. The Zeros did not break away to engage the P-51s. Shomo's wing man shot a couple more of them out of the sky. In all, Shomo himself took down seven Zeros in 15 minutes before heading away, low on gas.

Much later, after the war, it came out that the Japanese fighters were under orders not to break formation. The bomber was escorting Gen. Tojo, the Japanese war minister and prime minister.

Most pilots would have seen the 15 Zeros and flown the other way. Not Shomo. He had been crazy enough to take a whack at them.

Knocking down five airplanes qualified a pilot as an "ace." Shomo had knocked down seven in one engagement. His wing man had knocked down four.

Shomo related the whole thing to me back at base.

"S—, you oughta be court-martialed, Bill!" I said.

"What do you mean, court-martialed?"

"That Betty bomber had to have *somebody* important in it. Why didn't you knock down the Betty bomber, you dumb bastard."

The Air Corps brass had other ideas.

Shomo was named to receive the Congressional Medal of Honor, the highest award our nation gives one of its citizens. It was a political deal — the Army and Navy each had had one of their own awarded the medal; the Air Corps had not. Shomo was designated for the honor.

We were playing poker a few days after Shomo's one-sided dogfight with the Zeros. Somehow, he had gotten hold of a jug of booze. This was extremely difficult at that point of the war. On New Guinea guys flew back and forth to Australia, and returned with liquor. But now we were all the way up on Luzon. Still, Shomo had a jug with him at the table. He got pretty drunk. And then he started getting crazy.

"I'm going to fly a P-47!" he said.

The P-47 is a tough plane to fly. And he was going to fly one at night, and while drunk.

He left the tent and found a P-47 and took it for a joy ride. Then he returned to the poker table.

A military policeman showed up at our tent. He announced that Shomo was to leave at once for Manila. The theater commander was going to pin the Medal of Honor on him.

"Oh, tell that MacArthur to go f— himself," Shomo said, drunkenly. "I'm not going to Manila."

The MP left.

A few days later, we were playing poker

again. The MP showed up again. This time, he had his .45 drawn.

"Major," he said, "I have orders from Gen. MacArthur. You have 10 minutes to get ready. You're leaving with me to go to Manila. Throw a few things together and let's get going."

Shomo returned from Manila with the medal and a page-long certificate. It was quite a deal that came with the medal. No more combat the rest of his life was just one benefit. Shomo also was relieved of various tax obligations. Best of all: he was going home.

Shomo was a nice guy, but he was one of these cocky airmen.[20] I guess we all were kind of cocky. We were flying in life-and-death situations on a regular basis, so what the hell did we care about rank and medals, if the next mission, or the one after that, we were going to get killed?

As it turned out, after I'd turned down Col. Thompson's offer to bump me up to major if I'd hang around three more months, I was stuck overseas three months anyway.

I should have accepted the commission.

I MADE ONE OTHER unauthorized mission, in addition to the flights over Hiroshima and Nagasaki.

We had been told that under no circumstances were we to fly to Shanghai in China. We were told there was no food or fuel there.

That was enough for me to decide to fly there. It only was a couple hundred miles away. I had plenty of fuel to get there and back. I had no intention of landing, just to pass over and return to base on Ie Shima. But as I flew over the airfield, I decided to see if I could get radio transmission. I circled and tried a couple frequencies.

Finally, I got contact. "Shanghai tower, come on in, would you like landing instructions?"

"Yes," I said. Without even thinking I added, "I'm having trouble with my starboard engine. I'd like to land."

"Oh yes, land immediately. Clear to land."

I turned to my engineer — it wasn't my regular one, Morrow — and said, "The minute I cut the engines, get your ass out, take the cowling off, and make believe you're working on it."

"No problem," he said.

I landed. I looked out. A fire truck and an ambulance approached, which they do for emergency landings. This, of course, was no emergency.

It turned out the guys were from the 14th Air Force, and were curious about my plane. They'd never seen a Fifth Air Force patch. It was like being from Mars to them.

"I'd like to talk to your commander," I said.

They sent me over to him. He was a major.

"I'd like to get into Shanghai," I said. "You got any transportation?"

He laughed. "Hell, I've been here for a few days, and I can't get into Shanghai."

"Are you the base commander?" I said.

"Hell no, he's across the field," he said.

---

[20] When our outfit moved base from Luzon to Ie Shima, Col. Thompson told me to escort the P-51 squadron (27 planes), which Shomo would lead. No U.S. airman had been to the island yet, which was a mile or so west of Okinawa. I was to contact the Navy on a secret frequency to receive radio coordinates for a corridor to Ie Shima. The day was cloudy with little visibility. My navigator, Eakin, got us lost. Shomo finally broke radio silence.
"Link, little friends (our nickname for fighter planes) are running out of gas," he said. "You better find a landing field, quick."
"Bill, we're on radio silence. Just relax," I said. I didn't add that I was completely lost. I was mad at my navigator and took his maps away.
I looked down. There was an opening in the clouds and I saw land. It had to be Okinawa — occupied by the Japanese!
All of a sudden I saw nothing but ocean. I knew I was now north of Okinawa. I made a 180-degree turn to the left and found Ie Shima. I instructed the squadron to land.
On the landing strip I asked Shomo, "What were you nervous about?"
I never revealed we'd been completely lost a few minutes before landing.

I went over to him. I introduced myself to the colonel, and said I'd had an emergency and had to land. I added that I'd like to get into Shanghai if possible.

He treated me like I was from Mars, too.

"What outfit are you with?" he asked.

"The 17th," I said.

"What wing?"

"Seventy-first."

"Seventy-first?" he said. "Do you know Col. Sams?"

"I sure do," I said. Col. Sams was a mean sonofabitch. I'd only seen him two or three times.

"He's my brother-in-law," the colonel said.

Holy s—! There I was in Shanghai, against orders. This officer's brother-in-law is Sams.

The colonel got on the phone, and shortly after, two charcoal-burning limousines pulled up. I, my navigator and radioman were chauffeured into Shanghai. I'd won at poker the night before and had some money. I divided it among the three of us.

Shanghai was teeming with humanity — shoulder-to-shoulder people on the main streets. Items were so cheap. The Chinese port was suffering from tremendous inflation; the citizens needed foreign cash. A typewriter was $2. A camera was $2.50. What to do? We went to a bank to change currency. I handed the clerks $20 American. The clerks returned with a big stack of dog-eared, Chinese greenbacks, tied with twine. We stuffed the bills in our shirts.

I got a tap on the shoulder from a guy. He was a White Russian, a refugee from the

Col. Thompson and myself with three Japanese children in Tokyo, 1945.

Soviet Union. He spoke English. He took me aside. "You know, you made a mistake, " he said. "You didn't go to the right bank. You didn't get enough money.

"Don't cash any American money," he said. "If you buy one of my watches, I'll be your guide."

Just like in the comic books, he pulled back a sleeve to reveal an assortment of watches running up his arm. I bought one for $1. We had a guide now for Shanghai. He took us around. We loaded up on souvenirs, incredulous at the cheap prices. Oriental rugs for $40 or $50, which now would be worth thousands of dollars. A dress in a store window had a tag listing a price in Chinese money of $1,900,000, or so. Inflation was rampant.

The guide gave me some good advice. We loaded up on souvenirs. I bought several kimonos, and a miniature rickshaw, handmade of teak wood, about a foot long. We made out like bandits. We'd had found the market of paradise.

Immediately after I landed our plane back at base on Ie Shima, Col. Thompson informed me, "Col. Sams wants to see you."

I knew damn well what had happened. His brother-in-law at the base in Shanghai had contacted him. Sams had contacted my group commander. Now Sams was calling me on the carpet. I knew his type. He was a frustrated West Point graduate who could never make general, for whatever political reasons. He was a pissed-off individual. He was miserable to his subordinates.

Col. Sams was based on Okinawa, which

was so close to le Shima you had to radio for landing instructions when you were still on the ground before takeoff. I flew over and found his office, which was in a hut.

I knocked on the door and waited. No response. I knocked some more. Ten minutes passed. "Come in!" he finally said.

I walked in and stood at attention, saluting. Sams was at his desk, his head down. He chewed tobacco, and driplets rolled down his cheeks. He sat there, not looking at me or saying a thing, letting me stand there another 10 minutes. He did that with everybody. The guy was demented.

Finally, he looked up. "What are you doing here?"

"Capt. Piazzo, sir. You sent for me."

"Oh, yeah. One of our airplanes landed in Shanghai. I want you to send two airplanes over, pick up the crew and fly them to Manila. They ran out of gas, and here are the orders. They're being court-martialed, every one of them."

I was stunned. Here I was, having just returned from Shanghai myself. Now I was to ferry guys just like me who were being sent to the brig, all because, unlike me, they'd been caught.

I took the orders and flew back to le Shima. I told our squadron flight leader to go pick the guys up and fly them to Manila.

The next night I was playing poker at a table with some guys, including Col. Thompson. I never lied to my commander, but I did keep quiet about certain things. He was sitting to my left.

"I hear one of your airplanes landed at Shanghai," he said.

"Oh, is that right?"

Silence. Thompson was a man of few words. A tremendous man.

"Captain," he said, "I'd give anything to have one of those kimonos."

Some jackass had squealed on us!

"Colonel," I said, "you'll have one in about 20 minutes!"

I left the table and returned with the best kimono I had.

He could've court-martialed me for breaking regulations. But he must have respected me for doing a good job where it mattered — in combat.

Col. Thompson's adjutant was a guy named Duffy who disliked me.[21] I heard through the grapevine, after the war, that Duffy had gone into Thompson's office and said, "Piazzo is violating regulations." I'm not sure which violation he was referring to — I violated so many regulations. Perhaps it was my trip to Shanghai.

"Is that right?" the colonel had told his adjutant. "He's also helping shorten the war."

In other words, mind your own business.

Col. Thompson was that smart. He was a hell of a man.

THE WAR WAS OVER. We now were occupying Japan.

Our group's base area was to be in Yokota, a small town west of Tokyo. I had three officers and six enlisted men to help me get the base in order.

To fly to Japan we had to arrange our own transport. I went to an air transport command unit on le Shima and arranged with the C.O. for a C-46 cargo plane to take my personnel plus a Jeep to Atsugi airstrip in Tokyo. I looked at the pilot and co-pilot. They looked like they were each 14 or 15.

---

21   Most of us first and second lieutenants disliked Capt. Duffy. When we joined the 17th squadron, Duffy outranked us. We were told he preferred that none of us would be raised to his rank. Too bad for him. After I became a captain, I challenged him on occasion. When I became squadron leader I was able to raise my flight leaders to the rank of captain. Duffy would pigeonhole my requests to Col. Thompson. I spotted them one time and yanked them out of the bottom of the files, then had a heart-to-heart talk with Duffy. After that, Col. Thompson received my requests.

I asked the pilot how much flying time he had. Evasively, he answered, "Quite a lot."

Halfway over the China Sea I noticed the pilot and co-pilot were nervous. They were running low on fuel and didn't know how to switch the fuel tanks. I asked for a tech manual — they didn't even know what it was. I found the manual, ripped out the fuel system pages and found how to switch the tanks. It took me two or three minutes to find the information. We would have had to ditch the plane.

Close calls never ended.

I prepared to set up our headquarters. Gen. MacArthur issued a direct order, in writing, that we had come to Japan not as tourists but conquerors. We commanding officers were to commandeer *anything* to make our men comfortable. We drove from Tokyo to Yokota, our area, in two trucks full of our men, and went to a race track country club in the town.

I found beautiful teak furniture and other items in the club. I had it loaded in the trucks. As we were removing the furniture, an older Japanese man from the club came out screaming in Japanese. I put my .45 pistol to his forehead and pointed to a seat. He sat.

And so we were very comfortable at our new base. A week later, another directive came from MacArthur's office stating he hoped we'd made our men comfortable and there'd be no more commandeering.

Next thing I did at the base was request eight or 10 Japanese helpers.

"What do mean eight or 10? We'll give you 100 or 200," a guy in headquarters told me.

I opened up the little cabins on the base. The Japanese custom is to remove one's shoes before entering a home. Inside the cabins lay woven grass mats. I feared they were infected, so I told my workers to re-

ARMY AIR FORCES

Certificate of Appreciation

FOR WAR SERVICE

TO

LINCOLN E. PIAZZO

I CANNOT meet you personally to thank you for a job well done; nor can I hope to put in written words the great hope I have for your success in future life.

Together we built the striking force that swept the Luftwaffe from the skies and broke the German power to resist. The total might of that striking force was then unleashed upon the Japanese. Although you no longer play an active military part, the contribution you made to the Air Forces was essential in making us the greatest team in the world.

The ties that bound us under stress of combat must not be broken in peacetime. Together we share the responsibility for guarding our country in the air. We who stay will never forget the part you have played while in uniform. We know you will continue to play a comparable role as a civilian. As our ways part, let me wish you God speed and the best of luck on your road in life. Our gratitude and respect go with you.

COMMANDING GENERAL
ARMY AIR FORCES

My certificate of appreciation for war service, signed by Gen. "Hap" Arnold.

move the mats, put them in the center of the compound and burn them. Then I had the cabins fumigated.

I ordered my workers to remove the "honey buckets," containers in which the Japanese defecated. One of the Japanese boys who spoke a little English said, "No no, you get free vegetables and fruit for that." The contents of the honey buckets had been traded to the farmers, who needed fertilizer. I was insistent.

The man at headquarters who had assigned me the Japanese workers had told me one thing the workers couldn't stand were picks and shovels, because they were small people. "If you have any trouble with them, have them dig a hole, and then have them fill it, then have them dig it again," he'd said.

So I assembled some picks and shovels. I did run into trouble with having some workers produce, so I ordered them, through my Japanese translator, to dig holes.

I went back to headquarters a couple days later, and the guy who'd assigned me the workers said, "Jesus, you're all screwed up."

The commanding officer of Yokota Air Base named the control tower "Reno Tower" for me. Quite an honor!

"What do you mean I'm screwed up?"

"You're having window glaziers scrub floors. You're having labor guys glaze windows."

"Hell, I can't tell the difference!"

"Oh, Jesus Christ, didn't I give you a chart?"

The workers had Japanese designs on the backs of their shirts identifying their occupations: carpenter, bricklayer, and so forth.

With the help of my translator, I figured out what the designs meant, and reassigned the workers properly.

After that, things went much more smoothly. The Japanese were very hard workers.

Now that we were the victorious occupiers, some of our guys got a big attitude. The first night at the base, we were in the officer's mess. A Japanese kid, about 12, was carrying in a big tray of food. He walked down the aisle between tables.

The Japanese custom is to bow to those in authority. He bowed to officers before laying down his tray.

A major got up behind the boy and kicked him in the behind, sending food flying.

That precipitated the third occasion on which I clashed with someone of superior rank. I got up and went over.

"Major, I don't know if you know this," I said, "but the war is over. I'm certain this young man had *nothing* to do with it. But listen closely. Next time you do that, I'm going to knock your goddamn head off!"

A hush settled on the room. Here was this captain talking to a major this way.

We resumed our meal.

The next day, I was talking with the colonel who ran the base. I had met him a couple days earlier. He'd asked where I was from, and after I'd told him, he'd named the control tower "Reno Tower." The next day, "Reno Tower, Yakota Army Air Base" was painted on the tower. In fact, it stayed "Reno Tower" for a long time.

"I hear you had a little conversation with the major last night," the colonel said, standing in the tower with me now.

"Oh, we had a little discussion," I said.

"Anything I can do for you, just let me know," the colonel said. He was a terrific man.

I looked down. A squadron of B-24s were

parked on the hard concrete. The concrete lots — we called them "hard stands" — turned me on. On our bases on the Philippines, we'd been flying off mud and coral.

"Gee," I said, "when I call for my airplanes, colonel, I'd love to have part of that concrete."

"Don't worry," he said, "when the time comes, you'll get part of the hard stands."

The next night I went down to dinner. The major came over to my table and said, "You think you're going to get some of that concrete hard stand, you've got another guess coming." Unbeknownst to me, he was the CO of the B-24s parked on the hard stands.

"Major," I said, "your problem is not with me, it's with the colonel. Go talk to the colonel about it."

The next morning I went up into the tower again. "I hear you had another conversation with the major," the colonel said.

Again, I kind of pawned it off.

"Look down," he said.

I looked down. No B-24s.

"I made that bastard move them all over in the grass," the colonel said. "I was going to give you half of the hard stands. You get 'em all."

I don't know why the colonel liked me so much. I remember the first day I'd reported to him in the tower, he'd hugged me and said, "God, I'm glad to see ya." Jesus, I'd never had a bird colonel hug me. We had a nice conversation. He knew of my outfit's war record.

Indeed, the 17th had one hell of a record. As for myself, I'd flown 67 combat missions, and earned 13 medals, included the American Theater Medal, WW II Victory Medal,

Philippine Liberation Medal, the Asiatic Pacific Service Medal and the best one of all: the Distinguished Flying Cross. But though I'd earned them, I didn't have even one in my possession.

A sergeant sometimes would come to my crew's tent after a mission and say, "Piazzo, report to group headquarters, you just earned an air medal." He'd go through the list, naming other members of our crew.

"Piss on those medals," we'd say. "Give them to that sonofabitch Duffy. What the hell good's a medal?"

We didn't care for Duffy, Col. Thompson's adjutant. And we didn't give a damn about medals.

I didn't learn until 43 years after the war that the military kept records of the medals we'd earned. That's a subject for a later chapter.[22]

WHEN I GOT OUR base ready in Yokota, I was to notify Col. Thompson by teletype that we were ready for the airplanes and flying personnel to arrive. Rain was constant, and every morning the base commander and I would go out and step on the grass and dirt of the airstrip, to see if it was solid enough for the planes to land.

A week passed. Finally, one morning, I said, "Colonel, I'm going to send for the damn planes. We can't be here forever."

He questioned the condition of the airstrip. But I went ahead and sent Col. Thompson a teletype.

The next morning, the 28 B-25s from our outfit arrived. The base commander and I were in the control tower, watching. "Colonel," I said, "we're going to ask the lousiest

---

[22] I was given a physical when I was mustered out. My left ear was very hard of hearing, because of flying the B-25 with the window open. Ex-B-25 pilots are typically deaf in the left ear, while co-pilots are deaf in the right ear. The B-25 is one of the noisiest airplanes ever built.

The physician, a major, told me my deafness was "service-related" and advised me to go to a Veterans Administration hospital.

"Stick the 'service-related' in your butt," I said. "I want to get out of the service."

Now I wear two hearing aids, which I bought myself.

pilot to land first."

The pilot's name was Kilgore.

"If this guy can make it, they'll all make it," I said.

I radioed Kilgore. "Listen closely," I said. I gave him instructions to come in with little power and to keep the nose off as long as he could and gently put it to the ground.

Kilgore followed my instructions perfectly. The rest of the planes landed just fine.

That evening, in the officer's mess, Kilgore came up to me and said, "Link, thank you very much for giving me the honor to be the first to land."

I shook his hand with an earnest expression.

SHORTLY AFTER, I sent for the ground personnel and equipment. I met them when they arrived by ship at Yokohama, and established the convoy. Col. Thompson rode with me in the lead Jeep.

We drove in the rain the 50-some miles to Yokota. I got lost and realized I was driving in a circle. Finally, I stopped the convoy and asked a Japanese man sitting under a tree, sheltered from the rain, "Yokota? Yokota? Yokota?"

He pointed the direction.

We arrived shortly thereafter.

"Colonel," I said, "you might have thought that I was lost, but I wanted to give you a tour of Japan."

He laughed.

Col. Thompson was a hell of a man.[23]

I GOT BACK TO Reno before Christmas 1945.

I'd crossed the Pacific on a Liberty ship, landed in Seattle, and taken a train to Camp Beale in California. A major at the base was in charge of trying to persuade men to join the regular Army. For some reason, I wasn't called in.

I went to the major and said, "You know, I don't want to be in the regular Army, but you didn't ask me why."

"Oh, I looked at your records," he said. "The date that you enlisted, you were automatically regular Army."

This meant I could be called back any time after mustering out. It bothered me.

I returned to Reno. I walked into the kitchen of my mom's house. The whole family was there.

"Happy to see you," Mom said. The reunion was like thousands around America that fall. Not overwrought with emotion; but full of sincere gratitude and relief that a family member had made it home in one piece. Chet had survived combat, too. He'd spent some time recuperating in a hospital in Oakland, but he came out in good shape.

As for me, I didn't even have a nick on me, thanks to the good Lord — plus that metal frame that had stopped the spent .25 caliber bullet inches from my head in the cockpit.

I was ready to resume civilian life.

As for my remaining in the regular Army, I received a letter a few weeks later saying I had to appear for a meeting of the local Army reserves. There were monthly meetings, for which we were paid. We were to attend the meetings, and stay healthy, in case we ever were called back.

I never attended one of those meetings. Over the next year or two I received orders

---

[23] I really had only two lingering regrets from my war experience. One was not saving the piece of paper bearing the direct order from Gen. MacArthur telling commanding officers on Japan to commandeer whatever was needed to make their troops comfortable. The other regret is not getting the name of a man whose life I saved. Flying over the east coast of Luzon, I saw a crashed plane. An Air Corps pilot in tattered clothes waved at me. I dropped a lifeboat and rations, and radioed the Navy to send vessels to pick him up. The Navy captain I radioed said he'd send boats out the next day; I cursed him and told him if he didn't send the boats right away, I'd knock his head off. Unbeknownst to me, a general overhead the conversation. Boats were immediately dispatched and the downed pilot rescued.

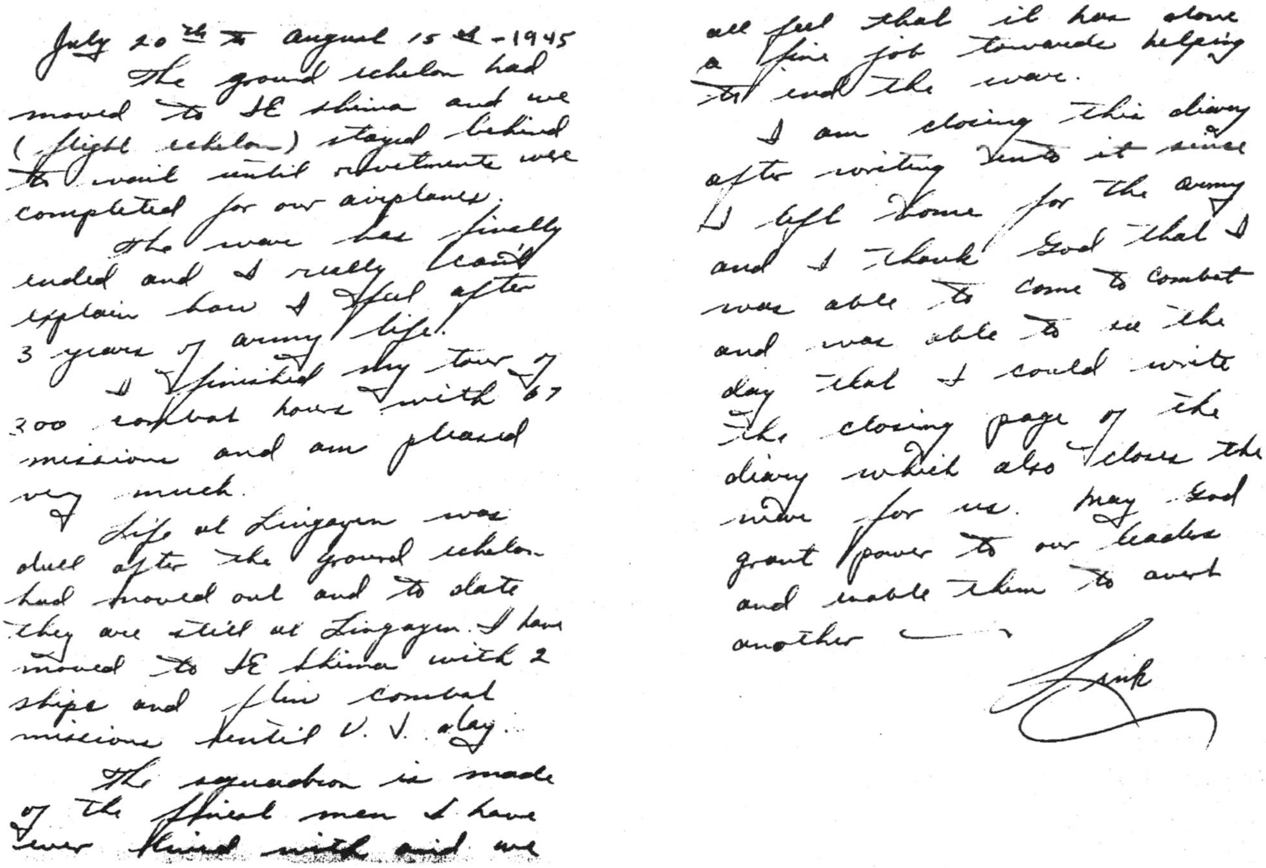

[Handwritten diary entry, reproduced as an image of the author's war diary. The handwriting reads, in part:]

July 20th to August 15th – 1945

The ground echelon had moved to IE Shima and we (flight echelon) stayed behind to wait until revetments were completed for our airplanes.

The war has finally ended and I really can't explain how I feel after 3 years of army life. I finished my tour of 300 combat hours with 67 missions and am pleased very much.

Life at Lingayen was dull after the ground echelon had moved out and to date they are still at Lingayen. I have moved to IE Shima with 2 ships and flew combat missions until V. J. day.

The squadron is made of the finest men I have ever flown with and we all feel that it has done a fine job towards helping to end the war.

I am closing this diary after writing into it since I left home for the army and I thank God that I was able to come to combat and was able to see the day that I could write the closing page of the diary which also closes the war for us. May God grant power to our leaders and enable them to avert another —

Fink

This is the last entry in my war diary.

in the mail to do this or do that, but I threw the letters in the wastebasket. I took the third such letter and wrote, "Deceased," across it and mailed it back.

I never heard any more from the Army reserve. I was taken off the rolls. I received no more reserve pay, either.

I didn't want any more of the military. I hadn't cared about rank or medals. I'd just wanted to do the best job I could possibly do, while I was there, then get myself back home.

That I'd done.

ON THE 50TH ANNIVERSARY of the bombing of Hiroshima and Nagasaki, a young television reporter in Reno had heard I had photographs of those cities. She showed up to interview me. At the end of our interview she said, "How did you feel when you heard the atom bombs were dropped?"

"Elated," I said.

"Elated?!" she said. "An atrocity like that?"

"I think," I said, "I'm voicing the opinion of everybody who was in the military, getting ready for the invasion of Japan. And another thing, young lady, why didn't you mention Pearl Harbor and the Bataan Death March and the atrocities performed by the Japanese?"

Boy, she cut me off in a hurry.

After the war I collected reprinted reports from Gen. MacArthur, the British, the Japanese. The enemy was prepared to fight to the last man if we had invaded the main islands. They were prepared to retreat all the way to Korea without surrendering.

It was estimated millions of lives would have been lost. All too often, things aren't exactly as they seem. It was the same way with the war, and with the men I fought alongside.

About 40 years after the war, I walked into Indian Wells, a country club I belonged to in the Palm Desert, Calif., area. Some guys were playing gin rummy. A friend of mine said, "Gee, play my hand, I got a friend in there I have to buy lunch for."

"OK," I said. I played his hand until the sheet was over.

I went into the dining room. "You won 10 bucks," I told him.

"Oh, meet so-and-so," my friend said. Neither I nor the stranger, a large guy about my age, caught each other's name.

We talked for awhile over lunch. "Now, do you want me to finish playing for you or are you going to go and finish?" I asked my friend.

"No, Link, I'll be in," he said.

The stranger jumped up. "Are you Link Piazzo?"

"Yeah."

He put his arm around me and started to cry. "If it wasn't for you I wouldn't be here," he said.

I remembered him then. His name was Ken Pultz. He had been a pilot in my squadron. He'd come to the flight line every morning, all gung ho, saying, "Let's go get 'em." I'd thought he was a guy like me, wanting to get up there and shorten the war. When mine was the lead airplane, I'd have him assigned as one of my wing men, flying on one of my sides, based on his attitude.

That day at the country club, he told me, "I was frightened to death on every mission."

9

Back in Business

Helen and I started married life at 613 W. 10th St., next-door to my mom's house, where I'd grown up, at 609 W. 10th. Mom, in fact, owned 613, too. She'd been leasing it out, but after I returned from the war, she gave the house to Helen and me.

Mom always was fair to all her kids. When she took Chet, Melba and me to Italy in 1935, she gave Louie and Olga the monetary equivalent of our travel expenses. After the war, she not only gave a house to me, but Melba got the house next-door to me and Chet got one just north of me. Mom had done quite well with the St. Francis Hotel. We Piazzos were spreading throughout the neighborhood.

Olga and Melba had done a good job managing the store. After Chet and I returned, our sisters couldn't leave the Sportsman fast enough. Olga went back to managing the hotel. Melba got married to a guy named Fran Cassinelli. They had two girls and one boy: Kevin, Julie and Dawn. They're still married.

Helen and I had a tearful reunion, but not overly emotional. "I knew he was coming home," she told people. I had come home on leave once in awhile before going overseas, and then, well, I'd gone overseas for awhile, and then

Family dinner, 1945, at the Club Fortune. From left: Louie Piazzo, Buddy Piazzo, Melba, mom, Olga, Carol, Alice. Clockwise from there: Chet, Darlene, Helen. I took the photo.

I'd come home. That was all.

The war matured many young men of my generation. I already was in business before the war, though, and a few years older than many of my colleagues in the Air Corps, and some of the other pilots used to call me "Pop." They'd come to me for advice.

What I gained most out of serving was reinforcement of my firm belief that the good

Lord is up above and I would never have gotten home without Him. That, and the philosophy that no matter what happened to me on this Earth, it can always be worse.

Just do the very best you can in an honest way, and what the hell, take what the good Lord gives you. You can't get much simpler than that.

Helen and I had no carefully drawn-out

Myself, Howard "Swede" Christiansen and Chet, 1971. Swede passed away 17 years later. He was still with the Sportsman (42 years) at the time of his death.

plans. We just wanted to stay alive. We knew we were going to raise a family. We didn't take time out to assess things. We just jumped right in to building our lives. That was the way our generation was.

I've said this so many times — U.S. industry played a terrific roll in winning the war. The factories churned out airplanes seven days a week, around the clock. In the brief period that I began flying B-25s to the end, we went from an A model to a J model. A can-do attitude permeated the country.

Olga and Melba couldn't get much merchandise during the war to keep the Sportsman stocked. Non-essential goods weren't being manufactured. Chet and I had left behind a good inventory, but when we returned, the store's shelves were nearly empty. The good news was that our sisters had $40,000 in cash from the store. That was the most money Chet and I had ever seen. We set about putting it to good use.

We gradually built our store's inventory back up. In a matter of months our shelves were well stocked. We also had cash to start

buying up property. We must have inherited the idea from our late, beloved father. Our first purchase was two lots on the corner of Fourth and Vine streets. The cost: $5,000. We constructed a building on the land to serve as our boat shop. The Sportsman sold boats and motors. After the war, there was a market for everything. As U.S. industry slowly geared up for a peacetime economy, companies rationed out products for sale. There was a great demand for everything available, including recreational goods. The Sportsman marine department opened on Fourth and Vine in 1946. Chet spent most of his work time out on Fourth and Vine; the taxidermy department was put on the second floor.

Soon, we had a tenant. Bill Lock of Hale's Drugstore wanted to open up a new store. He moved in and we moved our marine department to the back of the store building. The building was on the corner of Fourth and Vine. We tore it down after 20 years. The space is part of the Sportsman's parking lot now.

A typical birthday card from the Sportsman.

Right after the war, Chet and I hired our first full-time employee: Howard "Swede" Christiansen. Swede was known as the commissioner of softball in Reno; he supervised the leagues. His day job was for the *Reno Evening Gazette*, in circulation. We paid him a little more in salary — $150 a month — and lured him to the Sportsman. He was a little heavyset with thin blond hair, and a very kind, 100 percent honest person. He had a tremendous number of friends.

We hired Swede as a salesman, but made him a manager shortly after. He would stay with us 42 years. In later years we started a profit-sharing plan among our managers. Swede accumulated a tidy sum. One day I said, "Swede, why don't you take some of that profit-sharing money out?"

"Well, I want to leave $50,000 to my kids," he said.

I knew he didn't know much about finances.

"Fine," I said. "Tell you what we'll do. Let's take $50,000 out, and you put it in a separate fund for your kids. The remainder, I want you to invest it, and I'll show you how to invest it. And I want you to spend all of the interest. Promise me you'll spend it."

And he did. By golly, he would take occasional trips to San Francisco to take in baseball or football games. He thoroughly enjoyed it.

I can't say enough about Swede. He didn't want to retire, but we made him. "You can come in any time you want, we'll pay you, three hours a week or three days a week, whatever." The Sportsman was his life.

Chet and I knew 99 percent of our customers in those early postwar years. Reno was still a small town, though growing. We knew whose credit was good, and whose wasn't. We built up a very loyal following. Not long ago, as I write this book, another Swede — Swede Matheson, who was 94 — came into the Sportsman. He reminded me of things I'd done for him (most of which I did not remember). He had done very well in the catering business, and helped a lot of people, and he was the kind of person I helped. One thing I did remember doing for him involved .28 gauge shotgun shells.

Just after the war, ammunition was almost impossible to get. Swede Matheson had a .28 gauge shotgun. I brought him downstairs in the store and showed him shells I had in supply. "*You* can buy these," I said. "Nobody else can."

He never forgot that.

Chet and I really took care of our customers. The good ones.

Well, all of them were good ones.

NOT ALL OUR CUSTOMERS could be relied upon to make good on credit, and so not everyone got credit.

U.S. Sen. Pat McCarran had a reputation for not paying his bills. Gus Edwards, a friend of mine from Reno High who was managing Conant's supermarket, told me, "You know, Pat doesn't pay us. He owes us three-thousand and some-odd dollars." He also owed Herd and Short, a clothing store, a lot of money.

McCarran was a powerful senator on Capitol Hill and remains a legend in Nevada politics to this day. But that meant nothing to me as a business-owner. He'd come into the Sportsman to buy boxes of .28 gauge

Chet decorated the Sportsman with many trophies from his hunts. Here are a few of the mounted specimens.

shotgun shells. He'd ask for certain quantities, then say, "Link, would you like to have me pay for them, or would you like to have me charge them?"

I'd say, "I'd like to have you pay for them."

I believe we were the only business in town that got paid by McCarran.

The $40,000 our sisters had accumulated under their management got Chet and me going pretty well. It allowed us to get off and running. Well, not exactly running, at first. It took time. But we were, now, the only sporting goods store in Reno. Reno Sporting Goods on Virginia Street had gone out of business during the war. Frankly, this lack of competition made me uncomfortable. Some people would come into our store and grumble, "Geez, I've got to come in here, you know, because you're the only sporting good store."

This didn't last more than a few months, though. A fellow named Fred Brown had a little service station on the corner of Sierra and Fourth streets, not far from us, and he had a fish and tackle section. He became our first competitor. Then, in time, other stores opened up.

I've never paid a lot of attention to competition in business. A lot of people do, and I believe that's a tremendous mistake. You've got to run your *own* business, and run it the best you can, and you'll succeed. If you do the best job, provide the best service, you'll succeed.

AFTER I RETURNED FROM overseas, Helen quit her job at J.C. Penney and became a full-time homemaker. Our daughter, Suzanne, was born in 1947, at Saint Mary's Hospital. She had a cleft palate. Something else wasn't right with her. We had her examined by doctors in Reno and California. Suzanne, it turned out, was retarded. She suffered from health problems her entire short life; she passed away in 1961.

Our son Lynn was born in 1952 at Saint Mary's. I'd always wanted a son. He was a healthy baby. Our two-bedroom house at 613 W. 10th St. was getting crowded. In 1955 we moved into a larger house on Skyline Boulevard, on the corner of Moana Lane.

Lynn grew up to be a good-looking young man. He was a pretty good athlete. I had him outside playing catch as soon as he was old enough. We went fishing and hunting together by the time he was 5 or 6 and could keep up. He played Pop Warner football.

Lynn attended St. Therese the Little Flower Catholic school off Arlington Avenue. I liked the strictness of the nuns, and the good private education. Lynn attended Wooster High School. He was a very good student, and also loved animals. He took good care of our pet black Labradors. He ended up at Colorado State University, studying to become a veterinarian.

Drug experimentation plagued millions in Lynn's generation, and he was, unfortunately, one of the casualties. Drugs claimed his life.

Craig, our final child, was born in 1955. He was entrepreneurial practically from the get-go. By the time he was 7, he was wearing a little black-and-white striped shirt — the uniform for the Sportsman employees — and helping out at the store. He'd adjust merchandise on the shelves, he'd dust. He just was tremendously interested in the business.

One time, we had a display of Rainbow cluster salmon eggs. Craig came to me and said, "I think if you put that over here you'll sell more because people would see it."

He was right!

Craig liked sports. He attended Little Flower and then Wooster High. We hunted together a lot, especially around Lovelock. A good friend of mine, Smokey Quilici, knew every square inch of Pershing County. Craig, like his older brother, was shooting a gun by age 6. We hunted chukar, geese, pheasant, all upland game. We also fished, mostly in the Truckee River.

Craig earned a business degree from the University of Nevada, working at the Sportsman part time.

"Look," I said after Craig had graduated college and was job-hunting, "you don't have to come into the store, because I think I might want to retire."

"Oh no, no," he said. "This is my life. This is where I want to come."

Almost immediately, he took over as retail manager. He kept the store looking good, and was very good with the customers.

Chet had eased out of the business in 1978. I told Craig he could sell the store if he wanted to. But he didn't want to. He stayed as retail manager for 17 years, before I ended up selling.

At that point, 1994, Craig went full tilt into his own window-washing business. He does a beautiful, perfect job. When he started that enterprise, I told him, "Your best advertising is a satisfied customer."

Craig is a perfectionist. He always has been. Everything he does, he does perfectly. He supervises his employees very carefully. He handles buildings and homes. He cleans Helen's and my house, and when he's done, the windows are perfect.

He lives on Skyline Boulevard, in the house he grew up in. Helen and I practically gave it to him, continuing the Piazzo family tradition.

Craig hasn't married. He's had girlfriends, but never tied the knot. I guess Helen and I will never become grandparents, but we have plenty of nieces and nephews. Frankly, I don't give a damn whether Craig has kids or not, as long as he's happy. We're very close.

That's what a parent and child should be.

As for Helen and me, we've been married 54 years.

Helen is a very fine person. We've had our arguments. But I remember my mom and dad arguing when I was little. That was nothing; you're supposed to argue. The next hour, everything's OK.

A secret to staying married that long: Get in a good argument, then forget it.

That's about the best advice I can give.

Helen and I have taken tremendous trips together. We've taken care of each other. All in all, when it came to family life, I came out ahead.

10

How Bare was the Valley

The $40,000 cash Olga and Melba had amassed for Chet and me at the store during the war allowed us to plunk down $5,000 in 1946 to buy our first land — two 150-foot-square lots on the northwest corner of Fourth and Vine streets, where we constructed a building to house the Sportsman's marine division.

Chet and I must have inherited our father's yen for buying property. We always were borrowing money to buy land. In fact, we always owed money until we sold Lakeside Plaza many, many years later. But it ultimately worked out well. My philosophy is that real estate really is where you make money, much more so than in retail business, or in stocks.

In 1956, Chet and I bought property across the street on the northeast corner of Fourth and Vine, across the street from our first lot. We built a shopping center and named it the Plaza. When we built Sportsman's Corner in 1978, where the store is now, on the northwest corner, I took this property and Chet took the Plaza. The Gold Dust West casino stands on that lot, now, and Chet still owns the land, collecting rent from the casino's owner.

Most of the money Chet and I borrowed was from First National Bank, whose president was the legendary Eddie Questa. We'd started our relationship with this bank to expand the inventory for our store. We always were able to pay off our loans. Questa was a very influential man. Not only did his bank finance many businesses in Reno, but it provided the funds for the casino-owners who built the Las Vegas Strip. This speaks volumes for those who know the history. Questa, in short, was connected.

One time, he and I were playing golf, and I asked him, "What if one of those places foreclose?"

"I know who to call in Detroit," he answered.

He had a pipeline to money, Eddie did.

Questa was a slim man with light-brown hair, and very stern. Everyone kind of feared him, in fact. His banker's garb never changed: a dark suit and tie. His First National Bank office on the fourth floor of the Reno National Bank, on the northeast corner of Second and Virginia streets, had nothing in it except for a desk. If you had an appointment, you'd open the door and walk across 40 or 50 feet of empty carpet to reach his desk at the other end. The desktop was bare. If Eddie had to make a call, he'd reach in a drawer and bring out a phone. If he had to write something, he'd reach in a drawer and take out a pad of paper.

Questa always spoke very slowly, and accurately. He'd learned banking from A.P.

Giannini, who was head of the Bank of Italy (which later purchased Bank of America), in San Francisco. Giannini lent on character. If he knew you, no problem. Questa followed the same policy. He apparently had faith in Chet and me.

Sometimes he shook his head, sometimes he nodded. When Chet and I got the idea to buy the land on the northeast corner of Fourth and Vine to build the Plaza shopping center, we went to see Questa. Twenty or so houses were on this block between Fourth and Fifth streets and from Vine Street east, halfway to Washington Street. There was only one, small shopping center in Reno, the Village.

Questa should have thrown us out. Most bankers would have thought it a crazy idea. Chet and I had no collateral besides our store. But Questa thought the shopping center was a good idea. He lent us the money: about $450,000. We weren't surprised. We'd analyzed the plan, and believed we could make it work. In exchange, Questa tied up our store and the property we were buying as collateral. Chet and I went ahead with our Plaza.

IT NOW WAS 11 years after the war. A coffee klatsch of guys my age met every weekday morning at the Holiday Hotel downtown, sharing war stories and talking about the news of the day as well as how our town was growing.

Emmett Saviers should get the most credit for Hidden Valley. His family had the Westinghouse distributorship for the entire state. I used to kid him about being born with a silver spoon in his mouth. He had attended private schools and was a good golfer, having taken lessons. He was a bit younger than I, and one of my best friends at the time.

One morning, Saviers turned to me and said, "You know, we should have a private country club in northern Nevada. And I want you to help me find the property."

"Go to hell," I said. I was busy trying to keep our store going, as well as our real estate developments. I didn't have time for this.

"I think it's a crazy idea, anyway," I said.

Actually, it wasn't. The Washoe County Golf Course was the only course in northern Nevada. A private course could have plenty of local appeal. Las Vegas had a country club. Reno deserved one, too.

A few days later, Emmett repeated his idea. All of a sudden I found myself in a car with him, trying to find some property.

We checked out the Wheeler Ranch southwest of Reno (where Lakeridge Golf Course is today), and talked to old man Wheeler. He wanted to sell. The old ranching families who'd started their spreads nearly a century before were transitioning out of the old life. Their land, purchased very inexpensively in the 19th century, was very valuable. I don't remember the price Wheeler quoted us, but I told Emmett it was too much.

Another day, I found ourselves driving up Pembroke Drive, on the far side of the airport in southeast Reno. Pembroke was a winding dirt road leading up toward the edge of a little old ranch. There also was a gravel pit owned by Miller Construction company. I'd been out there before, because the Reno Duck Club was out there in a marsh. The whole area was way out of town. The boonies.

Emmett was driving. It was a foggy day, and the fog was so thick we couldn't see 10 feet. "Where in the hell are you going?" I said.

"There's a ranch out here I want you to look at."

"Hell, I know where it is, it isn't worth a

How Bare was the Valley

Hidden Valley, 1957. Peavine Peak is in the background.

Hidden Valley, 1965.

Hidden Valley, October 1998.

damn. Turn around and go back before we get killed."

He did.

A few days later, on a clear day, we drove out again. Two older men in our coffee klatsch — Delbert Machabee and William Kottinger Sr. — were with us. Saviers had talked us into going out to the Birbeck Ranch, to talk with J.A. Birbeck. He owned the 900-acre spread. He'd made money growing lettuce in Salinas, Calif., but foolishly had tried to raise carrots out here. The land was just awful. He couldn't make it.

The four of us sat down with Birbeck.

"Is your ranch for sale?"

"Yes."

"How many acres?"

"Nine-hundred."

"What do you want for it?"

"A hundred dollars an acre."

In 1956, that was dirt cheap. Most of the acreage was sagebrush. There was some lowland he'd tried to cultivate, but the results were terrible. He'd had enough.

"There are two stipulations," old man Birbeck said.

"What are they?"

"I want $400 down, non-refundable."

Birbeck had looked at four of us and decided on $100 apiece.

"What's the other stipulation?"

"If you pay it in 60 days, I'll give you a 10 percent discount."

Each of us handed over a $100 bill. We sealed the deal with a handshake.

Our idea was to develop a country club with an 18-hole private golf course, ringed by a 2,000-home community. It would be a completely residential community, with no commercial development. We'd sell the lots and people could build their homes on it.

Kottinger came up with the name "Hidden Valley." That's what the spread resembled to him, nestled as it was at the base of foothills of the Virginia Range, which formed the eastern barrier to the meadows that contained much of Reno and Sparks. To the southwest, the peaks of Mount Rose and Slide Mountain, in the Carson Range, seemed to rise very close.

The land of our residential community-to-be seemed like a hidden valley beyond Reno's city limits, on the opposite side of Reno's airport, seemingly forgotten by the forces of progress.

The details of the Hidden Valley story, including photocopies of original documents, are contained in a little memory book that Hidden Valley Properties put together in 1997. It recalls how the four of us — Saviers, myself, Kottinger and Machabee — formed a Founders Committee of 17 members to solicit charter memberships and operating funds. We really were starting from scratch.[24]

The whole enterprise seemed like a pipe dream; but we were fired up to bring it to reality. We found 13 local businessmen to join the four of us on the committee and a few weeks later — after knocking on friends' doors — we'd sold about 300 charter memberships at $1,000 each. Their venture-basis investments yielded each charter member an $800 note bearing a 5 percent annual interest, plus 20 shares of stock in Hidden Valley Properties, Inc.

With more than $350,000 raised by the corporation, we were more than ready to pay off Birbeck's $90,000 note, with the 10 percent off for early payment.

The remaining money in Hidden Valley Properties, Inc., was directed for the plan-

---

[24] The names of the 17 founders are on a bronze plaque mounted inside the entrance of Hidden Valley Country Club. As of this writing, of the 17, only three of us remain: Bob Bond, Prince Hawkins and myself.

ning and design of the golf course (at $10,000 a hole), a clubhouse (about $324,318.95) and a driving range, plus cutting the streets for the first residential lots to be sold in Hidden Valley Sub-Division No. 1. The country club was a subsidiary operation to solicit golf and club memberships; the buyers didn't have to purchase residential lots.

The next milestone was forming the first Hidden Valley Country Club Board of Directors. It was comprised of the Founders Committee members plus three others: Karl D. Breckenridge, Edward J. Questa and William K. Woodburn.[25] Questa also was one of the 300 investors. This probably helped us to be able to borrow the $350,000 we did from his First National Bank. In addition, we borrowed $250,000 from Nevada Bank of Commerce. Donald Bates, another of the 300 investors and a member of the Founders Committee, was president of Nevada Bank of Commerce.

Questa and Bates were kind of nervous. They knew their banks couldn't recoup their loans unless Hidden Valley Properties sold the residential lots. It wasn't long before their fears seemed justified. It turned out that this neglected stretch of land that was Hidden Valley was not blessed with good groundwater. In July 1956 we partners had a well dug about 150 feet east of where the 10th fairway of the golf course was planned. We put a pump on it and built a little shack. But the water from the well did not make the grass bloom. We had two ponds out there for irrigation. We called the University of Nevada, and experts came out. They tested the water: it seemed to have everything *but* water in it. It contained high con-

centrations of arsenic and boron-manganese. We capped the well. One of our Hidden Valley Properties shareholders, Frank Gaiennie, happened to be an officer of Sierra Pacific Power Co., which had absorbed extensive water rights throughout northern Nevada. Gaiennie arranged for us to acquire water rights from John Cavanaugh Sr., one of the casino pioneers in Reno. We traded him land for the rights through the Boyington Slough. The slough originates in ditches in the Truckee Meadows and empties into the Truckee River. We pumped the water to our two ponds.

It wasn't difficult for the course designer — a southern Californian named Billy Bell — to clear the land. There wasn't much vegetation other than sagebrush, given the arid climate and poor soil. The biggest challenge was keeping the grass from yellowing and dying in the alkali-rich dirt. Careful nurturing, including carting in special fertilizer all the way from Yerington, helped the course mature. Seaside bentgrass, which is tolerant of alkali, was planted. And with little annual rainfall, the course was watered frequently.

It wasn't long after plans for the golf course and clubhouse began to develop that we realized we were pinched for money. The Hidden Valley Properties board talked it over, and we members reluctantly agreed to buy one lot apiece in the proposed subdivision circling the golf course. We drew names out of a hat to determine the order of lot-selection. That got the golf course back on track. But tax bills and other expenses kept coming due, and so all the members who were interested put names in a hat again, and more lots were sold. The

---

[25] Nobody, including myself, wanted to be president. (We should have chosen Emmett Saviers — since the club had been his idea at the start.) We argued back and forth, and finally persuaded Hal Luce to take the job. I said I'd give him my No.1 membership in exchange for his No. 4. Years later, he moved to Scottsdale, Ariz. I wrote to him and said I was taking back my No. 1 membership.

buyers redeemed the $800 notes plus kicked in $100 to put toward the lot purchase price of $2,300. Now we had the money to build the clubhouse.

Sustaining the dream of developing Hidden Valley was a continuous battle. In fact, it was an improbable campaign. Lesser souls surely would have given up the ghost. The heavy alkali deposits and high pH content of the water seemed to mock our plans. The county health department condemned two of three wells we had sunk to provide water to residences, and even the third well was deemed marginal in water quality and insufficient in volume to meet residential growth. In 1956, the state Public Service Commission slapped a building moratorium on the land (which would last eight years) until we could provide an adequate source of quality water. That meant anyone interested in buying a lot also had to buy into the conviction that water eventually would become available and that the wait would be worthwhile. Eventually, home construction would be permitted.

The big sales sign we erected in 1957 at the entrance to the land on Piping Rock Drive — announcing such attractions as a "planned community," "spacious home sites," "unobstructed view," "school & parks," "country club adjoining" and "smog-free living" — met with extremely low response.

Our $300,000 loan from First National Bank came due and we hadn't sold anything near the amount of lots needed to satisfy it. We also owed $250,000 to the Nevada Bank of Commerce.

We appeared to be dead in the water.

In February 1959 the board authorized me to negotiate a seven-month time extension of the loan from First National Bank. Eddie Questa immediately telephoned me. I was treasurer for Hidden Valley Properties. In addition, we knew each other well by now, from all the loans he'd given Chet and me.

"I want to meet with your finance committee," he said.

We had no finance committee; but I appointed one in a hell of a hurry. I appointed Donald Bates, since he was a bank president and a good friend of Questa's. I appointed Paul Garwood, who was a member of the board of directors of First National Bank. I put some other board members on the committee, to round it out.

We showed up at Questa's office. Eddie, as I mentioned, was very stern. I was sitting to his right.

One of our guys didn't know Questa, or he wouldn't have piped up, telling the banker he didn't have to worry about the loan since we had plenty of collateral. We didn't have any money, but we had all this property, he said.

Questa turned around to me. "I want to talk with you in the next room," he said.

The two of us went into the next room.

"Who's that big fat blond sonofabitch making all that noise?"

"Gee, I'm sorry, I didn't introduce you," I began.

"I don't want to meet him!" Questa said.

That took care of that.

"Now tell me this," he said. "When September rolls around, will you be able to pay down on your note?"

"Hell no, Ed. Not unless we can sell some property."

Questa chewed this over in his head.

"That's all I want to know," he finally said. "Hell, I can't foreclose on you people. It would be like foreclosing on a church."

Indeed, he would have been foreclosing on most of the influential people in Reno. They'd each put in $1,000 for a share of

Hidden Valley.

We returned to the room and sat down.

"I just had a conversation with Link," Questa said. "He says when September rolls around, you'll be able to pay down on your loan."

I was stunned. I thought he'd confused the contents of our private conversation.

Questa excused everybody. I remained.

"Ed," I said, "did you misunderstand me?"

"No, goddamnit, get out of here."

With that, our corporation had a new lease on life. At least for the short term.

IN MAY 1960, BOTH First National Bank and Nevada Bank of Commerce demanded immediate payment of their delinquent loans to Hidden Valley Properties. That immediately forced us to sell valuable sub-divided lots and undeveloped acreage at bargain-basement prices considered less than 50 percent their value. Freeport Land Corporation bought 197 of the developed lots for $1,000 apiece and 427.69 acres of undivided land for $1,000 per acre. That settled our long-standing bank loans, and with the extra $24,690, our corporation became solvent for the first time.

Finally, Hidden Valley began to gain appeal as the new place to buy land to build a house (eventually). The golf course and clubhouse opened on Memorial Day 1958. A few homes lined Piping Rock Drive, built before the moratorium. At one point, the chairman of the Public Service Commission called me and said, "Look, we're working out a filtration plant for Hidden Valley."

"Great," I said, "who's going to pay for it?"

"Oh, the water-users," he said.

"How much is it going to cost?"

I took out a pencil and calculated the figures he gave me.

"Gee, that's wonderful," I said, "what moron figured that out? The water bill for these people will be much higher than their house payments. You're breaking the world record."

The filtration plant wasn't built. Nevertheless, the crazy dream that Saviers, Kottinger, Machabee and myself entertained in 1956 seemed to be approaching reality by 1964. Robert Helms, the local construction company owner, sunk two wells by the Truckee River. Naturally, I attended the public hearings when the Public Service Commission was deciding whether to permit Helms to pump water to Hidden Valley. The second hearing was at the Holiday Inn on South Virginia Street. The board voted to approve the plan. It was eight years to the day after the moratorium had been instituted.

Attendees had to sign their names on a paper in order to address the board. I didn't sign my name, but I raised my hand toward the end of the meeting. They allowed me to speak, so I stood.

"I'd like to compliment you people. You know, bureaucracy generally takes longer. But you guys solved this problem in *only eight years*."[26]

They weren't sure whether I was complimenting them — which I wasn't.

The water was piped in and stored in two tanks on the west side of the foothills. The biggest problem to selling lots, now, remained an obstacle presented by Mother Nature: mosquitoes. The insects swarmed the area day and night. Golfers were at their mercy — even insect repellent and swatters didn't keep the pesky blood-suckers at bay. The few residents kept their homes

---

[26] During my tenure as president, Jim Wood has been my executive secretary and righthand man. I could not be working with a more dedicated, honest and sincere individual.

tightly closed for days on end. At last, the county rescued us with an effective mosquito-abatement program.

The streets were nothing but packed dirt, and the legendary winds — Washoe zephyrs — howled through the valley, creating dust devils and sandstorms. The county created an assessment district and surfaced the streets. That took care of the swirling soil.

The country club had held its first formal dinner Sept. 29, 1957, at the Holiday Hotel, with a capacity crowd dressed in tuxedos and evening gowns. The golf course had opened in 1958. In 1963, Hidden Valley Properties sold the course and clubhouse to Hidden Valley Country Club for $500,000. The contract of sale called for a 20-year note, interest-free, with monthly payments of $2,083. The next year brought fantastic news.

With good water finally available in 1964, lots began to sell. Eight years of constant misery had been endured, and now we developers and shareholders were beginning to cash in. The dream of Kottinger, Machabee, Saviers and myself, hatched around a table sipping coffee at the Holiday Hotel eight years earlier, had become a reality. By 1982 the value of the property had increased to $15,000 an acre; this was the price for which the corporation sold 27 acres, at the north tip of West Hidden Valley Drive, to the Latipek Corporation, adding the condition that Latipek had to tie Mira

Loma Drive to West Hidden Valley Drive, providing a secondary access rode to the original one on Pembroke Drive.

As time went on, I bought as much property as I could afford in Hidden Valley, including all the property on the 10th Fairway. Historically, the most expensive property is oceanfront, lakefront, and fairwayfront. It's been that way for centuries.

Today, the property remaining under ownership of Hidden Valley Properties is in es-

Piazzo Circle in Hidden Valley Cove subdivision, under construction, 1999.

crow on a rolling options basis. I am the only remaining original partner of the four founders of Hidden Valley, and have, as of this writing, served on the board for 43 years, including 21 as president. Not an inch of land has been sold for commercial development.

The ironic thing is, we partners in Hidden Valley Properties had been bitterly disappointed about what became an eight-year building moratorium. However, the Public Service Commission had inadvertently done us a favor. Property values during that period kept steadily increasing. It's a funny way to get appreciated value in property, but had we been able to sell then, we would have let the lots go for much less than we ultimately did.

Shares — which cost $10 apiece with the initial venture offering in 1956 — had risen by 1996 to a value of $13,742.50. Dividends paid in 1996 were $50: five times the original share cost.

Some of the best ideas in business probably have started with idle chit-chat around a coffee table.

Of course, our gamble never could've gotten off the ground without the likes of an Eddie Questa. He was old school, and his old-school ways made our venture possible.

As I mentioned, Questa was the protégé of A.J. Giannini, head of the Bank of Italy. Imagine what officials with the Bank of America — the renamed Bank of Italy — would do today if faced with a loan application from a bunch of little guys in their 30s and early 40s with big ideas about selling lots on a proposed golf course.

"Go to hell," would be their response.

All banks operate that way these days — by the book. If you want to borrow $10,000, you'd better have $20,000 of collateral. Or something along those lines.

Questa, though, lent on character, as I said. He had faith in us and our project.

His faith was redeemed.

QUESTA WAS A BACHELOR, and he entertained a lot, first-class. One of his favorite places to entertain was at Hidden Valley Country Club.

Nobody wanted to serve as president of the country club. Hugo Quilici was manager of the main office of First National Bank. He was a very prominent banker. He agreed to serve as country club president for a term with one condition: I would be his treasurer.

"Holy cow," I said, "you're the banker, and you want *me* to be your treasurer?"

I continued: "I'll take that under one condition, that no money is spent, not one dime, without my approval."

Questa entertained at the country club one evening, and found there only was one size of wine glasses. When you serve three or four different wines, you're supposed to have a similar number of different wine glasses at each table setting.

I received a phone call from Hugo Quilici. "Link, Eddie Questa was out at the club last night and he was insulted because you only had one kind of wine glass."

Questa, of course, was Quilici's boss, as well as president of the bank we owed money to.

"He wants me to buy three other kinds of wine glasses," Quilici said.

"Bulls—, we don't have the money," I said. The country club was paying off its mortgage, and was on a shoestring budget.

"Tell Eddie Questa no," I said.

"Geez, I hate to do that, but I guess I'll have to," Quilici said.

It wasn't 10 minutes before the phone rang. Questa was on the line. "Link," he said in his slow voice. "This is Ed."

"Hi Ed, how are you?"

"Link, I was out at the club last night and there was only one kind of wine glass."

"Eddie, we owe you three hundred and some-odd thousand. I can't afford wine glasses. No," I said.

"Ed, I have an idea," I continued.

"What's that?" he said, slowly as always.

"We'll take 'em if you donate them to us." *Click.* He hung up.

We never bought the wine glasses.

IN 1955, WITH THREE children now in my family, I looked around for a bigger house.

There was a well-built house on a large lot on the corner of Skyline Boulevard and Moana Lane. It was owned by Joe Massinio, who was a very good builder and had built the house. The price seemed high, though: $69,000.

Joe and I were skiing one day on Mount Rose. We were having lunch at Sky Tavern, and he said, "Why don't you buy my house?"

"You want too much money for it."

"Well, I've cut the price."

"What do you want for it?"

"Forty-three five."

Quite a cut!

"I'll take it under one condition, that I can raise the finances."

We got in the car and drove to a title company, and I bought the house.

I only had $20,000 to put down. But I had a banker friend whom I'd known for years. I won't mention his name. He was a branch manager with First National Bank. I said, "I want to buy this house, I can put down $20,000."

"Nope, can't handle the deal," he said.

I thought that was ridiculous, so I got back in the car and drove over to see Eddie Questa, his boss.

"Eddie, I want to buy a house," I said. I didn't mention I'd already seen his branch manager.

"Where is it?" he said.

I told him. He knew the address.

"Yeah, that's the one Massinio built," Eddie said. He'd probably lent money to Massinio at some point. "Nice house, what does he want for it?"

"Forty-three five," I said. "I want to put $20,000 down."

"Keep the 20,000," he said. "I'll lend you the whole forty-three five."

He did, at 5 percent interest.

That's the kind of guy Eddie Questa was.

He never was easy about lending money. He always made you sweat. You had to have a very good reason to ask for a loan. But he was a terrific guy.

He'd make his decisions right away, yes or no. After making a decision to loan, he'd take his telephone out of his desk and call Hugo Quilici, or whoever the branch manager was, and say, "I'm sending Link down, take care of 'im. I'll give you the details later."

That's the way he was.

Questa was very savvy about business. As I said, he hardly was a soft touch.

Once I sought a loan and offered as collateral undeveloped land in Hidden Valley.

"We can't hypothecate that," he said.

"What the hell does 'hypothecate' mean?" I asked.

"It means we can't lend any money on it!" he said, angrily.

So I found out what "hypothecate" meant in a hell of a hurry. It meant he couldn't lend any goddamn money on the raw land.

In 1960, when the Winter Olympics were running at Squaw Valley above the northwest shore of Lake Tahoe, Questa came into the Sportsman accompanied by a man from Vegas we can characterize as being "a member of the club." He was one of the guys Questa had lent money to for a casino on the Strip. Questa introduced us; his friend's name was familiar to me from newspaper headlines. I wasn't bothered a bit.

"Outfit him in a ski outfit," Questa said. It was no big deal.

Questa helped a lot of people in business, in Vegas and in Reno. Our state wouldn't be what it is today without his bankroll and discretion.

It's a shame there aren't bankers like Eddie

Questa today, who lent on character, to people he knew he could trust.

THANKS TO QUESTA'S LOAN to Chet and me in 1956, we were able to buy the half-block of houses between Fourth and Fifth streets and from Vine Street halfway down to Washington Street.

We started a shopping center, and tore the houses down. You make much more money renting to commercial tenants than to home-dwellers, and collecting rent from residential tenants is a real headache, people moving in and out all the time.

A big supermarket — Washoe Market — and the Sprouse Reitz drugstore were our key tenants. A barbershop, a little clothing store, a bar at the far end were some of our smaller tenants. We leased out our plaza almost immediately. Reno was growing. Fourth Street then was still part of the Lincoln Highway, U.S. 40, the main east-west route from California to Salt Lake City. Interstate 80 wouldn't supplant it until 1970.

As I previously mentioned, Chet owns the Plaza now. The Gold Dust West casino occupies the entire area.

Our next plaza was Lakeside Plaza, on the northeast corner of Lakeside Drive and Plumb Lane. It was an apple orchard. We bought everything from behind the Continental Lodge on South Virginia Street to Lakeside, and from Plumb Lane north a half-block. We built the plaza and opened for

business in 1964. Albertson's supermarket became one anchor — the first Albertson's store outside of Idaho. Chet and I got to know chain founder Joe Albertson, one of the nicest people we've met. Thrifty Drug was the other anchor, on the east side of the plaza.

A decade later, after we'd paid off the loan on Lakeside Plaza, our lawyer, Bill Sanford Jr., called Chet and me into his office.

"You know it's paid off and completely depreciated," he said. "What you should do is sell it because the government's making all the money."

The Sportsman, in Sportsman's Corner, the year it opened, 1978.

Chet and I had never sold any of our property in our life.

"Hell no, we don't want to sell it," we said.

Sanford called is in a week later. He showed us the figures. It would be the first time in our life that we'd have money in the bank and not owe anybody.

So we agreed. We sold it.

Chet and I didn't develop our property on the northwest corner of Fourth and Vine until 1978. We named the new plaza Sportsman's Corner. The anchor would be the Sportsman; we were moving out of downtown, away from 358 N. Virginia St., where we'd been 40 years.

We needed more space. And the new location wasn't bad: a block away from Keystone Avenue and its business strip.

The Gold Dust West moved that same year to occupy all of the Plaza. The casino's done very well as a neighborhood grind joint. It's one of the few casinos where customers can park right in front of the door.

The Gold Dust West has been a great tenant for Chet. Sportsman's Corner has done OK, too. Lakeside Plaza put Chet and me into the black for the first time, debt-free.

Hidden Valley was more successful than I ever anticipated.

It was our dad's spirit — Santino's business sense to buy up property — that Chet and I inherited that made us financially successful. Retail alone would not have come close.[27]

---

[27] Here's one more business story — one that illustrates the "value" of education.

Through my contacts as president of the National Sporting Goods Association, I met the Dassler family (owners of Adidas). I was brought into a limited partnership with nine other men — eight of whom were Stanford graduates, and the other who was a Rice graduate. We landed the Adidas franchise for the 11 western states plus Alaska and Hawaii.

The general partner — who directed the partnership — called an emergency meeting. I didn't know what it was about. The partnership owned an Aero Commander, which was then a top-of-the-line plane. Even though we had a private pilot to fly it, I chose to pilot it on this trip. I flew it from Reno to Merced, Calif., where I picked up two of the partners, who were brothers. We flew on to the meeting in Santa Clara.

En route, one of the partners came to the cockpit, lifted my headset and said, "Link, don't you feel badly you didn't go to college?"

I got mad. "You dumb bastard," I said, "while you were cracking those books, I was making a living."

We landed. The general partner brought the meeting to order. He said the bank was foreclosing on one of the partners (the guy who had lifted my headset) and this partner wanted to borrow $40,000 from the limited partnership.

I lacked a degree but I was sharper than these guys. Immediately, I asked four or five of them if they needed any money. Each said yes.

"There's no way we can open this can of worms," I said. Then I made a motion that we wouldn't lend money to any of the partners. Another man seconded my motion. The proposal to lend the money was defeated.

Now I had to fly the brothers back to Merced. In flight, I suggested the cash-pressed partner sell his interest in a building in Santa Clara, that the partnership owned, to the rest of us for the $40,000.

He agreed. A few years later, the rest of us sold the building and we each received more than $100,000.

That shows it isn't important where you went to college. The best education is the school of hard knocks.

11

The Sportsman's Life

One thing I needed to learn when I got back from the service was to slow down, to downshift, and not be so surly and impatient. In combat, I'd had to be precise; there was no margin for error. Every detail had to be covered. But now it was peacetime. I was a civilian.

Chet and I hired a bookkeeper not long after we'd gotten back. I went up to the office upstairs one day, and she was reading a magazine and eating candy she kept in a drawer. I chewed her out in a hurry. (Later on, we got rid of her; that's all she did was loaf.)

After I got home, I'd been so accustomed to being combat-ready, I'd get mad easily at the store; but then I said to myself, "Now wait a minute here. You're not in combat now. Maybe you better settle down." It took a period of adjustment, but I adapted.

Still, even today, I'm hardly what you could call easy-going. My office is upstairs at the Sportsman, and if I see an employee standing around, arms folded, instead of doing something, it's grounds for me to take the person aside.

Swede Christensen, our first full-time employee, was a model worker. Later, as our work force grew, we'd hold weekly store meetings and assign each person duties. When our employees weren't waiting on customers, they straightened up their assigned departments. They arranged the inventory on shelves, or dusted. That kept them working; what's more, your help wants direction. They crave it. Another point: the employees play follow-the-leader. Chet and I set the example: we worked hard. We didn't stand around with our arms folded, waiting for something to happen, the way some employees do today.

We demanded our employees be honest, courteous and helpful. I had one employee, a big guy, who was a problem. A customer came in one time with a pair of Converse athletic shoes. "I have a problem with the sole of this shoe and I've only worn them twice," he said.

"Who are you kidding, 'only wore them twice?'" the employee said.

This behavior, evidently, was part of a pattern with this man. I hauled him up into the office. It was a store policy that, if a customer came in and wanted some adjustment, to always "roll out the red carpet." Say, "God, we're sorry you had to come back in. Come over to the department, we'll fix you up with a new pair of shoes." We had no problem with the manufacturers; they'd replace the product.

This employee, however, was arrogant. He'd insult a customer. I eventually had to fire him.

When a customer comes in to exchange or replace an item, and you satisfy him, you make a great customer. Why insult him?

Jobs were precious back in the 1940s and the 1950s; there was more unemployment in Reno, and not everyone had a job, but plenty of people were looking. Today, a kid can walk out of a job at a store and go to work at McDonald's. Help-wanted ads fill the classified section of the newspaper. But in those days, jobs were hard to find. And so when you hired an employee, he was likely to stick with you for some time.

We hired plenty of students for part-time work. Most of them were very good. I'm surprised sometimes how many worked for us. There was an article on the Sportsman in the local newspaper one time. Bill Thornton, the Reno lawyer and part-owner of the Club Cal-Neva, cut out the article and underlined a sentence about us hiring very fine, honest people. "Yes, including me," he wrote in a letter to me.

I'd forgotten he'd worked for us as a kid.

Many times I've encountered adults who've said, "You remember me?" One was a foreman for Sierra Pacific Power Co.

"Your face is familiar," I said. It's a line I've frequently used.

"I used to work for you," he said.

We must have been a very popular place for good kids to work at.

I guess we have been a Reno institution.

The Sportsman began sponsoring a junior ski program in 1955. The program still is going today, up on Mount Rose.

Marcy Herz, a ski instructor at Mount Rose, got Chet and me interested in sponsoring the program. Bob Law, the head pro at the Mount Rose ski resort, arranged for two hours of professional instruction and a lift ticket for $1. The Sportsman arranged for a bus to take the skiers to the slopes.

The idea was that if kids got interested in skiing, so would their parents. The promotion was good for the community, but it also developed customers for the store. It surprised me how many customers we developed through the program.

Today, the junior ski program runs several weekends in a row, unless there isn't enough snow. It remains very popular.

A parent will come into the store occasionally and say, "You know, my father skied in your program, and now my son's skiing in your program."

Yes, the Sportsman has been a strong part of Reno.

THE SPORTING GOODS BUSINESS always is in flux. The consumer determines what you keep in stock.

Take shoes, for instance. Our most expensive shoe, 60 years ago, was the Converse All-Star, which retailed for $4.95. Now athletic shoes cost way over $100 a pair. There are chain stores that sell nothing but athletic shoes.

I still can't get over how times have changed. A 10-year-old kid came into the store not long before I sold the business to one of my employees, Steve Humphreys, in 1995. The kid was with his mother, and he had a decent-looking baseball glove with him. "Mommy," he said, pointing at a glove on a rack, "that's the one I want." He wanted a $95 glove.

I recalled how the kids on my block had but one glove to share among us — an old, left-handed fielder's glove we decided the catcher in our pickup games should use.

"Ma'm," I said to the boy's mother, "I really don't think he needs another glove." She looked at me like I was crazy, and bought him the glove.

Prices of sporting goods have soared for

Here is a softball team I coached, 1949. They were the ninth-grade champions of the Rotary league in Reno. I'm at far left in the back row, in the suit. The guy at right in the sport jacket is assistant coach Hal West. Back row, from left: Blaine Hendrickson, Dick Blanchard, Howard Davis, Walter West, Bill Thornton, Jim Hessman, Buzz Meyers, Les Ede, Bob Arndell. Front row, from left: Ruel De Paoli, Ken Corica, Richard Jutkins, John Ferrari, George Fuji, Daryl Pelizzari, Dean Miller, Hank Derrico, Bill Eisele.

several reasons. One, labor costs have gone up, along with the cost of living. Two, the products are much better designed. The gloves we had when I was young are entirely different from the ones they have now. Finally, the consumer is welling to pay big bucks for products their children's friends have.

I remember when a Louisville Slugger baseball bat, the best you can possibly buy — made of second-growth ash wood, autographed by Joe DiMaggio or Babe Ruth — was $3.95. That was 60 years ago. Now, aluminum bats for Little Leaguers can cost more than $100.

The first skis we stocked were made by Northland. They were very stiff wood skis, and designed for the icy conditions of Lake Placid, N.Y. Groswold came out with a more flexible ski, and that changed the market.

Other manufacturers followed suit in making more flexible skis, including Northland. Consumer needs drive the market. As the skiing industry mushroomed, a line of products hit our shelves: boots, underwear, and so on.

Skateboards, in-line skates — these are other products that consumer crazes turned into large industries. Specialty stores, and chains, sprouted up and spread nationwide, generally selling only single kinds of products. But this never affected us. I never looked too much at competition. I knew the Foot Locker was in town, and Big 5 Sporting Goods. As I've said: you just run your own business the best that you can possibly do. You don't say, "Oh, Foot Locker's got shoes now, we're going out of the shoe business." Instead, you improve your shoe department. With that philosophy, you can compete with anybody.

Larger sporting goods stores, including those in advantageous locations, such as strip malls or large malls, have their weaknesses. Their biggest weakness is their help. Their employees haven't been trained to really know their product and really be honest with their customers. Jim Campbell, a friend of mine who's since passed away, called me one time from his home in Santa Barbara, Calif. Half-jokingly, he said, "Link, I heard a rumor, and it's true. Big 5 is coming to Reno. Ha ha ha."

"So what?" I said.

Big 5 opened up in Reno. The Sportsman's business increased. Big 5 is a chain, and its help is not as good as our help. Our employees are honest with the customer, know our product, and our store doesn't make too much of a profit, just enough. The larger stores are not magicians; they have their weaknesses.

Most of our employees have sports backgrounds. Therefore, they're interested in the products. I also learned something 60 years ago from Mr. Spiro, the owner of Spiro's, one of the largest sporting goods stores in the country, on Market Street in San Francisco. I got to know him through a friend of mine who worked for him. Each of his clerks wore a suit and tie and carried a little duster in the suit pocket. Mr. Spiro explained to me why: "When they're not waiting on a customer, they go and dust the merchandise, and adjust it."

In other words, his employees were working all the time. And there was another point: by cleaning and arranging the products, they were becoming familiar with the products, and therefore could do a better job selling. You pick up a canister of tennis balls, you read the label, and you absorb product knowledge.

I explained this to our own employees. That's one way how the Sportsman maintained an edge all these years.

Chet and I also instituted employee uniforms, a couple years after opening up downtown.

The gun department and our offices both were downstairs. One day I walked up the steps to the main floor and a man said, "Do you work here?"

"Oh, sure," I said.

"I'd like to buy a knife, but there's nobody here to wait on me."

I looked up. Two of our clerks were facing a wall, adjusting something, paying no attention to the counter.

I sold the man a knife out of our glass case.

I realized I'd have to put our employees in some kind of outfit, so customers could shake them out if they weren't being helped.

Powers, a manufacturing company, was closing out broadcloth referee shirts for very cheap: $1 apiece. I bought a bunch of them. They were a bargain to buy, and also tied into sporting goods. These black-and-white shirts became our uniform. Employees also wore black pants, Adidas shoes, a belt with a store logo and a bolo tie with a logo. They were very proud to wear this uniform. Chet and I wore it, too.

Steve, the new owner, does not require employees to wear the striped shirt. Times change.

IT'S FUNNY WHAT MAKES a business tick. Olga was quite an artist, and designed our first logo. It featured a tree and a fisherman standing in a creek with a trout hooked on the end of his line. She wrote "Sportsman" in script and our address, 358 N. Virginia St. Then Lew Hymers — a celebrated and highly skilled local artist — took the logo to a new level.

Hymers, an extraordinary caricaturist, drew a regular column, "Seen About Town," for the *Reno Evening Gazette* newspaper from 1938 to 1946. He was a contemporary of Robert Ripley of "Ripley's Believe it or Not!" fame, and at one point worked on the *San Francisco Chronicle* alongside Ripley. Hymers' Reno column depicted local luminaries, bankers, gamblers, politicians and the like. He also was a sportsman and fisherman who came into our store quite often. He was a real nice fellow. He knew Chet and I didn't have a hell of a lot of money. So he ended up drawing a new logo for Chet and me at no charge.

Hymers took the script-written "Sportsman," jettisoned the fisherman and inserted Chet's and my faces. That logo — depicting us in all our youth with our names, "Chet" and "Link," beneath — has remained on the Sportsman's advertising for nearly six decades, including the sign outside our store. We didn't realize how important that logo was and how it would affect our business. It became a recognizable mark — sort of a local version of the *Coca-Cola* trademark — giving us legitimacy and at the same time marketability. A customer scanning the pages of a newspaper would instantly distinguish the logo on an ad. Customers in the store would see Chet or me and identify us with the caricatured faces in the logo. Hymers' little sketches became our trademark.

Chet and I used to joke that we were as popular as the Smith Brothers — those two bearded faces on the packages of the cough drops bearing their names.

For years after Chet and I opened the store, locals would inquire whether we were Santino's sons. Then they'd lapse into the story about how our father had lent them $500 and never asked for a note in return.

. . . We'd finish the story for them: yes, he said that if their word wasn't good, their signature on a note wasn't, either.

Yes, our father had been very generous. Some of that trait rubbed off on Chet and me, I suppose. We cut breaks to a lot of kids who came into our store, but couldn't afford the full price of an item. We extended lots of "credit."

Two identical twin brothers, 10 years old, had designs on a model airplane engine that was in a plastic box. It cost $4.95

That was too steep. But they suggested a down payment.

"We want to buy that, and we don't have the money. Can we put down 10 cents apiece?"

"Sure," I said.

I marked the box "sold." I kept a slip of paper in the back to track their payments.

A week later the twins came in with another nickel or dime or 15 cents. This continued until they got up around $4.

"Here," I said, "you can have it."

Forty years later, I was upstairs in my office at the store. A man in a suit came in.

"Do you remember me?"

"Your face is familiar," I said, using my standard line. Actually, his face *was* familiar.

I looked at him, and looked at him.

"You know, you did me and my brother a terrific favor," he said.

"Do you have a twin brother?"

"Yes."

"Did you buy a model airplane engine?"

"That's what I wanted to thank you for! We're both in the computer business in California. We're very wealthy. And we still have the model airplane engine. And it's still in that plastic box. I told my brother that when I came to Reno I'd come to thank you for helping us."

That made me feel good.

Fishing hooks were about 15 cents a dozen. We had bins of hooks, and customers would take them out and lay the hooks on a piece of glass to count them. Often, I'd see these young kids count out a dozen, then put four or five back.

"What'd you put them back for?" I'd say.

"Well, we don't have 15 cents, we only got 10 cents," they'd say.

"Take the whole dozen for 10 cents," I'd say.

Many times, years later, I'd have the kids, now grown to adults, come in and thank me.

Today, for goodness' sake, every kid has $20 in his pocket. A kindly store clerk isn't needed. Kids today are kind of spoiled.

Chet and I weren't generous toward kids to build our reputation and bring in more customers. We simply were doing it to help the kids. We'd gone through the same thing as kids during the Depression.

CHET AND I HAD a local weekly television show, *Sportsman's Corner*, for 28 years. We started out on KOLO, and later moved to KTVN. We eventually renamed the show *Sportsman's Trails*.

Lee Hirshland, station manager for KOLO-TV Channel 8, an ABC affiliate and the only station in town back then, came up with the idea for the show. Chet already had a weekly outdoors show on the radio on KOH. He'd talk about hunting and fishing.

In 1957, we started our TV show. It turned out to be great advertising for the Sportsman. We got two canned commercials, free of charge, as part of the deal.

We broadcast the shows live from the studio. We'd mostly discuss hunting and fishing conditions for the week ahead. We'd run a five-minute film we'd shot with our own 16 mm cameras, showing footage of Chet or me hunting or fishing in a nearby area. We provided good information to viewers.

We had a mailbag segment. We'd put letters from viewers in a mailbag and pull one out. We'd award a prize to the writer of the letter we pulled out. We had no problem getting prizes donated from manufacturers. A fishing rod, a hunting knife, a pair of shoes.

We also had a game or fish recipe of the week, selected from what viewers sent in. We'd announce who'd sent it. Eventually we compiled a cookbook out of 1,500 recipes we'd received. It was very popular.

There was no rehearsal whatsoever for the show. Chet and I would have our film ready, and we'd grab our mailbag and head to the studio. We'd take our places on the set, and the camera would focus on one or the other of us, or both.

"Ten seconds," the cameraman would say.

"Are you going to open, or do you want me to open?" Chet would say.

We'd decide, then launch into local hunting and fishing conditions, and other pertinent information. We had good news sources. Archie Corbari, who ran the lodge at Wildhorse Reservoir near Elko, would send in the fishing conditions. We had first-hand information from all over the region.

A person with a Los Angeles advertising agency representing First National Bank in Reno called up. "We're told that you have an outdoor show," he said. "We'd like to have the president of First National Bank, Ernie Martinelli, and Dick Johnson showing outdoor paintings on your show."

Johnson was a very famous painter now, but I'd met him in Lovelock when he was a milkman. We'd hunted together.

"Sure," I said, "that's right down our alley, I know them both."

Two men and two women from the ad agency flew in from Los Angeles. One of the men said, "Now, Mr. Piazzo, we'd like to rehearse the show."

"Is that right?" I said. "We don't rehearse."

All these paintings were lined up in the studio. Beautiful oils of pheasant, quail, and so forth.

I had the studio manager set up chairs for the four of them.

"Mister," I said to the ad agency man, "all four sit down, and in 35 minutes the show is over."

"We better rehearse!" he said.

"We don't rehearse," I said.

He was pissed off.

Ernie Martinelli and Dick Johnson sat down, and Chet and I took our places. Martinelli and Johnson were wearing suits.

"Ten . . . nine . . . eight . . ." the cameraman counted.

We were on.

The *Sportsman's Corner* television show, New Year's Day, 1957. The guest on my knee is my son Craig.

I opened up. "Now you folks at home, you may not know these guys. One's a bank president, one's a famous artist. I'll give you three guesses. Which one is the banker, which one is the artist?"

Both looked like bankers in their suits.

"Have you guessed?" I said.

"OK, the guy over on the left is Ernie Martinelli. He's the president of First National Bank. This is Dick Johnson, who is now a very famous artist. And his first painting was a hawk. Many years ago I used to hunt with this guy. I told him, 'You better

take up another profession,' because you couldn't even tell it was a hawk."

"Thank God he didn't take my advice, because now he's a world-famous artist. And here are some of his paintings."

The camera flashed on the paintings lined up against the wall. First National Bank was displaying Johnson's artwork in their branches. They were holding a contest of some kind for customers, with a painting at each branch to be given away as a prize.

I explained all that to the viewers. Then we went through our regular segments: the hunting and fishing conditions, the recipe of the week, the mailbag, the five-minute film.

And the show was over.

The L.A. adman came over to me. "I can't believe it," he said. "At home, we would have to rehearse this show four times. It went over perfect!"

I knew there was nothing worse than rehearsing. Not only do you end up stiff, but you have to remember what you rehearsed. If you don't rehearse, it just comes out naturally.

I never was nervous in front of the camera.

Before the camera came on in the studio before each show, the station would play the lead-in tape: a series of goose calls. *Hoyk, hoyk, hoy-hoyk.* The lead-in became ingrained in the minds of many, many local residents.

People would tell us, "You know, at home, I'm out cutting the grass or working in the garden, and I hear that goose call and I run in to watch your show."

It could have been an actual gaggle of Canada geese flying overhead in formation that sent them indoors!

At first we aired Wednesday evenings, but then the show moved to Friday evenings, which was much better for us. It gained viewership, since outdoorsmen could then anticipate watching our show to plan their weekends.

The show was tremendous advertising for us. It associated our store with professionalism. If customers wanted to know about hunting and fishing and watched our show, where were they going to buy their sporting goods?

Lee Hirshland got a bunch of business partners together and purchased a TV station in town, KTVN Channel 2. It was a CBS affiliate. I was one of the partners, so *Sportsman's Corner* moved to Channel 2.

We later sold our station interests to Sarkes-Tarzian, a company in the Midwest. A new station general manager was hired. He ended up selling our 5 p.m. Friday time slot to another show.

He called me. "Now we're going to put your show at 1 o'clock in the morning."

"Take the show and stuff it," I said.

Thus ended our 28-year run on local TV. We canceled our advertising on Channel 2.

I was out playing gin rummy at Hidden Valley Country Club. Here came Lee Hirshland and Mr. Sarkes, owner of the station, and the station general manager.

Lee asked if I remembered Mr. Sarkes.

"Yeah, I remember him," I said, shaking hands. "How are you, Lee?"

"Have you met the manager?" Hirshland asked.

"Yeah, that's the guy who fired us!"

Lee put his head down and said in a low voice, "Well, I don't think he fired you."

"The hell he didn't, he put us on at 1 o'clock."

Hirshland backed up and didn't say another word. He knew I'm outspoken and very direct.

All kinds of people called the station wondering why we weren't on. The end of our show was written up in the newspaper.

Later on, the station GM was fired.[28]

THE BUSINESS TIPS I have to pass on haven't changed in 60 years:

Know your product. Deal honestly. And be very, very helpful.

When I see a business fail, the causes are very obvious to me. The failure can be traced to a lack of the three business principles above.

You walk into a business and if the help cares less whether they wait on you, well, that's a bad omen for the business.

The Sportsman has been in business continuously since 1938 — the longest tenure for founders to be involved in a business in our state.

Key personnel proved invaluable to the

---

[28] I don't regret being outspoken. Sometimes you have to hold your ground if you're right. Here are two incidents from when I was on the executive committee of the National Sporting Goods Association.

The executive director was a guy named Marvin Shutt. He was politically savvy but not the most scrupulous soul in the world. He and his executive secretary were standing at the entrance to the Morrison Hotel one evening during the 1960 association convention in Chicago, waiting to collar executive committee members. Shutt asked me to excuse Helen and accompany him to his suite for a private talk. In his room he told me he wanted to keep the current president on for another term. This went entirely against protocol. Throughout the association's history, each year the vice president from the previous year would be made president. The current president, however, was in Shutt's pocket, and Shutt was looking out for his own interests. "Marv, you can't do that," I said. "You're destroying the procedure." He raised his fist. "Link, I'm going to railroad this thing," he said. I raised my fist. "I'm going to stop it," I said. The executive committee met the next day to name the new president. Shutt made an eloquent speech on behalf of re-electing the current president. I stood up and spoke on the importance of maintaining procedure and making vice president Bob Brenaman the president. I also knew that the newspapers in Brenaman's hometown of Richmond, Va., had published big articles announcing he was to be the new president. Brenaman was a fine Southern gentleman. Fortunately, my

Sportsman over the years. No business can operate without good people in the important posts. The rest of the employees are part-time; they come and go. It's vital to a business's success to have the right people in the right places. They're the ones who stay.

Chet and I divided the store operation into the team department, industrial department and retail department. We put a manager over each department. That, plus an office manager, was all we needed as far as main employees; the rest all were part time.

The industrial department supplies Little League baseball, Pop Warner football, youth basketball programs and so on. The retail department covers goods sold off the shelves. The head also is in charge of part-time help. Swede Christensen was head of that large department for about 42 years. He was still working for us when he died.

The head of the team department was a traveling salesman in charge of selling uniforms and equipment to high schools and universities and various institutions.

We've supplied the University of Nevada Wolf Pack teams off and on since we opened. The university puts contracts out to bid, and sometimes we win, sometimes we lose. Other good customers have included the Nevada State Prison, which fielded baseball and basketball teams. Most of the area high schools have been good accounts.

Steve Humphreys was our team department man for a quarter-century. I ended up

selling him the business in 1995.

Chet and I ran the business as a partnership for many years, but our lawyers and accountants eventually persuaded us to incorporate. Incorporating provides another level of protection, since if a business is sued, the owners' assets can't be involved, only the corporation's.

Chet and I received great legal advice over the years. Our first lawyer, Harlan Heward, loved us. He shot skeet with us. He often did work for us for nothing. Later, as Chet and I bought property, he'd write up a lease document for $25. That's unheard of today.

We never turned the Sportsman into a chain. It would have diluted our competitive edge. The owners are supervising a store all the time; they cannot be in three places at once. Chains operate differently, but cannot provide the real specialized service of a local store with the owners on the premises. It's the same in most businesses.

It makes a big, big difference with a hands-on owner on site.

We moved the Sportsman from downtown to the new Sportsman's Corner in 1978. We needed the store to anchor our new plaza, and the store itself needed more space. Also, parking had become a problem downtown.

Chet and I split as partners in the Sportsman that year. I bought him out. He retired from retail and opened Sportsman Safari, a travel agency specializing in adventure trips around the world. He merged his outdoors knowledge with his passion for travel, and

---

viewpoint prevailed. Later on, Brenaman's wife, Jo, a Southern lady, took me aside with tears in her eyes and thanked me. She said not being made president would have destroyed her husband. But I would have stuck up for anybody in that situation. Right is right.

The next year I was president of the association. I knew that every year Shutt budgeted $200,000 for "convention expenses." No one ever challenged him to explain that extravagant sum. The executive committee met that summer in one of the cottages at the Ambassador Hotel in Los Angeles. After we finished the agenda items and moved on to old and new business, I asked Shutt for a breakdown on "convention expenses." "Do you realize what cost-accounting is, and how much it will cost?" he demanded. I said I wasn't asking for cost-accounting, just a simple breakdown of costs. He threw down his pencil, said, "Those ungrateful sonsofbitches!" and stormed out. We were shocked. I found him walking circles on the lawn. I put my arm around him and said, "You made a big mistake back there. There's only *one* ungrateful sonofabitch. That's me." I asked him to provide a breakdown of costs at the February meeting in Chicago. Guess what: I got the breakdown. And we cut expenses significantly. Which only goes to show that the extra money was going somewhere other than to cover "convention expenses."

hired his daughters, Christine Larsen and Gayle Stevens, to run the business.

Chet has led customers all over the globe: Alaska, South America, Africa. He's doing what he loves.

I stayed on running the store another seven years. Then I checked my birth certificate. I found out how old I was. I was almost 77.

Craig, my son, had worked at the store through high school and college and managed the retail department since 1978. I was going to give him the store, but he lost interest in retail and turned me down.

I sold the store to Steve Humphreys, who had been with the Sportsman 25 years. I'd hired him as a young guy from Idaho who had worked for a good friend of mine, Sib Kleffner, who owned Kleffner Sporting Goods and was on the National Sporting Goods board with me. Steve had moved to Nevada and was looking for a job. He fit in perfectly.

He'd done a good job at the Sportsman and knew how to run the business. I gave him a good price.

I wasn't sad to give up ownership. I've never been sad about any such turnings of the pages, I don't know why. After Chet and I left the downtown location, I was asked several times in interviews if I was sentimental about leaving the store my dad had built and which we had been in 40 years. I wasn't even a little bit sad. Life goes on, and you move on.

Today, I'm the store's non-paid "adviser." Steve demanded I stay on with an office at the store. I was going to move into a vacant space elsewhere in the plaza. I've since leased that space. My office is upstairs at the store. It works out for both Steve and me.

Steve and the managers don't always pay attention to me. But I show up every morning, seven days a week, at my office. I handle my various business affairs, including Hidden Valley Properties. I also have a hand in the Sportsman.

As I write this, Steve left a note on my mailbox this morning saying.,"I took my son deer-hunting, take over."

So I make sure the lights are on and the employees have come in on time. I'm sure they'd rather deal with Steve than with me.

The day before, three clerks were standing around, arms folded, bulls—ing. I walked in.

"You know something?" I said, "I'd like to have your job, I'd like to have *your* job, or I'd like to have *your* job."

They quickly broke up their chat and got to work.

I never did want to completely retire, ever. You've got to stay busy doing something. Your mind has a tremendous effect on your body. If you don't keep your mind working, for some reason or other your body deteriorates.

I've seen this phenomenon happen so many times in my life, it's amazing.

If the mind dies, the body dies.

I never expected when Chet and I opened the Sportsman in 1938, that it would last 60 years.

We owed money and we were having a hard time at the start. I still have my original books from the store. I've looked through them and seen that on one day we took in the grand sum of exactly $3.

But we never looked back.

12

Phantom Jet from Texas

Sometimes I think I did too much in my life. I always had something going. Hobbies, pastimes and community involvement have been major parts of my life.

How did I have time for it all? Easy. I just got up early and stayed up late.

I served as the official scorer and timer for high school zone and state basketball tournaments for 33 years. I'd begun before the war and resumed the job in 1946. I'd played for Reno High in the state tournament championship game in 1937, when we were up by a point with a second to go and, miraculously, lost after teammate Paul Seaborn tried to pass me the ball, then tackled the Carson player who intercepted it and was called for a flagrant foul. The Carson player hit two free throws.

After Chet and I opened the Sportsman, the state tournament director asked me to serve as the timer, controlling the clock. In those days, it was a volunteer job. The tournament always was held at the New Gym at the University of Nevada (now it's the Old Gym), and it was an all-day affair. We'd be served sandwiches and Cokes for lunch at the scorer's table. We'd work through the championship game at night.

I loved the tournament action, and it was a way for me to help out the community. It also was a way to see familiar faces once a year, such as Vic Arobio from Lovelock, who had played for the high school team there. In front of everybody, he'd give me a hug then go take his seat. It became tradition.

I built up seniority over the years. In one tournament, Las Vegas High was playing Reno High: a bitter rivalry. The Vegas coach, Harry Paille, was a guy I'd played with for Reno High. He came up to the two scorekeepers and complained about how many time-outs his team had left. One had charged him with two time-outs; the other had failed to record any. Harry decided he had two time-outs coming his way; he walked away to confer with his athletic director.

I leaned over to the scorekeeper who hadn't marked down the time-outs and said, "You put two time-outs there, real quick."

I called Harry over. "Where do you get that s— you have two time-outs coming?"

"Well," Harry said, "he doesn't have —" he stopped, looking at the scorer's sheet, and now noticing two Xes on it.

"I thought they were blank!"

My experience allowed me to handle many such disputes.

The tournament director ended up making me a scorekeeper as well as a timer.

In later years the tournament started paying the people working it, but I'd always send the check back. The rates rose to $500 per person. That was good money. Tournament directors changed every couple of years, and one came in who decided to hire his friends to work the tournament, given the good pay. After 33 years, in 1976, I was replaced. I was presented with a lifetime pass to all interscholastic games, as a reward for my service.[29]

MY BROADCAST CAREER STARTED on a night in 1947, as I kept score for the state high school basketball tournament. The play-by-play announcer for KOH was drunk. He was messing up the whole deal. Finally, the station engineer came up to me and asked me to take over the play-by-play.

I'd seen plenty of high school basketball, but I had zero experience in broadcasting. The engineer, Huey Keys (who later became station owner) pleaded with me. "Take over, I've got to get rid of this guy."

I moved over in front of the microphone. I was pretty good at it. Heck, I'd been around sports all my life. I told what the hell was going on.

Wayne Hinkley was head of Tidewater Associated Oil Co. in Nevada. He lived in Reno, and he heard my broadcast while he was sitting in a bar. Tidewater sponsored the KOH broadcasts of the big college games in the Pacific Coast Conference, and the University of Nevada's games. Hinkley got hold of me and said I should broadcast for Tidewater.

"I talked to Hal Deal," he said.

"Who's Hal Deal?"

"Oh, he's the head of all broadcasting and advertising for Tidewater in San Francisco. I want you to go down and talk to him."

I did. Deal was an older, gray-haired man. "You're in the sporting goods business and you know this is going to help your business," he said.

He offered me $40 a game to broadcast the Wolf Pack football and basketball home

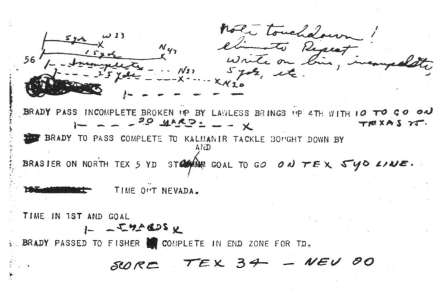

Here is an edited page of teletype for a re-creation broadcast.

games for Tidewater.

"What's Lee Giroux and Mel Venters getting?" I asked. They were the big-time announcers for Tidewater, announcing Stanford and University of California games in the Pacific Coast Conference.

"Why do you ask?"

"Because I'd like to make what they're making."

"Oh, we're paying them $80 a game," he said.

---

[29] One time before a tournament game, a fan in the stands — a big, fat guy — was blowing his nose and walking around during the national anthem. The minute the song was over, I walked across the court, up into the stands and said, "If these young kids by the hundreds can stand with their hands over their hearts, you can, too. Next time I see you do that, I'm going to call security and have you thrown out."

He didn't say a word. I walked back to the officials' table. Deloy Anderson, the scorer (and principal of Sparks High), said, "Link, I knew damn well that you were going to do that. And I thank you."

That was big, big money back then. The local guys were getting $5 a game.

"That's what I want to get paid," I said.

"Well you're not going to get that kind of money."

"Mr. Deal, I've been told about you. If I don't do a perfect job you're going to fire my ass. And if I do a perfect job I want to get paid as much as Lee Giroux and Mel Venters."

Four of us traveled from Reno to a sportscasters conference in San Francisco in September 1950. Left to right: Wesley Craig, KOH technician; Hugh Kees, KOH station manager; myself, the sportscaster for University of Nevada games; and Myneer Walker, the station's producer. At the time of our visit, KOH could boast of having built up a statewide network of stations to air our sports broadcasts. Stations in Reno, Las Vegas, Elko and Ely aired the games to every town in the state that had a radio station.

By God, he agreed. Deal used to tape segments of a broadcast to review it. A week later you'd get a letter. I'd called the Cal Aggies the California Aggies, and he wrote me a blistering note about it.

I worked with another fellow who did the commercials during the breaks. During halftime I'd have an interviewee. I interviewed many celebrities; one time it was the widow of Dr. James Naismith, the inventor of basketball.

I never did much commentary. And I detest the announcers today who do all the damn commentary, what they call the "color." I just kept the information flowing. The show had a producer, Myneer Walker, a friend of mine who was associated with Tidewater. He'd hold up white cards saying, "Score," or, "Commercial," to prompt me.

I worked hard to do accurate broadcasts. When a basketball team was coming to town from the coast, I'd have someone drive me to Truckee. I'd board the train into Reno and, roster in hand, meet every one of the players. I'd find out their stories, idiosyncrasies, and store the information in my mind. When they got out on the court, I'd know every name.

Dick Trachok, athletic director for the University of Nevada, told me I had the greatest memory for names.

During one football broadcast, Nevada was on the 1-yard line, ready to score. Walker held up a card saying, "Commercial." He wasn't paying attention to the game. I waved him off, but he flashed the card again. I hit him in the ribs, but he persisted.

So I had to turn over the mike to the color man to do the commercial.

I looked up after the commercial. I didn't know what had happened on the field.

"Now Walker, what happened?" I said. "We were on the 1-foot line."

He never called again for a commercial at a crucial moment in a game.

I got all kinds of phone calls after that fiasco.

Once a year I'd go on the road with the Wolf Pack basketball team to Las Vegas, when Nevada played Villanova. But I never went on the road with the football team. The way I broadcast the away games was by using teletyped updates of the plays. This involved what we called "recreation," calling the game from within the station studios back home. We were supposed to fool the audience. Isn't that terrible?

One time, Nevada's football team was in Denton, Texas, playing North Texas State. The teletype machine, a big, noisy thing, was in the next room. One of my men manned the machine, tearing off periodic updates and handing them to another guy who edited the report for me to read in the broadcast booth. I'd have to wing it between reports.

I had the team rosters nailed in front of me, with tongue depressors to help me keep track of the play. If the teletype report said that so-and-so for North Texas carried the ball over right tackle, I'd look over and see who was left tackle on defense for Nevada. Then I'd announce that he had made the tackle.

If I ran into a snag, unable to make sense out of the teletype information, I'd announce Nevada had called a time-out. But only three time-outs are granted per team per half, so if I used up the time-outs I'd have to come up with something else. "Gee, a dog just ran out on the field and he won't get off."

I even used a "drunken sailor" once.

Improvisation was the key to recreating broadcasts. A report might tell me the Wolf Pack had the ball on their own 30-yard line, second down and 8 yards to go. The next teletype might say North Texas had the ball. I had to either announce a fumble or intercepted pass — "Stan Heath fades back and throws a pass, 10 yards. Oh! It's intercepted by North Texas State. They run it all the way back to —" wherever the teletype said they

had the ball.

It was a hell of a job. It kept me sweating. You had to make it sound like you were there.

I never was found out, though. One time, I finished the broadcast of a Nevada game in North Texas, then left the KOH studios, got in my pickup truck and drove out to Lovelock for pheasant hunting. It was about a 90-minute drive.

Felix Turillas, owner of a restaurant and bar in Lovelock, saw me. I'd gone to Reno High with him. I went into his bar to meet my hunting buddy.

"Jesus Christ," Felix said, "I just heard you on the radio. How come you got home so fast?"

"I took a jet airplane."

He believed me.

My broadcast job lasted from 1947 to 1951, the year Tidewater quit sponsoring broadcasts.

It had been fun.

I STARTED FISHING AND hunting as a kid, as I mentioned, at the reservoir in northwest Reno owned by Sierra Pacific Power Co., and where old man Whiting was the caretaker, spotting us from his house on the hill and driving down in his Dodge touring car to chase us away.

I used to hunt religiously. When duck season was open, I'd hunt three days a week, Wednesdays, Saturdays and Sundays, at the Stead Ranch in Spanish Springs. The owner, Jim Stead, used to have me out as his guest. One day he told me he'd had so many requests he'd decided to organize an exclusive duck club. I helped him get the members — including my brother, Chet, George and Al Solari, Swede Matheson, Wally Rusk, Mike Scherupp and Art Smith, Bob McDonald — and he made me secretary of the club.

Chet liked big-game hunting. I liked upland game hunting. I became good friends with Smokey Quilici, who was born and raised in Lovelock and knew every square inch of Pershing County. We hunted chukar, pheasant, quail and ducks, many, many times together.

Jim Olin was head of the Nevada Bank of Commerce in Elko, lending ranchers money. He shot skeet for the Elko team, and I shot for the Reno team. We competed against each other a lot, and became good friends. He invited me deer-hunting one time.

"I don't like to hunt deer," I said.

He talked me into it. I didn't even own a rifle; I don't like to hunt big game. I don't like to kill large animals.

I borrowed Chet's 30.06 with a big scope on it. We went north in Elko County, to hunt on the land of a rancher named Dewy Moore. Of course, Olin was a very important person in those parts. Moore wanted to do a good job as a guide.

In the morning we got up, and the rancher said, "Now what do you guys want? Do you want a big deer with big horns? Do you want a young deer?"

"I don't want to kill a deer," I said.

The other ranchers looked at me like I was crazy. There I was with a big 30.06.

We went out to an area, and Moore drove me to higher ground in his jeep and said, "You sit up at the end of this canyon, and I'll go down and dog for you." He ran through the canyon to flush the deer out.

I sat on a big rock and waited. Here came the deer. One came to within 15 feet of me, and looked at me.

I shouldered my rifle.

The deer blinked its eyes at me.

I put the rifle down.

The deer looked at me again, and scampered off.

Twenty-two deer came by me. I counted them.

Moore came up, all out of breath.

"Link, Link, didn't you see them?"

"Dewy, you won't believe this. There were 22 of them."

He was pissed off.

We got back to camp. Venison liver is delicious. "All I want is a deer liver," I said. "The hell with these deer."

Once the others knocked a deer down, they gutted it.

All the ranchers had walk-in ice boxes. The ranchers in our group ended up giving me three deer livers. Of course, they were still pissed at me for not knocking down a deer myself.

I got home, and three days later, a driver with the Oregon-Nevada-Cal transportation outfit came into the store and said, "I got something in the alley for you."

It was a big old, gnarled buck, a 300-pounder. On its horns was a big tag that read: "To Link Piazzo from Jim Olin."

I called a few guys, and managed to give it away. Someone came and got the buck.

I don't hunt or fish any more. Smokey Quilici died and after that I hunted only twice more. You hunt for the comradeship as well as the game. Smokey mentioned many times that I was the only hunter he felt comfortable with hunting quail. They fly in all directions.

I remember hunting quail with Smokey right outside Lovelock, where the Humboldt River makes a big bend. There was a pasture. We were at opposite ends. We were shooting quail to beat hell, because Smokey had a lot of guests and we had to fill their limits, too.

"Link, Link," he yelled. A quail was coming my way. I was in his sights so Smokey put his gun down and yelled. He was in my sights so I put my gun down, too. The quail was coming right at me. I turned my gun around and struck it, left-handed, with the barrel.

I looked at Smokey. He was lying in the meadow, laughing. He told that story a million times.

He was terrific. Hunting wasn't the same without him, and so I quit.

Smokey knew of a secret canyon, which he called Dead Horse. We were having trouble filling out our chukar limit one day, so we got in his pickup and drove out to Dead Horse. He kept a big juniper branch in his truck. We drove into the canyon, and he washed out our tracks with the brush.

A beautiful spring ran in the canyon, and about 3 p.m. the chukar would come to the water by the hundreds. We'd flush them and fill out.

One of the two times I hunted after Smokey passed away, I went out to Dead Horse. Motor homes, trailers, dune buggies were parked there. There wasn't a chukar within 500 miles. The visitors were camped right on the spring water, which you're not supposed to do. There must have been 50 people there.

That's what happens when the population grows.

I drive off the 18th tee at St. Andrews, Scotland. The Royal and Ancient Building is at left in the background, with Swilken Bridge at right edge of photo.

I did a U-turn and left.

Boy, was I sad that day.

I'VE PLAYED LOTS AND lots of golf. I learned myself, just hitting balls at Washoe County Golf Course, while I was still in high school.

One time I took Dick Trachok, the athletic director at the University of Nevada, out to the course. He'd never golfed. I was giving him pointers on putting his weight on his left leg, lining up the putt, and so forth. Dick was having trouble putting.

At the third hole I said, "Look, you're an athlete. You've got that piece of metal in your hand. And there's a golf ball on the green, and there's a hole over there. Try to get it in the hole."

He putted perfectly after that!

He still laughs about that day.[30]

I had a 10 handicap in the mid 1950s. I had never in my life shot in the 70s. I was

---

[30] Through the years I have had to associate thousands of uniform numbers of basketball and football players with the athletes who wore them. But I recall only one of these numbers — No. 21, that of Dick Trachok, who was a great running back for the University of Nevada and later became the Wolf Pack's athletic director. Trachok is a man of good character whom I consider a good friend.

in the Reno Golf Club Championships in 1956. To qualify for the championships, they put you into "flights" — you had to score well enough in a round of golf. I shot a 79.

They put me in the first flight — with the best scores. I figured I had no chance.

There were three rounds over the next three days: I shot a 78, 79 and 79, and won the trophy!

Right after that tournament, I went back to shooting in the 80s. In the championship flight I'd tried harder and concentrated more.

That reminds me of something Bud Beasley, the former baseball coach at Reno High, told me. Beasley coached me in American Legion baseball. He had been a great pitcher for the Sacramento Solons in the Pacific Coast League. We used to drive out from Reno to watch him. He'd fill the stands; he was that good.

Beasley was kind of a comic. One game, he got on the mound. He had a big glove with holes in it. The palm of the glove was full of talcum powder. He pounded the glove and a cloud of talcum formed around him. The umpire tossed him out of the game.

The Oakland Oaks were Sacramento's bitter rivals. They were managed by Casey Stengel, before he became a famous major league manager for the Yankees, among other teams. Stengel would coach third base and try to psych out Beasley by having the batters use different antics.

One night not long ago, I was at a dinner with Beasley. "There's something I could never figure out, Link," he said. "We had a big field in Sacramento, and a short outfield in Oakland. I always pitched better in Oakland."

"Simple, Bud. You worked harder in Oakland because it was *a short outfield*."

I present Casey Stengel with the Sportsman of the Year award at the National Sporting Goods Association convention in Chicago, 1962.

"You know something, you're right," he said.

When faced with a big challenge, you just bear down.

I MET MANY PROFESSIONAL athletes in the course of my business or service associations.

I was president of the National Sporting Goods Association in 1962. Once a year we'd name a Sportsman of the Year. That year we elected Casey Stengel. We had a big plaque made and engraved a baseball diamond on it. On the bases we engraved the years and places he'd managed.

There were 1,500 people in the audience at our awards ceremony in Chicago. I made the big presentation of the plaque. Stengel came and accepted it. He looked at the plaque and said, "Whoever engraved this plaque engraved it wrong."

There was dead silence.

"Yeah, yeah," he continued, in his vintage Stengelese. "First base, yeah that's right, 90 feet to first base . . . and from first to second, that's correct , 90 feet . . . and from second to third, 90 feet, that's right . . . but it's got to be a mile-and-a-half from third to home, because I could never get anybody

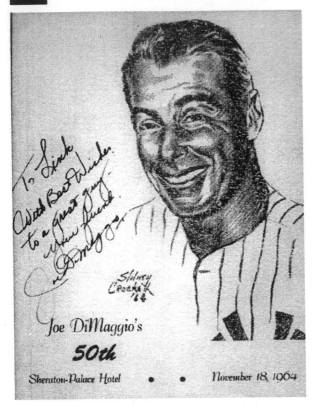

The program for Joe DiMaggio's 50th birthday party, at the Palace Hotel in San Francisco.

This autographed photo reads: "To Link, Best Wishes, from your pal 'Dizzy' Dean."

Autograph from Lefty Gomez, on a card commemorating his 70th birthday.

home!"

The place roared in laughter.

When it was over, I said to Stengel, "We had a guy in Reno that we used to go down and watch years ago in Sacramento when you managed the Oakland Oaks. He was a left-hander, you probably wouldn't remember his name."

"Bud Beasley," he said, just like that.

I KEEP THINKING ABOUT getting back into golf again. When Helen and I traveled through England and Scotland in 1963, I made it to the most sacred course in golfdom: St. Andrews.

The Royal and Ancient Building is behind the 18th green. I thought it was the clubhouse, so I went up and found out it is an extremely exclusive club. I couldn't get in (although years later, a friend got me in).

But I did get on the links. St. Andrews is a community-owned golf course, as are most of the courses over there, since golf is a way of life for the Scots. The doorman pointed me out to the little round shack. The starter scheduled me for a tee-time the following morning. I was paired with a Swedish doctor who'd just won a tournament in his country. Green fees were 85 cents.

The green fees today at Pebble Beach are $325. I and seven friends went down to Pebble Beach for a week every year for 17 years. We first went down in 1949. For lodging, three beautiful meals and green fees, the bill came to a total of $28 a day.

The third year, the manager came to the desk as I was signing in our group and said he had bad news. Before, guests staying at the lodge had no green fees. But the board had changed the policy; now guests had to pay a half-rate for green fees: $3. I screamed like hell.

The fees rose from $6 in 1952 to $325 in

The four golf marathoners and our wives, after we finished 73 holes in one day. From left: Dike Canak and Ruth; Dot Depaoli and Holly; Dan Canak and Mary; Helen and I.

1998. Golf has become so incredibly popular.

Northern Nevada used to have one golf course. Now the area has more than 40, with more on the way.

I used to play two-three times a week at Hidden Valley. But from the first day of hunting season, Sept. 1 for dove season, I wouldn't touch a golf club until hunting season ended in April.

I have great memories from golf. When there only was the Washoe County Golf Course, I'd have a standing $5 bet that I'd hit an 85 or less. I never lost.

One time, Dan and Dike Canak, Dino Depaoli and myself went to dinner. "Let's try to break our record and play 72 holes in one day," someone said.

We agreed. It would be a true golf marathon. We would pack our bags and putt in every putt.

Pete Marich, the pro at Washoe, told us to show up before dawn on a Sunday. We'd take off at sunup, and when we came through after finishing 18 holes he'd hold up whatever foursome was on the first tee and wave us through.

Our team finished second at the 1963 Mug Hunt. To my left are Reno Barsocchini, Mel Decker and Joe DiMaggio.

We made it through the first three rounds. Dan Canak was in great shape. He was a tough guy, with a terrific war record. We got on the 16th tee of the fourth round, and he hit his drive. His leg straightened out. He had a severe cramp. He lay down and said, "Fellas, go on without me, go ahead and play your 72."

"Oh, no," we said. We massaged his leg and got him back up.

We finally finished. It was dark out.

"You know," I said, "somebody will want to play 72, so let's play one more."

Our wives were waiting for us. We sent them down to the street behind the first green and had them turn on the car headlights.

We played another hole — 73 in all, all in one day.

John Petranovich, a restaurant-owner and good friend of ours, heard about our marathon golf match. He'd called the clubhouse and said to send us down with our wives for a complimentary dinner. So we got something out of our kooky effort.

I WAS CHAIRMAN OF the prestigious Mug Hunt Golf Tournament. We'd invite Hall of Fame baseball players. The Holiday Hotel, owned by Newt Crumley Jr., sponsored the event, which was held at Washoe County and Hidden Valley golf courses.

One tournament we had Luke Appling, Dizzy Dean, Bill Dickey, Joe DiMaggio, Lefty Grove, Gabby Hartnett, Carl Hubbell and Heinie Manush. I was in the photograph with these gentlemen. The photograph hangs on a wall in my office.

Someone figured out that was the largest number of hall of famers ever to sit at one table in the history of baseball. A copy of the photograph is in the Hall of Fame in Cooperstown, N.Y.

I became friends with Joe DiMaggio through this tournament. He came to it for several years. He was very shy and reserved, and hated publicity. He consistently came to me, as tournament chairman, to ask me not call on him to speak at the tournament banquets and awards ceremony.

"Joe," I said, "I've got to call on you. I'm going to call on Dizzy Dean and Carl Hubbell and Heinie Manush. If I don't call on you they're going to think what's the matter with me.

"Just get up and say three words and sit down."

So he'd get up and say, "Thanks for being here, nice seeing all you guys," and sit down.

I played a lot of golf with Joe. One day I said, "Joe, will you answer a question for me?"

"Yeah, what's that?"

"You stand before 65,000 people and you hit home runs, and you can't stand in front of 200 people, for Chrissake?"

"Link, that's different," he said.

He was right. You're face-to-face with people at a banquet. It's harder to do than perform, as part of a team, in a stadium full of fans in the stands.

I remember when DiMaggio went from the minor league San Francisco Seals in 1936 up to the New York Yankees. The first thing the sportswriters thought was that he was a snooty, aloof man. The truth was: he was nervous and bashful; just very shy.

He started hitting home runs and all of a sudden they got to liking him. They found out then that he was bashful. He remained that way until his death in March 1999.

Here's the head table at a Mug Hunt golf tournament. Jack Dempsey is the speaker. To Dempsey's right is Lon Simmons (head in hand), Carl Hicks, Ernie Nevers, Crazy Legs Hirsch. To Dempsey's left are myself, Emmett Saviers.

One other year we were playing golf at another tournament. A friend of mine, a young kid whose dad I knew, was breaking into radio. The kid, Jack Cafferty, told me he'd love to interview DiMaggio. He had a remote in his car, about 50 feet away.

I told Joe. He always said the same thing: "Is he all right?"

"Yes, he's a young kid breaking into radio. Go sit with him in the car."

Ten minutes later, here comes Joe, madder than hell. "You said he was all right. You know what he asked me? He asked me how old I was."

"For Chrissake, Joe, don't you know how old you are? Why the hell didn't you tell him you're old enough to play golf, if you didn't want to tell him your age?"

"I didn't think about that, I didn't think about that," he said.

I never kowtowed to Joe or treated him

like a celebrity. I always talked to him directly, and I think that's why he liked me.

Many years ago, Helen and I were vacationing in our motor home down in Mexico, just north of Puerto Vallarta. There was a fellow there I'd meet once in awhile from Idaho, named Ott. One day he came over and said,

Here is the committee of the 1961 Mug Hunt golf tournament.

"Why don't you come over and meet a friend of mine, a Mexican. He owns a banana plantation."

This plantation-owner turned out to be a complete baseball nut. He'd never left Mexico, yet he knew the players, their batting averages, everything.

Ott said to him, "Link knows Joe DiMaggio."

The man gasped. "You know Joe DiMaggio?!"

"I sure do."

He went on and on in amazement. He ended up giving me a stock of bananas for free.

I wrote to Joe about the Mexican fan. "Here's a guy who's never been to the United States, he knows all about baseball, he knows about you. I told him I knew you. If you have an old picture lying around, will you autograph the damn thing and send it to me?"

A few days later, here comes the picture from Joe. He autographed to the guy, "To José so-and-so, my friend to the south, from your friend from the north, Joe DiMaggio. I wish you good luck."

I sent the picture to Ott. Ott gave it to José. He was so thrilled, he framed the photo above his fireplace, and lots of people stopped in to see it. He was a big shot in town.

That's how generous Joe could be. But he was very shy.

Harrah's Tahoe held a golf tournament every year. At the banquet at Harrah's, I sat in the first of two tiers. At a table behind the railing was a table of 10 gray-haired women. I reached over the railing and said, "You know, I'm kind of curious. Is this a convention of some kind?"

"No no," one of them said. "We're all widows and Bill Harrah invites us up every year for a free weekend." Their husbands must have been high rollers.

"Gee," one of the women said, "there's a lot of celebrities out there. Do you know Ernie Nevers?"

"Sure," I said. He was a big football player in his day.

I told Ernie they wanted to see them. He went up and talked to them.

I asked Lefty Gomez to go up and talk to those girls. He really loved people. He went

Here is the head table at a Mug Hunt golf tournament. The photo depicts the most baseball hall of famers to sit at one table in the history of the sport. They are Luke Appling, Dizzy Dean, Bill Dickey, Joe DiMaggio, Lefty Grove, Gabby Hartnett, Carl Hubbell and Heinie Manush. A copy of the photo hangs at the Hall of Fame in Cooperstown, N.Y. Another copy hangs in my office. I was chairman of the tournament; I'm in the photo at far right.

up to their table, too.

I asked three or four more celebrities to go up and talk to the women. They did. Then one of the woman asked, "Is Joe DiMaggio here?"

I looked down. Reno Barsocchini, Joe's friend who always went with him on these trips, was sitting there, but the seat beside him was empty. I asked him, "Is Joe going to be here?"

"Oh yeah, he'll be down pretty soon."

"Well, tell him when he comes down, come see me because these gals want to talk to him."

"OK, Link."

Two minutes later, here comes Joe down the aisle.

I got up. "Joe, these gals would like to say hello to you."

"Link, why didn't you warn me?"

"Joe, how much warning do you have to

have to talk to some old, gray-haired gals?"

He gave me a stare. Then he went over. It was very brief. He talked to them for about two minutes. Then he came back, gave me a dirty look and sat down at his table.

That's the way he was.

LEFTY GOMEZ IS MY No. 1 favorite celebrity, along with golfing great Arnold Palmer. I'll discuss Palmer first. One incident in particular stands out in my mind.

Several years ago I was attending a sporting goods convention at the Kahala Hilton Hotel in Honolulu. It so happened that the Hawaiian Open golf tournament was taking place, and many of the touring pros, including Palmer, were staying at the hotel.

I had met Palmer on many previous occasions, such as golf tournaments and in Palm Desert, where I have a home in Indian Wells, and where Arnie has played in the Bob Hope Classic. One morning after breakfast at the Kahala Hilton, I found myself visiting with Arnie outside.

A large, deep moat surrounds most of the hotel. A gentleman dressed in a suit and tie recognized Palmer. Obviously the man was a fan, for he couldn't take his eyes off Arnie, who had his back to the man. The man was about 50 feet from us, not watching where he was going, and he fell into the moat. He made a huge splash.

"What happpened?" Arnie asked, turning.

"You caused that, " I said. "That man was gawking at you and fell into the moat."

We dashed over and helped him out. He

was so pleased to be able to shake hands with Arnie he wasn't worried a bit about getting sopping wet.

Lefty Gomez was a tremendous man, a kind man, a man with a great, great memory.

Monte Pearson was a house-painter in Reno. His brother, Vern, played for the Yankees, and in 1939 he pitched a no-hit, no-run game. Monte came in the Sportsman one day and said, "My brother Vern's coming to town. And he's going to bring Lefty Gomez with him."

I'm at left. Next to me is heavyweight champion Rocky Marciano, Lew Spitz, and Rocky's manager, Al Weil.

Lefty at that time was very famous. He had pitched in six World Series games, and won every one.

I met the two pitchers. Lefty took me aside and asked if I could fix him up with some booze and women. A guy named Jack Evershaw had Evershaw's Tavern on Second Street just east of Center Street, on the north side. Evershaw was a tremendous baseball fan. I called him and said, "Lefty Gomez is here. He wants to get fixed up."

"Send him down!"

A couple days Lefty showed up at the store, all bleary-eyed.

Lefty was an alcoholic, but he ended up straightened out completely, and became a great inspirational speaker on the subject. His after-dinner speeches for Wilson sporting goods were incredible.

About 25 years after I first met him, I went to Chicago to attend the National Sporting Goods convention. I went into the Wilson room. I knew the president and vice president of Wilson. We said hello.

"We want you to meet a celebrity," they told me.

The room was full of people. I went to the end of the room. A couple minutes later, here comes the celebrity: Lefty Gomez. He said, "You want to introduce me to Link Piazzo, for Chrissake? He fixed me up in Reno and took me duck-hunting."

He came over and put his arm around me. A tremendous memory!

Another year, Newt Crumley approached me before our big banquet for the Mug Hunt golf tournament, of which I was the chairman. "You know," he said, "we tried to get Lefty Gomez for our speaker, but he was tied up."

"Who'd you call?" I said.

He'd called the division manager of Wilson, whom he knew in San Francisco.

I called the president of Wilson and said, "Gee, we'd like to have Lefty come."

Minutes later, I got a call from Lefty. He lived in Connecticut. "Link, for you, hell yes, and no charge!"

He came in and did a terrific job at our banquet. Everybody loved him.

Dizzy Dean also was a great guy. I met him through the Mug Hunt tournament. He called everybody, "Padnuh." He didn't want to remember names.

He was a great pitcher, and after he retired he had a broadcast career. His English was terrible. "He slud into third," he'd say. A lot of people thought he talked that way on purpose, but that's just the way he spoke.

He was a very good shot. He and I were part of a hunting group one day in

Gardnerville. Coming back to Reno, I was sitting next to him in the car. He'd had a cataract operation. "Diz," I said, "how're you doing with those eyes?"

"Oh, gettin' along fine, padnuh, but my peri — my peru — my pehoo — !"

"You mean, peripheral?"

"Yeah, how in the hell did you say that?"

He was trying to say his peripheral vision was distorted.

He moved his hands to the right and left to explain. "My perinshal, whatever the hell vision that is, is bad."

That's the way he was. Nice man.

Dean was the opposite of DiMaggio on speaking. If you called on him, hell, he'd talk for an hour if you wanted him to.

He was very entertaining.

I knew Jack Dempsey. He sometimes lived in Reno. He built the Dempsey Building out by the state fairgrounds.

One thing many people don't know is that Dempsey had a high voice. He talked like a woman. He endorsed Bulldog Beer. They had another person do the voice for the commercials.

Dempsey was a nice, nice man, kind of quiet.

I could go on and on about the famous athletes I got to know, like Lefty O'Doul, a close friend of DiMaggio. Whenever Joe would get into a batting slump, he'd talk to Lefty and Lefty would straighten him out.

He was the opposite of Joe, very outspoken, entertaining. One night we were having a drink before a banquet, and he said, "Goddamnit, Link, if I'd have known I was going to live this long, I'd have taken better care of myself, for Chrissake. And I'd have saved some of my money. I blew all my money."

He used to say that all the time.

ONE OTHER CELEBRITY I should mention is Richard M. Nixon.

In 1939 the Reno 20-30 Club chose me as its delegate to attend the national convention in San Diego. The first evening a few of us — including Nixon, a delegate from Whittier, Calif. — ventured across the border into Tijuana, Mexico, and returned late that night. We didn't know that the

The cover of the 1947 PGA golf tournament.

hotels locked their doors at midnight.

Faced with being stuck on the street, we went to the rear of the hotel, turned over garbage cans and used them as step-ladders to reach the rear windows. We climbed inside and proceeded to our rooms.

Flash ahead 24 years, to 1963. Helen and I were on our way to Europe and stopped in New York. We dined at the 21 Club, where we ran into Nixon. By this time he was a lawyer in New York, following his failed bid for the presidency against John F.

Kennedy in 1960. Before that he'd been vice president under Eisenhower.

Nixon had a great memory. He remembered me and the garbage can episode. I had forgotten whom we'd elected national 20-30 president at that convention 24 years earlier, and he immediately mentioned Abby Strunk.

Five years later, in 1969, Nixon was elected our 37th president of the United States.

THERE WAS ONE OTHER hobby that I've had: getting people to quit smoking.

I used to smoke, from age 14 to 16. My mother didn't know, or she would have knocked my ears off.

In those days the top cigarette brands were Chesterfield, Camel and Lucky Strike. Fifteen cents a pack. Wings, which weren't supposed to be as good, were 10 cents a pack.

We smoked because the movie actors and big shots smoked. Unlike today, nobody knew back then what smoking causes: cancer, lung disease, heart disease. Today, before a young man or woman starts to smoke, he or she knows that.

I was a pretty good swimmer, especially underwater. I'd swim at the old Moana Pool. One day I was swimming underwater and I got about 20 feet from the end and my lungs felt like a bunch of needles were stabbing

I hand money to actress Constance Bennett during a 20-30 Club fund-raiser. At right is Pick Southworth, who was national president of the club.

them.

I tried to figure out the cause. You know, I thought, it could be smoking. I have no idea why I hit on that explanation. But I went into the dressing room and threw away my pack of cigarettes.

That was the last of my smoking for the rest of my life.

Years later, I became something of an anti-smoking crusader. And I've succeeded in getting about 10 people to quit. Kicking the habit is very, very difficult. But I have a folder of letters from people I've turned around.

Those who've successfully given up cigarettes for six months get a brand-new silver dollar in a plastic case from me and a note: "Keep that to remind yourself that you're doing what millions of people would like to do, but don't do."

I also give a silver dollar to any young person who doesn't smoke and is in his or her late teens or early 20s. I make them promise, in writing — including their name, address and age — that, "Link Piazzo, I'll never smoke as long as I live."

To turn around a smoker, you have to be real rough with them.

A few years ago, I went to buy outdoor carpet at a store in Palm Desert. The kid who helped me was good-looking and well-built. Halfway through taking the order he reached in his breast pocket and took out a cigarette and lit it up.

"Oops," I said, "maybe I don't want to buy this carpet."

"Why?"

"You've got to be the dumbest sonofabitch who ever lived."

That's the way you've got to talk to them.

"What do you mean, dumb?"

"How old are you?"

"Twenty-four."

"You're spending good money to destroy your health, you've got to be pretty goddamned stupid."

He reached into his pocket and tore his pack of cigarettes up.

I handed him my business card.

"Look, if you quit for six months, I'll give you a silver dollar."

A few years later he wrote me a letter, which I have. His name is Robert Smith. "Maybe you'll remember me, maybe you won't. I live in Palm Desert, Calif., and I work at Chuck Silva's Carpets. I think I sold you some outdoor carpet a few years back. You caught me smoking a cigarette outside the store and promptly lectured me on the evils of smoking. You offered me a reward if I ever quit smoking for at least six months. I believe the figure was a United States silver dollar. Well Link, I quit for four.

"Link, I appreciate your concern and want to give you a reward for looking out for the best interest of a young stupid kid. Thanks

I teach actress Constance Bennett to shoot skeet. She didn't learn too well.

a million, I wish I had that much to send."

He sent along a paper dollar with the letter. That was in October 1992.

I wrote him back: "I'm in receipt of your recent letter, and the good news that you are in your fifth month of kicking the habit. Also enclosed is a dollar that I am framing with your letter. I am anxiously awaiting your letter telling me that you have quit for six months and forever, so I can send you the silver dollar. Robert, the silver dollar is insignificant compared to the reward you will be giving your health, a memento that will remind you that you had the courage to quit."

I didn't hear from him again, so I wrote him again. I told him I polished a silver dollar and it was ready to be mailed.

He wrote back: "I just celebrated my 10th month without cigarettes. In 10 months I've gone from an unhealthy smoker to a health fanatic." He was exercising regularly.

I wrote back and sent the silver dollar. "Robert, there are millions of people throughout the United States who would like to accomplish what you have done. Enclosed please find the dollar. You earned it through sheer willpower. Try to use it as a constant reminder not to smoke again. If you're ever in Reno, please let me know, I'd like to take you out to lunch or dinner."

That was my best conversion.

I was down in Palm Desert waiting for my car to get out of the car wash. A young guy sitting next to me lit up a cigarette.

"What do you do for a living?" I said.

"I'm a contractor, I build homes."

"I wouldn't want you to build a home for me."

"Why?"

"You got to be one of the dumbest bastards I ever met."

If you don't talk with them that way — if you say, "Look, gee, don't you think it would be nice to quit?" — you get nowhere. They won't listen. They'll listen a little bit if you really chew their ass out.

He threw his cigarette away.

I HAVE OTHER GOOD Samaritan hobbies.

I give away Swiss Army knives to those who've done a good deed.

Jim Wood, my executive secretary at Hidden Valley Properties, went with me one day to Jack in the Box. A bunch of high school kids, about 10 of them, were sitting at a table.

I walked up to them. "Does anybody have any extra food they can give me?"

Most of them looked at me, and kind of smiled. One kid got up, "Oh, yes sir," he said. "I ordered too many french fries, and you're welcome."

I shook his hand. "Young man," I said, "I don't really need that food. I just want you to know that you're a fine young man, and you're going to be a fine man the rest of your life, and I have a gift for you."

I handed him a Swiss Army knife. He passed it around the table. The kids said, "I wish I had said that," "I wish I had said that."

I talk to strangers all the time. In elevators, anywhere. It all depends how you talk to them.

In another fast food place, I ordered a small meal, and it was a small bill. I pulled out a dollar and said, "That's the tough part," just joking. I reached in for more change.

The cashier thought I didn't have any more money. "It's OK, mister," he said. He reached in his pocket and put the money in the till.

I shook his hand and gave him the coins for the rest of the bill, and gave him a knife.

It gives me personal satisfaction. I always say, "You're a fine young fellow, and you're going to continue to be that way the rest of your life." The knife will remind him of that.

Can you find a better hobby?

13

The Roots Spread

Who has more influence on how you turn out than your parents?

My mother, Emma, died Thanksgiving Day, 1979. She was 94. She died knowing she had fulfilled her mission as a mother. Her five kids had turned out pretty well, including the three of us alive today — Chet, myself and Melba — who were still very young when our father was killed.

Mom always helped us out, both financially and with emotional support. She was the pillar of our family. She was made of stern stuff, indeed. Like so many immigrants, she passionately believed in America and the American system. She never missed voting in an election. Twice in her later years — at age 82 and 92 — she had a broken hip on election day, yet still got to the polls. "It's voting day today, and I'm going to vote!" she'd say.

We children would put her in the car and load in the wheelchair, and take her to the Veterans of Foreign Wars building on Ralston Street. We'd have to carry her up the steps. She was going to vote, period.[31]

When Chet and I were younger, we chafed

Mom on her 75th birthday.

at our mother's discipline, the chores, the rules, the curfew, the switch she kept on top of the stove. But later on, when we matured, we thanked her for the way she raised us. There was no gray area with my

---

[31] After mother broke her hip the first time, at age 82, her physician, Dr. Herz, took me aside and said there was a good chance she wouldn't walk again. Mother asked me what our conversation had been about. "He said you may have a little trouble walking," I said.

When she was released from the hospital, a walker was brought to her bedside. Mom was told the hospital's regulations required she leave in a wheelchair in order to be released. She folded the walker and threw it against a wall, then reluctantly sat in the wheelchair.

At home, she recovered and walked perfectly again.

Ten years later, Mom broke her other hip. Again, Dr. Herz told me she wouldn't be able to walk without help. But the same thing happened. Not many days after coming home, Mom was walking perfectly.

mother, period. It drives me crazy to hear people equivocate: "Well maybe this . . . maybe that . . . " With Mom, it was either right or it was wrong. It was very, very simple. Her universe was black and white.

She had to raise five children after Dad was killed. She raised us, and she raised us properly. She didn't have time for a whole lot of dialogue. Curfew: 9 o'clock you were home. Period. If it was three minutes after 9, that switch came off the stove. She didn't hit you too hard. If it was five minutes after 9, you got hit pretty hard. After that you came in at 9 on the dot.

One night I said to her, "You know, the Marinis have a 10 o'clock curfew."

"You know," she said, "the Marinis don't live in this house. It's 9 o'clock. Period."

We were taught that. And we lived that. It's a simple way to lead your life. Period.

And, oh boy, we were taught to be 100 percent honest.

This gray area business drives me crazy, especially in politics.

When her kids started school, as I mentioned earlier in the book, Mom laid down the three rules:

1) If you ever have to stay after school;
2) If you get into a fight;
3) If you get into trouble with the law;
that was grounds for the switch to come off the stove.

I know why she gave us Rule No. 2: we used to fight. A *lot*. But we took great pains to conceal this, including washing our faces at the Orr Ditch and applying cold pebbles to swollen lips. Mom only found out about two of my fights. There was the time I beat up Junior Vietti and his mother knocked on our door; and there was that Easter Sunday when Doddie Zunino knocked on our door and I had to fight a kid, and I came back with my nice white shirt bloodied.

Rule No. 1? Mom knew education was the ticket to getting ahead in America. She in-

Mom's 75th birthday party. From left: Chet, Melba, mom, Olga, myself.

sisted all her kids finish high school, and she would have loved it had we gone to college, as well.

Rule No. 3? Hell, we didn't even *think* about getting in trouble with the law.

I passionately believe that Mom's switch was the proper tool with which to raise us. This non-discipline bulls— they have now in the public schools is terrible. Kids are not stupid. They weren't in my day and they aren't today. If we knew we could get away with acting out and not be punished, we would have torn the school down. Corporal punishment would restore order in our public schools today, if only it were allowed.

Mom instilled so many values in her children. She had, as I've said, lost two fingers and part of her left arm when she was 10 and fell into a fire. This never held her back. She still had eight fingers, after all. It can always be worse. She did more with the three fingers on her left hand than most people do with a full set. How she'd harangue people who favored injuries! The family friend, for example, who limped into our kitchen one day, saying he'd lost a toe. "Well, why do you think God gave you 10 toes?" Mom said. "Can't you get along with nine?"

She told him to quit limping and get along with nine toes. After his visit, he walked out — without limping.

That was my mom.

She taught us that family always came first. Every day for years after our father was buried, Mom walked the mile-and-a-half to his gravesite and laid flowers. Chet and I, on a windy or blustery, wintry day, would say, "Mom, you don't have to go up every day."

She'd give us a look like, "Just forget it, kid."

Mom was a very determined person, very strong-willed. She taught us to be tough. Chet and I and the other boys in the neighborhood used to throw rocks and glass at each other and sometimes we'd get conked

Our beautiful daughter, Suzanne. She passed away at age 14.

pretty good on the head, but Chet and I never would go home to lick our bleeding wounds because we knew Mom would get the old whip out. Instead, we'd go down to Mrs. Zunino. Boy, we thought she was a magician. She'd apply baking soda on our wounds and fix us up.

Then we'd have to hide the scar from our mother.

Mom never showed pity for our stupidity. And I thought that was terrific. It taught me a terrific lesson in life.

Chet and I would horse around the house, and sometimes we'd get cut. Mom would say, "Naw, we're not going to waste a Band-Aid on that little cut." Maybe we'd sprain a bone, but that wouldn't elicit compassion from Mom, either. We'd just go off and the wound would heal on its on. And it worked!

Today, a parent would have a kid all taped up, and the injured arm put in a sling, and so forth. But we never dwelled on our bangs and bruises. Mom deliberately taught us a lesson:

It can always be worse. You can get along all right.

Mom taught us that you make your nest, and you sleep in it. She was completely accepting of the women Chet and I married, even though they weren't Italian or Catholic. She was ahead of her time in tolerance. Our family had to endure the "Dago" and "Wop" bigotry of our times, but Mom never got into any of that. Of course, she associated mostly with Italians and probably never heard ethnic slurs against Italians. Still, she never succumbed to ethnic animosity. Everyone, of whatever background, was a nice person unless the individual proved otherwise.

Mom gave her children the moral foundation to lead good, honest, productive and meaningful lives.

IF I TRACE VALUES Mom passed onto me and that I passed onto my surviving son, Craig, one is his commitment to perfection.

Since he was a little kid, if I assigned him something to do — he'd carry out the task to perfection.

I'd assign him an area of my garden to pull weeds from. I'd come home from work and his work space would be perfect. Until the job was completely done, he wouldn't leave it. He's been that way his whole life. He's in the window-washing business now, and he does an absolutely perfect job.

"When a task is once begun, never leave it until it's done. Be the tasks both great and small, do them well, or not at all."

I made a plaque out of that saying, and hung it on a wall of my office. I have lots of

Son Craig, when managing the Sportsman, showing the Sportsman softball trophy.

sayings on my office walls. Here's a saying I made up myself:

"True satisfaction does not come from success, but from what you have had to endure and overcome to succeed."

My son, Craig, is honest. And he is optimistic. And he has learned that one must rely on oneself to overcome obstacles and succeed.

He's overcome three bad habits, conquering each, and I am so proud of him for it.

I have another favorite saying: "The greatest conquest of man, is that of self."

During World War II, when my outfit was based on Ie Shima near the end of the war, a typhoon absolutely leveled our base. It looked like the city dump. Some of the younger guys were crushed: "Oh my God, what are we going to do?"

"You can always go over in a corner and die," I said.

"You want to go over and put your hands down and die? Or should we pick this crap up and find out if there's something usable, and build our tents back up and get back in business?"

We rebuilt the base.

Today, kids by-in-large aren't self-reliant. It's not their fault; they weren't raised to be.

They are raised in a different era from my generation. We went through the Depres-

Smokey Quilici teaching hunter safety to my sons Craig (with the gun) and Lynn, in Pershing County. On other side, blocked by Smokey in this frame, are his sons, Brad and Kip.

embezzled from his boss's business. The boss had deeply trusted the man, for he was a key employee, a manager. His embezzlement really hurt the boss financially. At the moment I'm writing this, the now ex-employee is sitting at his home, brooding, afraid.

If he worked up the gumption to come into the business, I'd tell him: "Grab yourself by the seat of the ass and solve the problem yourself. It can be solved. It will be a little bit tough, but it can be solved."

He can take concrete steps to overcome his addiction. He can work out a plan with his boss to pay back the giant losses. He probably can avoid the full brunt of judicial prosecution.

Instead, he's waiting for something to fall out of the sky and save him. Terrible.

sion. "If you want to eat," my mother used to say, "you got to work." It was simple. Kids today have $30, $40 in their pockets. You can't enjoy the virtues of spring unless you've endured the rigors of winter.

I teach Lynn about gun safety.

I thank my lucky stars my mother instilled true values in her children.

Kids today don't have discipline; they get everything they need. When adversity strikes, they don't know how to handle it.

They haven't learned that it can always be worse.

Members of the younger generation of Piazzos occasionally seek me out for advice. Mostly it's when they're in financial straits. I try to help them out. I may help them financially. I also try to counsel them how not to get into such a situation again.

Problems — even seemingly impossible ones — always can be worked out. There's a man I know who is a gambling addict and

MY OLDEST BROTHER, LOUIE, was killed in 1955 in an automobile accident.

He was driving home from his store, the Model Fruit Market on the ground floor of our hotel downtown. He was passing the university campus on Virginia Street when a large truck ran into him. He left two children: Carol and Buddy.

Louie was killed the same way my dad had died: the accident crushed his head. He also was the same age Dad was when he died:

49.

You can imagine how Chet felt when he got to be 48 or 49. He couldn't help but wonder if there was a curse on our family's males.

Olga married Dario Dibitonto and raised two children: Sam (who was elected mayor of Reno) and Darrell. She managed the St. Francis Hotel for many years. She passed away in 1965. Melba married Francis Cassinelli. She raised two kids — Julie and Dawn (who became schoolteachers) and Kevin (who became a Reno police officer).

Chet served as a Naval Air Force gunnery officer during WW II. Before going overseas he married Darlene Gilmer and raised two children: Christine and Gale. The daughters helped him out with his travel agency at the beginning.

Our family roots have sunk deep into Nevada, the land my parents came to from Italy. When Chet and I were kids, our relatives would get together every weekend — uncles, aunts and cousins — at our house or their house. It was normal. Or we'd go to Lake Tahoe together; it would take all day to get there, and we would spend the whole weekend camping on the West shore near Homewood and never see another person. The family was tight.

In today's society, the pace of life, and the mobility, and the dispersion across great distances, and with both parents of a family working, and television, too, all have separated relatives, disintegrating family lives. I've had young people come into the Sportsman and say, "I'm related to you." I'll say, "What's your name? What's your father's name? What's your grandfather's name?" Then I associate the relationship.

Isn't that terrible? Once upon a time, family ties were clear.

Chet organized a family reunion several years ago. He had T-shirts made up bearing the family crest. The clan gathered together on Sept. 15, 1996, at Chet's house on Lakeside Drive. About 80 of us crowded together for the group photo — three generations of Piazzos: spouses, children, grandchildren.

There we were, all because 91 years earlier, an Italian immigrant named Santino Piazzo had walked 42 miles through the snow to Reno, after his train ticket ran out 200 miles shy of San Francisco.

The Piazzo family reunion at Chet's home, Sept. 15, 1996.

Here are kids in the Sportsman's junior ski program, 1962. My son Craig is in front, holding the skis and wearing the pointy ski cap. My son Lynn is at right, in front.

14

Couplehood

Helen was my first, and only, love. I made a lot of big decisions in my life. My decision to marry Helen was one of the best I ever made.

She was pretty. After we were married, she'd model for functions for the 20th Century Club. She served as queen of the 1947 PGA golf tournament at Washoe County Golf Course, posing with $15,000 of silver dollars stacked on the practice green to show the prize money.

She was a trooper.

Helen was two years younger than I, and strong-willed, like me. And what has impressed me the most about my wife — she always has been very, very honest. Many times in conversation, she'll correct me. "You know," I may say, "we went about two miles to the west." She'll say, "No, it was about a mile-and-a-half."

Now, it wouldn't make any damn difference whether it was two miles or a mile-and-a-half. But she is completely devoted to accuracy. I admire her for that.

We have our arguments. People have told me I have a strong personality. I don't back

Helen, queen of the 1947 Reno PGA Tournament.

down. Well, Helen handles me just fine. She doesn't back down, either. She's outspoken. Once in awhile I'll criticize something, and she'll tell me to shut up.

We were in Fresno, Calif., at an organizational dinner of the California Indians, a very exclusive skeet- and trap-shooting group. I was the first to be elected to the board outside the state of California. It was just one more board I was on. I had been president of the 20-30 Club, president of the Sierra Nevada Sportswriters and Broadcasters Association, president of the National Sporting Goods Association, on and on.

So there we were, sitting at the head table in Fresno. Helen turned to me and said, "When are we going to get the hell out of these goddamned head tables and sit down there with the ordinary people?"

Helen modeling for our 20th Century Club.

She was kind of joking about it, but not joking, either. It would be better to enjoy the evening than sit up at an elevated table, looking like a fish in a punch bowl. I appreciated her opinion. It's just that, for whatever reason, whenever I get involved in something, I end up president later on.

Helen has been a great companion. She golfed and hunted with me. We'd boat together at Lake Tahoe and Pyramid Lake.

I learned as a young child that couples argue. Mom and Dad did, but when the argument was over, it was over. I learned that when you're married, you're married for life, for better or worse. Thank God Helen's and my marriage has been a good one.

YOU TALK ABOUT HOBBIES — Helen and I have taken some great trips together. She's as adventurous as I am.

In 1963, we went to Europe. I went to Vernon Durkee Sr., a travel agent in town. I told him I wanted to buy a car through Triple-A, for delivery in Portugal. I wanted to drive across Europe.

"No, no, nobody's ever done that and I don't want you to do it," Durkee said.

"Is that right?" I said. "Well, I'm still going to do it. Furthermore, I want no reservations."

I bought the car, a Renault. It was delivered from Paris to Lisbon. I bought plane tickets all the way to Lisbon.

Durkee called me the night before we were to leave and said, "Link, you said you didn't want reservations, but you don't have any in Lisbon! I won't get confirmation but I'll try to make them at the Ritz Hotel."

We did get rooms at the Ritz Hotel. Then we went to get our car, despite the language barrier. A smile and a handshake gets you by. With my English and Italian, and the Spanish I've learned to speak given my Italian, I manage to get along pretty good. I find somebody who speaks one of these languages.

Helen and I drove across the continent, visiting 13 nations. We got along great.

In Italy, we worked with Company Italian Travel — C.I.T. — the biggest travel agency in the world at the time. If we liked Venice, we would stay there as many days as we liked. We went at our own pace. We made plans as we saw fit.

We wanted to visit Austria. Looking at the map, we would have to go through Yugoslavia, a Communist country. We went to the U.S. embassy and were told we'd need a special visa, and that it took a long time to get one. So I talked to the people at C.I.T.

"Do you have your passport?"

Couplehood

I surreptitiously snapped this photo of Chinese soldiers on the Great Wall of China, 1997. We weren't supposed to photograph soldiers.

Here's the traffic in Beijing. Our tour bus had a police escort (note the car at bottom right).

Helen and Sunny, our tour guide in China, in Beijing. Sonny spoke perfect English, which she had learned at college. She was 27, and had never left China.

The Forbidden City in Beijing.

Helen in Tiananmen Square in Beijing.

Here is a group photo of the around-the-world trip passengers, with the Concorde. Helen and I are standing at far right.

"Yeah."

"You go to the Yugoslav border, and you show them your passport, and they'll charge you a couple of dollars."

We stood on the Italian side of the border. The Yugoslav border police didn't speak Italian, Spanish or English. But they were very polite. I understood they wanted some money, so I pulled some out.

I was escorted into a little room on the Yugoslav side. The customs agent spoke a little Italian. "Would you do me a favor?" he said.

"Sure, what do you want?"

"Can you tell me how to say 'thank you' in English?"

"I'll do that if you tell me how to say 'thank you' in Yugoslav."

So I said, "Thank you."

He said, "Fala."

We're shaking hands, and he's saying, "Thank you. Thank you," and I'm saying, "Fala, fala."

I only wanted a visa for two days. Now he wants to make me out a visa for a *month*.

In the Yugoslavian town of Celji, nobody spoke English. At the hotel desk I asked, "Parle Italiano? Speak English? Habla Español?"

The clerk said, "Sprechen sie Deutsch?"

In Italian I said I wanted to make reservations, not for the hotel, but for lunch.

A man walked over. He spoke Italian. "I understand you want no lodging, just lunch," he said.

"Yes."

He told the clerk in Yugoslavian.

We were led into an open courtyard for lunch. On the public address system the hotel people played *San Antonio Rose*.

A young employee who spoke English came up and said, "Sir, we are playing this in your honor."

Attitude makes all the difference in human relations.

We continued on to Austria. It was a great trip, 13 countries, no advance reservations, just working with C.I.T. whenever we planned to go to a new city and needed to book a hotel room.

Attitude makes all the difference when traveling.[32]

OF OUR MANY TRIPS, our one on the Concorde supersonic jet plane, a 24-day trip around the world, was one in a lifetime.

Everything was well organized, 100 percent first class, and we met great, great people.

Everywhere we landed, there was a guide who spoke perfect English.

In China, our guide's name was Sunny. She was 27, born and raised in Beijing, never left China, but spoke perfect English. She answered every question we asked.

I asked plenty of politically sensitive questions. Washoe County Sheriff Dick Kirkland is a friend of mine, and he had issued me a deputy sheriff's card. It's an honorary title, but the card doesn't say "honorary" on it.

I used the card in China to indicate I was an official of some kind, and to be taken seriously when I asked questions.

Sunny would serve as interpreter with

---

[32] On that trip we visited the Forum in Rome. I saw the caretaker sitting on a bench under a tree. In Italian I said, "Do you get paid for sitting on your ass?" We started chatting amicably, and he took a liking to me. He got out his keys and asked if I'd like to go into the Senate building, which was off limits.

"God yes," I said, "if you wait until my wife gets here."

He opened up the wooden building for us. There were marble steps and marble seats. He told me where I was standing was where Julius Caesar was stabbed by Brutus, and he was standing where Brutus had been.

It gave me a weird feeling.

"We better get out of here," the caretaker said. "This is against regulations."

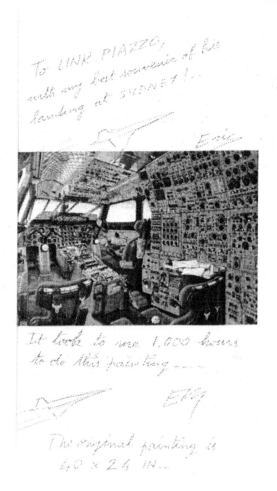

On Helen's and my Concorde trip around the world, I was allowed to fly as co-pilot when we landed at Sydney, Australia, on Sept. 22, 1997. It gave me a great feeling, and the crew was great. The letter at left is from the French pilot, Jean Rossignol; the picture at right depicts Rossignol's painting of the cockpit, which he noted in his letter took him 1,000 hours to finish.

Chinese police and military officials. My inquiries always were answered.

Human rights is a big issue in U.S.-China relations. Frankly, I admire the Chinese system of law and order. For a misdemeanor, a prisoner is put in a desert prison surrounded by barbed wire, and works seven days a week for the government. There are no visitors, television, letters from anybody. When the sentence expires, the prisoner is released.

China, the most populous nation in the world, has the lowest crime rate in the entire world. Isn't there a reason for that?

I criticize our own judicial system. It has to be tightened up. There are people who murder others in cold blood, multiple homicides, and are sentenced to 26 years, or whatever, in prison at tax-payers' expense. *Three meals a day, television, library*, etc.

That's wrong.

HELEN IS A GREAT cook. She learned French cooking from her mother, and Italian cooking from my mother. She also is a very sympathetic person, to every little thing.

She loves birds. She buys big bags of birdseed for the birds in our back yard. Sparrows, doves, quail show up. Our little dog, the minute we let her out, chases the birds. Helen yells at the dog to stop. You can't kill an insect around her; she's sympathetic to any living thing, which I admire her for.

Helen is very close to her siblings. Her older brother and younger sister are still around. Her sister had a stroke several years ago. Helen will take her shopping, buy things for her. She's also close to our son, Craig. They're always calling each other.

Helen suffered a stroke herself, 10 years ago, but she's recovered. She's very strong-willed. A friend of a friend serves as a health aide, and even though Helen really doesn't need her services any more, she keeps her on for company.

I came home one day a few months ago and Helen was using a cane. "What the hell's that?" I said.

"It's a cane I bought."

"What the hell for?"

"Well, my knees hurt once in awhile."

"Throw the cane away and don't limp!"

By golly, she put the cane up in a corner and hasn't used it since. And she isn't limping.

Helen has faced adversity, but had the courage to keep plugging along. There was our little daughter, Suzanne, the most beautiful thing in the world, who was born retarded and died at age 14. There was our son Lynn, who died at 22.

Though it may not seem so at the time, it can always be worse. Helen picked up the pieces and moved on.

What's it like growing old with a woman? It's better than not growing at all. It's just great.

I'll tell you one thing: in 54 years of marriage you better learn each other's habits!

I play gin rummy in the afternoons at the Prospector's Club. Helen should say, "What the hell you playing gin rummy for? You could be home doing this or that."

She doesn't complain, though.

Helen and Punkin in our courtyard at 3 Craig Court.

I don't need to give her any leeway on anything. She's so honest and good, whatever she does is OK with me.

She's been my anchor.

15

Deputy Piazzo

If you're going to exist in a community — regardless of your occupation — you should be involved in volunteering. You get tremendous satisfaction out of contributing.

The National Sporting Goods Association asked me to give several lectures at the Chicago convention to dealers across the country. So I selected a committee of top dealers to give me input. In one of the lectures I said: "It just occurred to me that basic business principles never change. Today, before we were born, and after we die, it always is the same. You have to work hard, be very honest with your customers and treat them like they're the greatest people on Earth. And above all, have community involvement."

If you're living in a community, why don't you help it? The community is helping *you*, after all. It's just that simple.

It's the same with the industry you're in, or any organization you're in. It's larger than you are, and you, as a member of it, deserve to keep it going.

I'm so impressed with the volunteers who clean up the Truckee River. They get more done in a week than the city council or county commission get done in a year. And they do it sheerly out of a sense of civic responsibility.

The 20-30 Club — for members between the ages of 20 and 30 — is active again. Every Christmas, when I was in the club, our members would go to grocers and get goods free of charge, make Christmas baskets and deliver them to those in need, whose names we collected from area

The Reno Rodeo Committee, 1953. I'm fourth from left in the top row.

ROTARY INTERNATIONAL

Service Above Self

JERRY L. HALL
GOVERNOR 1993-94
DISTRICT 5190

16 SUDA WAY
RENO, NEVADA
89509-3046
U.S.A.

(R) 702-323-7610
(F) 702-329-5404

May 4, 1998

Link Piazzo
Three Craig Court
Reno, NV 89502

Dear Link and Helen:

I was very pleased that the District and the Rotary International Foundation were able to honor and recognize your generosity during the District 5190 Conference. Your thoughtful contribution will have a significant impact in many ways. Through your donation and the work of the Foundation you will be helping improve lives of the less fortunate. Equally important, your donation sets a positive example for others to follow.

I tried to get over to congratulate you after the ceremony but missed you in the crowd. I hope the enclosed picture will serve as a remembrance of the occasion.

I know Norm Olsen expressed the sentiments of the district and Rotary International, but please accept my congratulations and thanks as well.

Best wishes to both of you.

Yours in Rotary,

Jerry L. Hall

Believe In What You Do — Do What You Believe In

A Rotary presentation to Helen and me, 1998, at the district conference at Lake Tahoe.

churches. Boy, what a feeling! To go to a home with a big box of groceries and candy — and the people would cry, they'd be so thankful.

Giving to others, contributing to one's community, gives one a tremendous degree of satisfaction.

I've belonged to so many organizations, my wife has asked me how I ever found the time. I remember attending three meetings one night. One was for the board of Hidden Valley Properties, another was the board of Hidden Valley Country Club, the other probably was the Sierra Nevada Sportswriters and Broadcasters.

I served on the Reno YMCA board for three three-year terms (and I'm still a member, exercising every weekday morning). I was on the local United Way chapter board (it was originally called Community Chest) for 19 years.

I helped found the Reno chapter of the National Italian-American Sports Hall of Fame. I was one of four guys who organized the first Reno Little League, in 1951. Dick Taylor, who managed the YMCA, was chiefly responsible. He was very community-conscious. (The other two guys were Bud Beasley and Al Landsdon.)

I was on the Reno Rodeo Association Executive Committee 19 years. Back then, the board members would perform much of the manual labor — raking the arena, sweeping the grandstands, stenciling numbers on the seats. If we needed extra help, I'd go to Ted Berrum, chief of police, and say, "Ted, we need about 10 prisoners to work."

He'd call in one of his officers. "How many guys we got behind bars?"

"Seven."

"Well, go out and pick up three more, we need 10."

So they'd go out and pick up three guys. This is no exaggeration. And the prisoners would be good workers.

That was the old Reno.

Here's another story. When I was president of the Western Sporting Goods Dealers Association, we had a board meeting in Reno, at the Riverside Hotel.

One of our board members was a guy last name of Ward, from Stockton, Calif. He was a successful businessman, president of that city's chamber of commerce and also of the Little League. He got gassed up in Reno the first night, and the police picked him up, booked and released him.

I went down to see police chief Berrum. "Look, this guy is head of the chamber of commerce, head of the Little League, head of everything in Stockton. If this gets in the newspapers . . ."

Berrum went over to the arresting officer, Cavallo. "What'd you pinch him for?" the chief asked.

"He was a menace to himself. I found him on the Virginia Street bridge, he could

This is my plaque for the National Sporting Goods Association's Hall of Fame, presented to me in Chicago in 1991.

hardly walk."

Berrum dismissed Cavallo.

"Link," he said, "the newspaper guys come every morning at 10 o'clock, and go through the files. I'll take this file and put it on the bottom, and hope they don't find it. It's in the drawer, isn't it?"

He turned the sheet upside down and put it on the bottom of the drawer, under the file of the police reports.

Talk about good common sense.

Berrum called me at 11 o'clock and said, "Link, I got the job done."

He saved the guy's reputation, which would have been sullied because he'd had a few drinks in Reno and had gotten picked up by the cops before he could make it back to his hotel room

Many of the organizations I've belonged

to, I've ended up president at some point. I guess when I've joined something, I've gotten deeply involved. I've been president of the Sierra Nevada Sportswriters and Broadcasters, president — "High Chief," they call it — of California Indians, president of the Western Sporting Goods and National Sporting Goods dealers associations. I've been president of Hidden Valley Properties 22 years, and on the board 43 years. We have 53 acres — out of 900 original acres — remaining to be liquidated. We plan to give the mountain we own behind Hidden Valley to a non-profit zoological society.

One time I had to turn down a presidency. I was made president-elect of the Reno Main Rotary chapter in 1981. I told the chapter members I'd have to refuse the office. It was the year I had a chance to bring my son, Craig, to Europe to meet his relatives in the village of Piazzo. It was a beautiful trip.[33]

I've been in Rotary 50 years. Rotary has meant a lot to me; Rotarians do so much for the world. I've contributed quite a bit of money to our Rotary chapter's foundation. Ten years ago, Rotary decided to stamp out polio in the world. Around the globe, Rotarians volunteered help free of charge to administer the polio vaccine. In 1998, in India, in one day, 125 million children were given the vaccine.

If that doesn't impress you, I don't know what does.

AWARDS AND HONORS HAVEN'T meant that much to me. But one that did was induction into the National Sporting Goods Hall of Fame, in 1991. Only one sporting goods dealer is elected a year. My selection came as a surprise to me.

To be considered by your peers as No. 1 in your industry is quite a compliment. It was validation I'd done a good job in business. I also received a National Leadership award from Sporting Goods Dealer magazine.

Another honor that meant a great deal to me was the Washoe County School District's Outstanding Graduate award for Outstanding Community Service. It recognized my community service. I'm proud to be a product of our public schools.

I've felt great loyalty to my alma maters, especially Reno High School. I've contributed a $400,000 gift to help the Reno High School Alumni Association build an alumni museum. It will contain memorabilia, both academic and athletic, and even a computer data base to research when students graduated and even their grades. The $400,000 is the biggest gift ever made to Reno High, and I am so pleased I am able to do this. The Link Piazzo Alumni Center will be attached to the high school building, on the east side, north of the circular driveway, facing Booth Street. At Bud Beasley's request, there will be a bronze plaque of me inside.[34]

Reno High, as the oldest high school in

---

[33] On this trip, we visited the Berlin Wall, passing through the several checkpoints into Communist East Germany. Craig had a camera with him. This did not please the Soviet guards. They confiscated it. Craig asked me what would happen. Any of three things, I said. One, they'd take his film. Two, they'd expose his film to the light, then return it. Or three: he wouldn't see his camera again. Well, his camera was returned to him, with the film in it, and the film wasn't even damaged!

When we were driving from Frankfurt to Paris, we stopped in Lyon, France, around noon, at a roadside restaurant. We couldn't interpret the French menu, but I told Craig not to worry — if I had to, I'd step into the kitchen and point out to the waiter what food we wanted; I had done this in other countries. First, however, I stood and said, "Does anyone here speak English?" There were about 50 French people eating there, but no one said anything. A couple minutes later, an elderly Frenchman came to our table and said, "I speak a little English." I said, "If you can help us order lunch, we will be very thankful." He helped us — but refused my offer to pay for his meal. He did accept a glass of wine.

When he returned to his table, several people came up and shook his hand. He had a big smile and had enjoyed helping the Americans.

[34] I also made a large contribution to Rotary. If a Rotarian contributes $1,000 to the Rotary Foundation, he becomes a Paul Harris fellow; the name comes from the founder of Rotary. In 1997, I went to the Reno Rotary Club's foundation chairman and said I wanted to make every member a Paul Harris fellow. It cost me $100,000.

The cedar arrowhead I carved by hand, presented to the California Indians in 1971. It's placed at the foot of the totem pole.

Here I am, high chief of the California Indians, 1971.

A rock and plaque presented to the California Indians by me and Mike Scherupp, 1969.

the area, has many alumni who've served the community as prominent members. So much local history is connected to it. As for me, it taught me the trade skills I needed for my first job as a carpenter, and which I've used throughout my life. I had some great teachers. I remember most all of them. Kilpatrick taught me bookkeeping. Randall Ross taught me English. And there were Sgt. Skeen in R.O.T.C.; Herb Foster in mechanical drawing as well as my basketball coach; Nathaniel Gray, my shop teacher.

I'm presented the Distinguished Flying Cross by Major Gen. Dale Smith (ret.), right, and Col. Clarence Becker, at the Reno Rotary Club, 1988.

As of this writing, I can't wait for the ground-breaking for the alumni center.

I NEVER PICKED UP my war medals. As I mentioned, during warfare, we pilots just didn't give a damn about them. We figured we'd be killed, anyway, so who needed them?

I knew I'd earned the Distinguished Flying Cross, because I'd received copies of the citation, describing the two missions that had yielded me it.

One day in 1988, Air Force Major Gen. Dale Smith (retired) came into the Sportsman to buy a fishing license. I knew he was born and raised in Carson City, and had commanded one of the groups in the Eighth Air Force in Europe. He was a great big guy, and I knew of him, but he didn't know me.

When we had a sale at the store, we'd shift the selling of licenses to the upstairs office. I overheard my office manager ask,

"Have you been in Nevada six months?"

The customer was very polite. I looked up from my desk. And there he was. I recognized him.

"Mae," I said, "that's Gen. Smith. Make him out a license and quit asking all those stupid questions."

When his license was made out, he came over. "Whose picture is that on the wall?" he asked. He was looking at me wearing my wings, in uniform.

"That's me," I said.

"Boy, you've changed a lot."

"General, I got news for you. You've changed a lot, too, in 43 years."

We got to talking. I said, "I know that you commanded a group in the Eighth Air Force."

Later, I said, "You know, I was awarded the DFC and never got it."

"What? We oughta do something about that!"

"What?"

"We've got to get you the DFC."

"No, I don't care."

"Do you have any information on it, your war records?"

"Yes I do, but forget it, general."

A couple days later, Air Force Col. Lawrence Becker (retired) called me. I knew him through Rotary. He wanted information from me to get me the DFC.

"No, forget it," I said.

"No, I can't forget it," he said. "The general told me . . ."

So I got him the information.

Every now and then I'd get a note from Smith updating me on the progress. Information was being passed along.

All of a sudden I got a phone call from a major at Randolph Field.

"Is this Capt. Piazzo?"

"No, this is Mr. Piazzo."

"Well sir, I have information from Gen. Smith . . ."

"Since when does a major call a captain 'sir'?"

He was terrific. "We appreciate what you people did during World War II, and the honors that you bestowed upon military history. And I want you to know that we have finally gotten all your records together, and you have earned and we are sending the Distinguished Flying Cross."

I had three options: I could have a formal or informal military presentation, or a simple informal presentation, the major said. "But a general must pin the medal on you."

"Just send the goddamn medal," I said.

The medal arrived. I passed it on to Col. Becker. And Gen. Smith pinned it on me at a ceremony at Rotary.

Local TV covered the story, there was a big article in the newspaper, President Reagan sent me a letter.

I received a standing ovation. I started to say a few words, but I just choked up. All I could think about was my buddies who had not made it home.

The only way I'd made it home and they

hadn't was that the good Lord was looking out for me.

Bill Farr, the WW II veteran and former fire chief of Sparks, as well as a dear friend of mine, was at a book-signing with me for *War Stories*, published in 1995 by the University of Nevada Oral History Program. The book contains chapters on 21 of us veterans, including Farr and myself.

"You know," Farr told me, "I lost a lot of my medals, and I wrote to Barbara Vucanovich and she got them for me."

I knew the congresswoman from my district, Barbara Vucanovich, quite well. She was a conservative Republican, and lived in Hidden Valley. She'd been secretary to Paul Laxalt when he was a U.S. senator for Nevada. I'd known her for years.

"I don't have my medals," I told Farr, "but I've got the records."

Funny. Although I could not care less about the medals during the war, now I felt like having them. That's what the years do to you.

I went to visit Congresswoman Vucanovich at her office in the old Federal Building across from Reno High on Booth Street. I had to empty my pockets before passing through the ground-floor metal detector.

Vucanovich wasn't in, but her secretary took down my information. The congresswoman wrote me asking for my military records. I sent them. She ended up securing 12 medals (one with an Oak Leaf cluster, indicating I'd won the medal twice) for me. I received a big package in the mail.

The DFC meant a hell of a lot to me, after 43 years. That's what time does to you.

Norm Holland, a good friend of mine who's on my board of directors of Hidden Valley Properties, was in the Navy during WW II and earned the Philippine Liberation Medal, but never did get it. He gave me permission to get him his medal. I got the phone number of the people handling the medals, and mailed them a copy of his records. I sent in the required $25 myself on a MasterCard and gave the medal to Holland for Christmas.

He was delighted.

IN 1993, CHET AND I left a lasting testament to our father in his native village of Piazzo.

The little church in Piazzo had no pews. The parishioners knelt on the marble floor. So, in 1993, Chet and I — successful descendants of the village — had pews built and the church painted. We made our contribution in our father's name; a marble plaque commemorates Santino. When Chet and I arrived for the dedication, people arrived

The marble plaque attached to the face of the church in the village of Piazzo, in memory of Santino Piazzo, who was born there.

from surrounding villages, as well as priests and nuns.

In the course of the ceremony, they mentioned that long-ago ancestor who had stormed the marquese's castle. Eight-hundred years had passed, yet they were appreciative of him to this day!

Few Americans can trace their familial roots so far back. Throughout my life I have felt bonded with that ancient ancestor of mine, that medieval Robin Hood of northern Italy. I feel connected in history. I look at my relatives in Italy: our mentality is so similar. No gray area — one must be completely honest. Right and Wrong. No stretching of the truth. No equivocations. No fly-by-night mentality.

I know who I am, and who came before me.

I feel rooted in the world. This gives a person strength.

DICK KIRKLAND, A FRIEND of mine, made me an honorary deputy sheriff shortly after he was elected Washoe County sheriff. He gave me a card saying I was deputized. I carry it in my wallet.

"Certificate of Appointment of Special Deputy, Washoe County, Nevada," the card reads. It doesn't empower me to do anything, but I've used it.

I was eating in Jack In the Box around the corner from the Sportsman one morning. There was a commotion, and I looked up.

A big, husky Latino man, probably an immigrant, was running out the door. I thought there was an emergency of some kind. I stood up and looked out the window.

There was a kid, maybe 5 at the most. The man picked him up and was shaking and beating him. He carried the boy back into the restaurant and threw him up against the back of the fiberglass booth.

The child was sobbing. His nose was bleeding. I stood up and walked over.

"What's going on here?" I demanded. I took out my sheriff's card and handed it to the man. "Read that," I said.

The man did.

"Oh, he's a pest," the man's wife said about her son.

"I think *I* was a pest when I was his age, but my parents didn't want to kill me," I said.

"If I catch you hitting that child once more, I'm going to throw you in jail for child abuse."

"Yes sir, yes sir," the man said.

I watched them drive off later. The car had a California license plate.

One of the restaurant customers, an older woman, came over and thanked me. "I don't know what you did, but you sure stopped him," she said.

I told Dick Kirkland about the incident. "You did the right thing," he said. "All you had to do was call us and we'd have sent a deputy down."

It may not seem easy. But it's important to be involved in your community.

Here's Chet's and my coffee klatsch at the Little Waldorf on North Virginia Street, 1972. Chet is in the striped shirt in the back row; I'm two to Chet's right.

16

It Can Always Be Worse

I have printed up a lot of my favorite sayings, and fixed them on plaques, and put them on the walls of my office. One of the sayings I made up myself:

"True satisfaction does not come from success — but from what you have had to endure and overcome to succeed."

I've given plaques with sayings on them away to a lot of people. One day I walked into a lawyer's office and saw one of these plaques. "Boy that's a nice-looking plaque," I said.

"Yeah," he said, "somebody gave it to me."

Ever since I've put my initials, "L.P.," at the bottom of the plaques.

Getting to be an Army Air Corps pilot, I had to clear a number of hurdles — and, boy, it seemed like every time I just made it by a hair. One thing I haven't mentioned in this book is that I used to get airsick. In those days, the World War I tradition endured; if you puked in the cockpit, you had to clean the plane up with a brush and bucket after you landed.

The other guys used to sort of laugh at this, but I was the kind of guy they didn't laugh at too much, or I'd knock them on their ass.

R.J. Lehmann, my tough-as-nails instructor during primary flight training, stopped the plane one time at an auxiliary field and said, "Piazzo, I don't know how in the hell you're doing it, but you're advancing."

I hadn't known I was!

I'd just throw up and keep flying, day af-

The American flag flies proudly from its pole in front of 3 Craig Court, our home in Hidden Valley.

ter day.

I guess that's enduring.

Let me say something else about success.

I guess I've done everything I set out to do in life. I am comfortable financially. I feel I have respect in the community. I helped grow a business, and contributed to a number of civic and fraternal organizations. But now, looking back, it isn't the enjoying of success that is satisfying: it was the getting. And the giving. The ability to give.

Thank God I'm able to give. The $400,000 for the Reno High School Alumni Center; and $100,000 to the Rotary Foundation, to help Rotary International stamp out polio around the world and make many other contributions.

I don't pat myself on the back for making these generous gifts. Rather, I appreciate that I'm very fortunate that I'm able to do it.

There are people I know who have a hell of a lot more money than I do, who won't part with 10 cents. I feel sorry for those people.

Success means helping others. And helping others get their success.

THERE ARE THINGS I have stood steadfastly against. One is unions.

Some unions, I know, serve a tremendous purpose. Protecting coal miners' rights, for example. I had the pleasure of meeting John L. Louis, head of the miners' union in the East, one time. He organized those miners who worked for very low wages underground and often got miners' consumption — mostly immigrants, they were. Louis started the United Miners Union. He did a terrific job.

I met Louis when he was at the Palace Hotel in San Francisco. "Mr. Louis," I said, "I want to shake your hand."

"Why?"

"I don't believe that a person should rely on a union. But you have done wonders for these poor miners. Congratulations."

There's a hell of a lot of difference between workers trying to achieve a civilized existence, and workers making $40 an hour going on strike because they want more money and less work and want the union to get it for them.

I am very much opposed to forcing an employer to go down to the hall to hire people. I am very much in favor of a guy earning a living on his own merit, without having to rely on a union.

On the television not long ago, TV reporters interviewed striking United Auto Workers. One of the guys had an on-strike sign on his shoulder. "You know, I can't make my car payments, I can't make my house payment, I'm broke. I gotta go to work," he said.

In the meantime, he's on strike! If I had been the one interviewing him, I would have said, "McDonald's is looking for some help. Why not work for them?"

These guys, making $30 or $40 an hour, on strike!

When the issue of right-to-work cropped up in Nevada politics, I voted with a majority on the board of our local Rotary chapter to circulate a petition to put the issue on the state ballot. The measure would prevent closed shops — jobs open only to union members.

I called Tate Williams, our board secretary, and said, "I want to come early, have the petition ready for the members to sign. I want to be the first to sign it."

After the petition got the measure on the ballot, a fellow came into my store. His name was Hicks. He was head of the local culinary union. Hicks wanted 12-dozen baseballs and league uniforms. I worked like mad for an hour getting it all together for him.

"By the way," he then said, "you didn't sign the right-to-work petition, did you?"

"I not only signed it," I said, "I was the first to sign it."

I knew he'd walk out. He did, the sonofabitch.

I heard he went over to Patterson's and was fitted with suits. Then he asked the same question. Patterson had signed the petition, too.

Hicks went all over town doing that. Now, that's a hell of a way to operate, isn't it?

I needed that money for the team uniforms in the worst way. But I had guts enough to tell him that I was the first to sign the petition.

A man should succeed on his own merit.

The way I've lived my life is that you have to be better than the next guy to get ahead. Today, too many workers fold their arms and let the union take care of them. I'm opposed to that, completely!

Period.

Shortly after I got back from the Pacific after the war, I was in the airport in San Francisco. American Airlines pilots were on strike. They had their uniforms, caps and ties on, and were picketing in front of the terminals.

"Whatsa matter with you assholes?" I said. "You're overpaid *now*. And you want more money?"

They kept marching, back and forth. And I kept talking.

"I was in the war. And I was flying an airplane. I was being shot at. And I got $250 a month. And you guys are getting a hell of a lot more than that. And you put that goddamn plane on automatic pilot and you go to sleep. You ought to be ashamed of yourselves."

Nobody had guts enough to challenge me.

They kept marching. *On strike, on strike. More money. Less hours.*

I was talking loudly, and a couple of other guys heard me. And when I got through they came over and shook my hand.

I was a staunch baseball fan. I'd known so many great players. But when the Major League Players Association went on strike in 1994, I lost interest in the game.

Millionaires going on strike!

WHEN IT COMES TO politics, I describe myself as a conservative.

To me, a conservative is someone who has good common sense.

My favorite conservative was U.S. Sen. Barry Goldwater of Arizona. He was 100 percent honest — no gray area — and as a result, how far did he get in politics?

His opponents lied about him when he ran for president against Lyndon Johnson in 1964. They said he was going to drop the atom bomb on Vietnam.

He didn't care. He just spoke honestly. Period.[35]

If you're completely honest in politics, you're not going to get very far. The mudslinging and lies in campaigns in our own state is just sickening, and, in fact, voters have gotten sick of it.

Lawrence Jacobson, the Republican from Minden, was elected to the state Senate for the first time back in 1962. He's won every election since.

I got to know him several years ago. My B-25 crew had a reunion in Reno, and Jake took us on a tour of the state Capitol, through the Senate and Assembly. Then Jim Wood, my good friend, invited Jake to our Rotary chapter meeting, and I had the pleasure of sitting with him again. He's a Goldwater-type of man. He was running for re-election.

"Link," he said, "my opponent is telling everyone I'm too old."

I almost threw up. That man has done

---

[35] Years later, Goldwater made a speech at the old State Building downtown. I walked up afterward, shook his hand and showed him my 1964 campaign button. He smiled.

A wall of my office upstairs at the Sportsman. All four walls are "momento walls," covered with memorabilia.

more for the state than just about any other senator. An honest, 100 percent, no-gray-area man.

That's all I ask out of anybody.

In my opinion, liberalism stretches the truth a lot. The conservative faces the facts.

Period.

SO MANY PEOPLE DON'T honor their wedding vows.

They take an oath to protect each other, through sickness and health, until death do they part.

Today, a couple have a little spat, they go get a divorce. It's crazy. What they have to do is learn to live together. It's a give-and-take situation. To learn the habits of each other, and live with them, and it works out perfectly.

I've seen so many people get divorced, I could write a book about them.

"What happened?"

"Oh, we had an argument."

Can you imagine that?

Parents never should argue in front of a child. They can avoid it, if they have the guts. It makes a child feel uneasy and insecure, and they're defenseless.

They also should have the guts to stick out the tough times, and stick to fulfilling their vows to each other.

Too many people seek what they think is the easy way out.

RELIGION IS ANOTHER TOUCHY subject.

I have absolute religion: I don't go to church.

I've told several priests this: I don't need a middleman to talk to God. Period. I talk to God often. God saved my life so many times, I'm a firm believer. It's got to be God that did what happened to save my life all those times.

Religion is a broad word.

God is some force that we have no effect on ourselves. He has effect on us.

Why do bad things happen to innocent people? We used to say, "The good die young."

The Lord moves in mysterious ways, and don't try to out-figure Him. Play the hand the good Lord deals.

No way you're ever going to figure out why the innocent, including the young, are killed in places such as Hiroshima, or Nanking.

OUR NATION'S FLAG IS a symbol of our country, and everything it stands for. Flag-burning has become a controversial issue because those who support the act of flag-burning say that part of what the flag represents is freedom of speech, and burning the flag is freedom of speech.

I remember during the Cold War, a Communist announced he was going to burn the flag on the courthouse steps. He was tossed in jail; the case went all the way to the U.S. Supreme Court. The justices studied the case, and analyzed it, and voted 5-4 that burning the flag was freedom of expression.

To me, that's plain bulls—.

Those five Supreme Court justices, we should burn their pants.

Common sense. There's right and wrong, no gray area.

The day I heard the decision, I called Judge Lew Carnahan, a county judge in Reno, and said, "Judge, that goofball Supreme Court voted 5 to 4 it's OK to burn our flag."

"Oh yes, Link, that's freedom of expression."

"Now what if I go back and kill those five guys, is that freedom of expression?"

I was just kidding, of course. But it's so simple. My mother taught me that: no gray area. Right and wrong. It's wrong to burn our flag.

We protected our flag in the war. We put up our lives for it. On Ie Shima, the typhoon destroyed our flag. The pole was bent. We were all distraught: we'd lost our flag.

We hunted over the whole island and found a Marine outfit that had an extra flag. Everybody was happy. We straightened out our pole and put our flag up.

Now it's OK to burn the flag? Bulls—. And I'll tell any Supreme Court justice that.

The flag represents every U.S. citizen. It represents, despite our faults, the greatest country by far in the world.

The mistake we made, when the guy burned the flag on the courthouse steps, we should have sent a couple of Marines who served in World War II down to watch. They would have killed the bastard.

THE U.S. POSTAL SERVICE wanted to issue a stamp in 1995 commemorating the 50th anniversary of the bombing of Hiroshima and Nagasaki. This offended the Japanese government. Clinton decided not to have the stamp, bearing a mushroom cloud, issued.

I wrote a letter to the editor of the local newspaper, saying I was in favor of issuing the stamp, because it might send a message to other people about starting another war, and furthermore, why don't opponents of the stamp mention Pearl Harbor, the Bataan death march and the Japanese atrocities that were committed in Nanking, in the same breath?

I wrote to President Clinton in support of the mushroom stamp. In my third paragraph I wrote: "Mr. President, if we would have shown in World War II the lack of courage that you've shown with this stamp, we certainly would have lost the war."

I got a letter back from the White House saying, "Thanks for being interested in our great country," etc., etc. He simply signed it, "Bill Clinton."

The day after my letter to the editor appeared, a man called me in town and said, "Did you know that the Japanese had a stamp commemorating their bombing of Pearl Harbor, and the Bataan death march?" I went down to his store on California Avenue. I bought a stamp of each — they had been issued in 1942.

I wrote back to Clinton: "Maybe you're not aware of the fact that they printed a stamp of Pearl Harbor and Bataan?"

No answer from the White House.

AS I WRITE THIS, Nevada remains the fastest-growing state in the nation, largely because of the incredible growth in Las Vegas and surrounding cities in the southern part of the state.

Reno's leaders, in contrast, continue to bemoan the decline of the local casino industry, and the downtown core, and fret about the future, since California has made it easier for Indian reservations to have large casinos.

What's the future of my hometown?

I was born in Reno 13 years before gambling was legalized in Nevada, and I already was in business before gambling became such an important industry.

I used to know all the casino-owners, during Reno's heyday as a gambling mecca, and they did a good job. They were given a license to gamble, period. They followed through.

But I'll argue this with anybody: gambling destroys a lot of people. A lot of *families*.[36]

When the Sportsman was in the St. Francis Hotel downtown, I'd walk to the bank four or five times a week. I'd often see a distraught couple walking out of a casino, sometimes with children in tow, and the woman saying something like, "Why did you gamble all our money? How are we going to make our house payment? How are we going to make our car payment?"

I heard that so many times!

They should eliminate those short-skirted gals with their boobs hanging out, serving free drinks in the casinos. A person who is sober seldom gets crazy about gambling. But

---

[36] One of my good friends was Dr. Kenneth Maclean, a prominent Reno physician. Our families often went boating together. Maclean, unfortunately, had a terrible gambling problem. Several times casino employees approached me to counsel him about his frequent financial hemorrhages. On three occasions I went to his office on Ryland Street, next to the county hospital (now Washoe Medical Center), locked the doors, then laid into him. "Ken, you dumb sonofabitch, what the hell are you doing?!"

He eventually joined Alcoholics Anonymous and straightened himself out. He called me one day and asked me to come see his new home. I said I was busy, but he insisted. I drove over and found him alone. In his beautiful new house, he thanked me for having chewed his ass out about gambling.

"Link," he said, "I never knew I was making so much money." He had a hothouse where he grew flowers, and he handed me a red orchid as a token of his esteem.

When Maclean had finally overcome his addiction, he had his lawyer, Bill Woodburn, write letters to the casinos telling them to forget about collecting the $250,000 debt he still owed. Back then, casinos couldn't legally collect. But several years ago, the Nevada Legislature passed a law enabling the gambling houses to legally pursue debts. That indicates how much money the casinos put into the pockets of our lawmakers.

ply him with alcohol — he loses control. All of a sudden, he's got a $5,000 worth of credit, but he gambles $25,000 at the tables.

I'm not in favor of destroying people and destroying families.

It hurts too many people. I'll argue that with anybody.

People say to me, "Where would Reno be without gambling?"

I *lived* in Reno when there wasn't legal gambling. It was one hell of a fine town.

Gambling has destroyed a lot of families, brought in a lot of bums and homeless people. Period.

The expanded fast growth in the Truckee Meadows has brought in a lot of people, mostly from California. Our better tax structure has lured many of them. One of these days there isn't going to be one square inch of meadows. It's all going to be houses and buildings and strip malls.

All you have to do is open your eyes.

I'm for managed growth.

Reno still feels like my city. I can drive around the old neighborhood, on 10th and Bell streets, and feel like it's home. But it's not the city it used to be.

"Holy cow," I'll say to Helen as we drive around, "look at that building, and look at *that* building!"

When you get into politics, and the politicians are paid off, you have a problem.

Uncontrolled growth.

Still, this is my city. I'm not moving to Beowawe.

WHAT ABOUT THE FUTURE of the human race?

I flew over Hiroshima and Nagasaki on my secret, unauthorized mission right after the "big bombs" were dropped.

I saw the devastation.

Today, hydrogen bombs are capable of

12/12/1994

Japan deserved it

Print that A-bomb stamp

I read with interest the article, "Japan opposes Atomic Stamp," wherein Mr. Hiroka of Tokyo states, "Whatever reasons there were, the use of nuclear weapons is not forgiven" (Prime Minister Muryama is also protesting).

I can give both gentlemen at least four good reasons why the bombs were dropped and the stamp should be printed:

1. Pearl Harbor — which forced us to war with Japan.

2. Bataan Death March.

3. Ended war with Japan.

4. Saved estimated 2½ million lives if U.S. was to invade Japan as planned.

Having served in the U.S. Army Air Corps for 3½ years during WWII and flown 67 missions as pilot against the Japanese in the South Pacific, I feel certain that I am expressing the feeling of not only the military but millions of patriotic Americans when I ask our Postal Service to print the "Mushroom stamp."

The stamp that the Japanese are protesting will serve to warn them and other countries to refrain from another "sneak attack" on the U.S.A.

Link Piazzo, *Reno*

This is my letter about the A-bomb stamp, printed by the *Reno Gazette-Journal* .

such destruction that they make those first atom bombs look like firecrackers. And atomic bombs have proliferated.

The uncontrolled leaders in the world will eventually get their hands on these bombs. All you have to do is read the newspaper to see the writing on the wall.

Iraq is a very small country. Saddam Hussein is uncontrollable. He's told the United Nations, the United States and Britain to go to hell. And there are many like him around the world, waiting to climb onto the world stage.

Until the world gets together, emphatically, and decides to eliminate nuclear weapons, one day one of these crazy bastards is going to decide, "All I have to do is push these two buttons and I wipe out the United States of America."

Isn't that frightening?

I'll argue that with anybody.

Until the rest of the world thinks like we do here in our country — where the Jews can get along with the Italians, and the Italians with the Irish, and the Irish with the Poles — we're in a lot of trouble.

Period.

LIFE HAS ITS UPS and downs. Why do some people get down in the dumps, and others pick themselves up and keep on going?

It's amazing. I feel sorry for those who get down in the dumps. Life happens to be that way. Not every day is going to be a bowl of cherries. You have to take it as it comes, and do the best you can with what God gives you.

Back to the sayings on my office wall. Here's a good one from Abraham Lincoln:

"I am not concerned that you have fallen. I am concerned that you arise."

Here's a long one, which is a fitting way to end this chapter. It's titled *The Man in the Glass*:

"When you get what you want in this struggle for wealth, and the world makes you king for a day, just go to a mirror and look at yourself, and see what that man has to say.

"For it isn't your father or mother or wife whose judgment upon you must pass. The fellow whose verdict counts most in your life is the one staring back from the glass.

"Some people may think you a straight-shooting chum and call you a wonderful guy. But the man in the glass says you're only a bum if you can't look him straight in the eye.

"He's the fellow to please, never mind all the rest, for he's with you clear up to the end. And you've passed your most dangerous, difficult test if the man in the glass is your friend.

"You may fool the whole world down the pathway of fears and get pats on the back as you pass. But your final reward will be heartache and tears if you've cheated the man in the glass."

Conclusion

I wrote this book for my son, Craig, and my extended family, and my close friends, including Jim Wood, who told me to write a book, and my community.

Maybe it will induce those who read it to become more community-oriented. Perhaps the positive things I've done in my life will serve as good lessons.

Looking back at age 80, certainly there are things I've done that I regret to this day, but a person can't dwell on such things. You just go on to the next page of your life.

I've led a pretty full life. And, frankly, I have no call for regrets, seeing as I survived what I call "near-misses," and should have been killed 30 times or more.

I achieved what I set out to achieve. I'm not sure that I set any high goals, but I do have some goals now.

One is to see that the Reno High School Alumni Center is built. Another is to completely sell out the remaining acreage held by Hidden Valley Properties, after 43 years.

Another is to complete my subdivision in Hidden Valley: Hidden Valley Cove.

Another is to complete this book. I guess when I reach the end of this concluding section — in a few more paragraphs — I'll have at least reached this goal.

TWENTY YEARS AGO, A friend of mine, John Cerveri, came into my store. He had tears in his eyes.

"What the hell are you crying about?"

"The town's getting too big and I'm going to move to Lemoille." That's outside of Elko, in northeast Nevada, about 300 miles away.

"I want to say good-bye to my good friends," he continued.

After that, he'd come periodically into the store, perhaps after five years or so, and each time I'd miss him. I'd be out of the store.

I found out he was now living in Kingman, Ariz. Then he visited the Sportsman again. This time, he waited for me to return.

I walked in and recognized him. I had not seen him in 20 years. He'd aged quite a bit. Again, he had tears in his eyes. We hugged each other.

We went up to my office and talked.

"I want you to know that you've been my best friend," he said. "You took me into the 20-30 Club, you paid my dues and you bought my dinners (they were only 75 cents) because I did not have any money."

He saw piles of manila folders and photographs scattered around my desk. "What's this stuff?" he said.

"I want to write a book," I said.

"Do you mind if I write a letter?" he said, "and would you use it in the book?"

He did write a letter. This is how it began:

Rare People

It's a rare person who doesn't get discouraged. Whether it happens to us or to an associate we're trying to cheer up, the answer centers around one word: perseverance.

The value of courage, persistence, and perseverance has rarely been illustrated more convincingly than in the life story of this man (his age appears in the column to the right):

Failed in business	22
Ran for Legislature (defeated)	23
Again failed in business	24
Elected to Legislature	25
Sweetheart died	26
Had a nervous breakdown	27
Defeated for Speaker	29
Defeated for Elector	31
Defeated for Congress	34
Elected to Congress	37
Defeated for Congress	39
Defeated for Senate	46
Defeated for Vice President	47
Defeated foe Senate	49
Elected President of the United States	51

That's the record of Abraham Lincoln.

I have many inspirational messages on my office wall. Here is one about Abraham Lincoln. It illustrates the value of persistence.

"My family's an old-time pioneer family who came to Reno in 1914. I lived in Reno 65 years and I've known Link Piazzo since the 1930s, personally as a friend and also as a ballplayer on our team where he played excellent ball.

"I can't say enough about his good character, and I consider him my best friend. When I was playing ball he helped me in many ways. He paid my 20-30 dues, bought my lunch and dinner on numerous occasions. I played for 20-30 after I was too old,

through his efforts . . ." And he went on to tell what a great guy I am.

I told John I'd use his letter in this book. And so I have.

Here's a postscript: I was looking through my old war diary, and I found an entry from Nov. 25, 1942, when I was at pre-flight training:

"I went to see 'Gentleman Jim' with Errol Flynn, and I received a duck from John Cerveri today, and we ate it."

That's the kind of friend he was.

I SAW DODDIE ZUNINO — the kid Godfather from the old neighborhood — six or seven years ago.

I was driving up Keystone Avenue, near his block. I knew he had bad knees, although he never complained about anything, because I'd seen him a month earlier hobbling into the Gold-N-Silver Inn's café.

"What the hell's the matter?" I'd said.

"Ah, these goddamned knees are bothering me." That's the way he was.

As I drove up Keystone in front of his house, I saw him outside, on his knees, planting something. I stopped the car.

"You can't give me that crap your knees are bothering you," I said. "Here you are on your knees."

"Christ they hurt, help me up," Doddie said.

I helped him get up and said, "I'll see you later."

I drove to the store and got a pair of knee pads.

I gave them to Doddie. He thought they were great.

He took me around to his back yard. Doddie was a great gardener. He gave me a gallon can with a little peach tree in it, about 6 or 8 inches tall.

I just happened to have a spot for it in my

back yard, where a shrub had died. A drip system watered the spot.

The peach sapling grew real well.

I saw Doddie another day. "When that thing has peaches on it," I said, "I'm going to have you and Olga (his wife) out to dinner and we'll eat the peaches off of your tree."

"Oh, we don't go out much, Link," he said.

"You're going to come out that night," I said.

About three years later, Doddie passed away. The next year, I had peaches.

The past year, I had hundreds of them.

Every time I look at that tree, I think of him.

MAYBE, IN SOME WAY, this book will become a legacy, like Doddie's tree.

Near Misses

The following is a list of brushes with death I've had. In all, I believe I should have been killed more than 30 times in my life, including before and after the war. Here are notes on most of those events:

1. In August 1924, when I was 5, I was walking to the store with my sister, Olga, and brother, Chet, when we heard an airplane overhead. A local pilot, Billy Blanchfield, was making his annual flight to drop a wreath on the grave of a friend of his at the nearby Knights of Pythias cemetery. He crashed his plane into the McKinley house on the corner of Ninth and Ralston streets, tearing down telephone wires that wrapped around me like snakes. Firemen untangled me.

2. When I was 10, a neighbor, Angelo Pardini, took Chet and me for a ride in a buggy without a tongue, and the horse bolted, overturning the buggy. I was caught between the buggy bed and the spinning wheel. Spokes clobbered my head — red flashes — and knocked me unconscious. I recovered at a rancher's house, then ran home. My head was pretty banged up, with skin missing, but I hadn't been killed.

3. In 1940 I was driving to Fallon with Jake Hook at the wheel and five other passengers in his new Buick, to attend the annual 20-30 Club dinner. Jake's family owned Reno Brewing Co. and Jake was known to drink more than he should. Driving nearly 100 miles per hour, he reached Hazen, where the old highway made a sharp right turn and elevated. Jake missed most of the turn and rolled the Buick end over end twice, then barrel-rolled three times. Only Howard Christensen was seriously hurt (and recovered). The car wasn't worth towing back to Reno. We all should have been killed.

4. Stationed at Lemoore Army Air Base for basic training, two Reno friends of mine visited — John DuPratt and Jack Hargrove. We drove to Hanford for dinner in my 1939 Buick and after dinner, returning to Lemoore, I fell asleep and drove off the highway. We all got out and didn't know where the highway was or where we were. We managed to get back on the road and return. A few days later I drove back to the site and saw I had barely missed a large culvert. Had I driven off 50 feet sooner we would have all been killed.

5. Stationed at Florence, S.C., I was buzzing cotton fields in an A-20, about 10 feet

above the ground, and saw several black people running from the fields; I was frightening them. I felt bad, so I pulled up and barely missed hitting a large, high-tension electric line. Had I not felt sorry for the cotton-pickers, I would not be here today.

6. Flying from Australia to New Guinea, I ran into the edge of a thunderhead hidden in the clouds. Tremendous currents tossed the plane out of the thunderhead, or we'd have been torn apart. We lost the right engine and the Plexiglas in the canopy above our heads. I had absolutely no control of the plane.

7. Diving straight down from 16,500 feet, trying to reach 400 mph in an A-20 over the ocean off Lae, New Guinea, I couldn't pull out after hitting 400; the ocean looked like it was rising up fast to meet us. With all my strength, about 100 feet above the ocean blue, I pulled out.

8. I was the first plane to land on Mindoro as a replacement for the 17th squadron; the tower instructed me not to land because the runway was slippery as ice and full of craters. Low on fuel, I landed on the coral anyway, skidded off the runway and ended up in sand dunes. No one was hurt.

9. Three of our four planes were shot down on a mission to north Luzon. My plane was the only one to return to base, and was shot up pretty bad. I lost one engine and the bomb bay tank was hit and ruptured. Had I not asked our line chief before takeoff to fill the tank, even though we needed no extra fuel, we would have been blown out of the sky when the bomb bay tank was hit; the fumes would have ignited.

10. On a China Sea mission with a new crew, I found the co-pilot couldn't fly and the navigator couldn't navigate. During the flight the radioman burned his hands and the tail-gunner lost his mind. It was night, I was flying on instruments and running low on fuel. The man in the control tower gave us incorrect information. He also wouldn't turn on a spotlight for us. I told him to talk with our group commander, Col. C.T. Thompson. He did, and Thompson ordered the light turned on. By the grace of God I found our way to our base on Mindoro.

11. Returning to Luzon after a mission, I found our base socked in by a large rain squall over the landing strip. Our planes had broken formation and all of us had to land on the strip. As I came in to land and hit the end of our runway in the heavy rain, I saw one of our planes just a few feet in front. I yelled over the radio for him to give it some throttle and still be able to land, but this did not happen. I came within inches of chewing that plane's tail off; we both would have crashed. I locked my brakes while still in the air, knowing I would probably run into the plane after we hit the runway. The maneuver worked and as I was taxiing, I could feel a *thump-thump-thump*. My crew got out of the plane and we found what the thumping had come from. The tires were worn through several plies, but had not blown out. Locking the brakes in the air had saved us.

12. On a mission over Formosa, I was so intent on destroying the target that I did not pay attention to what was beyond it — cloud cover over the rugged mountain range. I found myself flying on instruments, expecting to crash any moment as I

was making an 180-degree turn. Why I did not hit the mountain, I will never know.

13. On a mission to Canton, China, I was leading the second flight. We came in at tree-top level, as always. As I hit the target the plane received a tremendous jolt that made us sink even lower. Somehow, we didn't hit the ground. It turned out that bombs from the planes ahead of us had knocked mud high into the air, and tons of it had cascaded down onto our canopy. I immediately opened my window to be able to see, and luckily found some clouds with water in them; I flew through several times and washed most of the mud off, or it would have been difficult to land.

14. I was sent from Luzon to Mindoro to check out the new A-26 and give a recommendation on whether the military should purchase it. A few days later, I flew the A-26 to Luzon; our guys, of course, had never seen one and a crowd gathered around the plane. I asked my commanding officer to go up with me, and he was happy to oblige. When we were about 50 feet off the ground, the left side of the nose came open and the plane started to do a slow roll just off the ground. I hit the right rudder and skidded the plane to the right to keep the nose from opening further. I skidded the plane around to the end, and we took off and made a very bumpy landing. What had caused our nose to open? Our armament people had been curious about seeing nose guns and had opened up the nose, which I had not realized. They forgot to fasten the nose back in place with the Zeus fasteners. We fastened the nose back and I asked the C.O. to get back in for another flight. But he had had enough.

15. I was duck-hunting in the late 1940s east of Fallon with a friend, Vic Teglia. We were walking through a swamp in about two feet of water when, all of a sudden, I found myself blasted into the water. Vic was to my immediate right, shotgun in hand. Both of us were wearing waders. The small rope that served as a belt for his waders had worked its way through his 12 gauge trigger guard. His gun's safety was off; the knot at the end of the rope had hit the trigger, and the gun had gone off. His gun was pointed across the front of my chest and the concussion of the blast had knocked me into the water. Had I been a few inches farther, that would have been the end of me.

16. In the late 1940s I was Scuba diving at Lake Tahoe with a cousin, Roy Pizorno. He was an expert diver; I was a beginner. We were diving at Hidden Beach. It was a rainy day, with a strong wind blowing. We both went underwater. Roy went to the west and I to the southeast. When the weather was good, we would look at the large boulders that weren't far from shore, the tips of the rocks jutting out in about 20 or 30 feet of water. We would swim to the top of the water line and sit on top of a rock. I decided to do this; when I reached the top of the rock I dropped my mouth piece. That was a beginner's mistake; an experienced diver holds it in with the edge of his mouth. Just as I reached the top of the rock, a huge wave hit me and drove me off. I reached for my mouth piece, which was underwater, and could not find it. Now I was gasping for air. I tried two or three more times to reach the top of the rock. But as I breathed some air, I again would be washed off the

rock. I yelled "help" to Roy, but he did not hear me. I decided to duck underwater and try to swim to shore, without air. I knew that I could not last too long, but it was my only chance. I reached shore completely out of breath. My diving suit was ripped open from trying to stay on top of the rock. My mouth piece was gone and the air unit was destroyed from pounding on the rocks.

17. I went on a hunting trip for wild turkey to Mexico about 1950 with my brother, Chet, Ralph Cardinel, Dr. Bob Lock and Glen Turner. Our Mexican guide was terrific. We were gone several days on horseback through some of the most rugged country one can imagine. As a horseman knows, a horse will eat and drink in the morning; then the rider saddles it up and takes off. Late in the morning we were going up a very narrow trail at the top of a sheer cliff that dropped at least 500 feet. It was a steep climb, and all of a sudden my saddle began to slip to the rear of the horse. If the saddle reached the horse's flanks the horse would immediately begin to buck — and Link would be tossed down a 500-foot cliff. The guide saw what was happening and yelled for me not to move. He then slowly walked up to the horse, speaking in Spanish. He stroked the horse's head to calm it. He held the reins and asked me to slowly dismount. The reason I mentioned that a horse eats and drinks in the morning before being saddled is that later in the day the horse's stomach shrinks and the saddle cinch loosens. The guide was mad at himself for not tightening the cinch. I, too, should have known better. Had the horse been a little spooky, I would have ended up at the bottom of the cliff.

18. In 1975, Helen and I were in Guatemala for a few days' vacation. We decided we'd seen all we wanted and planned to leave a day early. We drove to the airport terminal the day before our departure, but the young woman there said there only was one flight per week. The flight was the next morning, but was full. She said the best she could do was to notify us if there were a cancellation. She asked us to return to the terminal at 6:30 the next morning. We did. We had a rental car. We turned it in, and put our luggage in the terminal. We would re-lease the car should we not be able to board the flight. The young woman periodically got on the phone, then would hang up and shake her head at me, meaning no cancellation had occurred. As departure time approached, she yelled, "Two, two," meaning we were able to make the flight. We flew to Mexico. That night at the hotel in Merida, a few hundred miles north of Guatemala, we felt an earthquake. The next morning we learned that a devastating temblor measuring 7.5 on the Richter scale had hit Guatemala and several thousand people had been killed. The hotel we had stayed at had been leveled. In all, some 22,000 people perished in the quake.

19. In 1991 I was crossing McCarran Boulevard at Pembroke Drive, the inlet to Hidden Valley. My car was stopped at the red light. When it turned green I began crossing. I looked to my left, which I always do; however, I was almost halfway across when I saw a pickup truck coming with no intention of stopping at the red light. Without exaggeration, I can say it was going at least 100 mph. Of course I hit my brakes; the pickup swerved slightly to the left and missed me by inches. Had I not looked left I would not be here today.

This list, as I said, is not complete. I've merely listed the occasions that come readily to mind. Had I recalled every instant during combat that nearly claimed my life, this list would stretch a mile.

Correspondence

The following is the report I wrote on the A-26. I added the last paragraph after my commanding officer. Col. C.T. Thompson, objected to the tone of my first draft:

HEADQUARTERS
17th Reconnaissance Squadron (B)
APC 70

19 July 1945

SUBJECT: Test Pilot's Report of A-26-B Airplane

TO: Commanding Officer, 71st Reconnaissance Group, APC 70

1.   The following is a complete report of the undersigned Pilot who conducted tests on the A-26 type airplane:

After six (6) flights and a total of eight (8) hours in the A-26 type airplane, which included one ride with Mr. Morresey, Douglas Test Pilot, I find the airplane to be maneuverable and easy on all controls, however, it requires a great deal of back elevator pressure in a bank, and pressure increases as the bank increases. This I believe, is caused by loss of wing lift which causes a greater force of gravity pull on the airplane.

The A-26 has a nose heavy characteristic which is noticeable while banking, taking off or landing.

With a 3,000 pound bomb load, 1,050 gals of fuel, at cruising power settings, the A-26 is recorded to have fuel consumption of 115 gals per hour and an IAS of 215 MPH----- altitude 5,000 ft.

I find the A-26 difficult for formation flying and especially true for low altitude, due to poor visibility caused by the design of the aircraft. A good formation can be flown to and from the target with a limited amount of flexibility, however, flexibility is practically nil for low altitude formation over the target.

A high speed can be accelerated over the target in the A-26 which is a definite advantage to low altitude work.

From compiled reports of the 3rd Attack Group who had flown three (3) missions to Formosa from Mindoro, I find that the Max. bomb load is 3,000 lbs with a fuel load of 1,050 gals. This gross load is considered an overload by the Douglas Factory and I am lead to believe that the factory is discouraging a gross weight that exceeds 34,000 lbs. With the bomb and fuel load mentioned the gross weight totals 35,650 lbs.

With the present A-26 design, it is possible to remove the turret gunner's escape hatch and take photographs from this station. The right side being the only side accessible. The hatch opening is located aft of the bomb bay and I do not believe that a K-17 can be operated from this position.

From a pilots standpoint, due to maneuverability and speed, I find it to be an excellent ship, however, I feel that it's limited visibility for formation flying and limited stations for photographic work greatly hinder the tactical value of the A-26 for the type of work that this Squadron has done in the past.

It is understood that the above report is my personal opinion of the A-26 type airplane and does not necessarily express the opinion of any other member of the 17th squadron.

LINCOLN E. PIAZZO,
Captain, Air Corps,
Ass't Operations Officer.

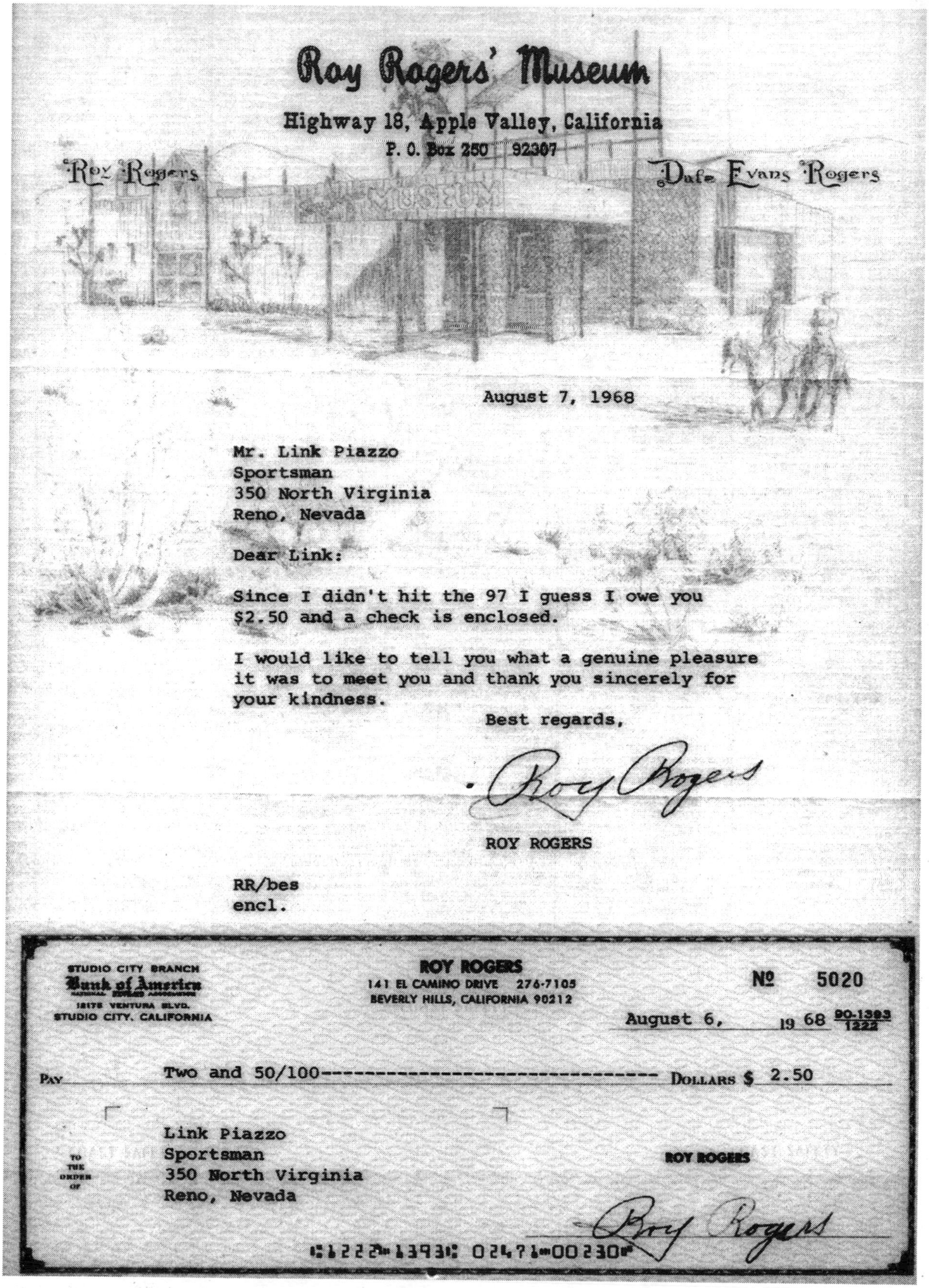

Roy Rogers' Museum

Highway 18, Apple Valley, California
P. O. Box 250 92307

Roy Rogers — Dale Evans Rogers

August 7, 1968

Mr. Link Piazzo
Sportsman
350 North Virginia
Reno, Nevada

Dear Link:

Since I didn't hit the 97 I guess I owe you $2.50 and a check is enclosed.

I would like to tell you what a genuine pleasure it was to meet you and thank you sincerely for your kindness.

Best regards,

Roy Rogers

ROY ROGERS

RR/bes
encl.

STUDIO CITY BRANCH
Bank of America
12175 VENTURA BLVD.
STUDIO CITY, CALIFORNIA

ROY ROGERS
141 EL CAMINO DRIVE 276-7105
BEVERLY HILLS, CALIFORNIA 90212

№ 5020

August 6, 19 68 90-1393/1222

PAY Two and 50/100------------------------------ DOLLARS $ 2.50

TO THE ORDER OF
Link Piazzo
Sportsman
350 North Virginia
Reno, Nevada

ROY ROGERS

Roy Rogers

⑆1222⑉1393⑆ 02471⑈00230⑈

My letter from Roy Rogers … and the check I kept as a souvenir.

THE WHITE HOUSE
WASHINGTON

March 31, 1986

Dear Mr. Piazzo:

Congratulations on your recent award of the Distinguished
Flying Cross! While I realize it comes 42 years after the
fact, the honor and recognition bestowed upon you is by no
means diminished. Your extraordinary flying achievements
and service to your country during World War II have
earned the lasting appreciation of all Americans.

Again, congratulations on this high honor, and please pass
on my thanks to General Dale Smith for rectifying this
situation.

With best wishes for every future happiness,

Sincerely,

Ronald Reagan

Mr. Lincoln R. Piazzo
1801 Skyline Boulevard
Reno, Nevada 89509

A letter from President Reagan.

Newspaper Clippings

Air Cadet from Reno Honored

L. E. Piazzo, air cadet from Reno, was one of a group of outstanding cadets at Lemoore army flying school in California to receive awards. Pictured left to right are Col. Donald B. Phillips, commanding officer at Lemoore school; Air Cadets Robert E. Sheriff of Cleveland, Ohio, John S. Volkert of Bangor, Me., Thomas J. Reading of Forest Park, Ill., Robert J. Auer of Syracuse, N. Y., Michael J. Furey of Chicago, L. E. Piazzo of Reno, John H. Singleton, cadet commander from Eaton Park, Fla., Jack G. Yancey of Tampa, Fla., and Avery T. Cashion of Hickory, N. Y.

L. E. (Link) Piazzo of Reno was awarded outstanding cadet honors last week at the Lemoore army flying school in California where he has completed his basic flying training.

Since becoming an air cadet last August, Piazzo has served as a cadet officer in all phases of his cadet training. At primary school at Rankin Aeronautical academy, he was named flight lieutenant, and at Lemoore he was appointed a squadron commander and finally was promoted to group commander of his class.

On conclusion of his flying training at an advanced army school, Piazzo will be commissioned an officer.

Piazzo, twenty-four years old, is the son of Mrs. Emma Piazzo of 609 West Tenth street. Before joining the air forces, he and his brother, Chester (Chet) Piazzo, operated The Sportsman, sporting goods store here. He took an active part in amateur athletics here, and also was an expert skeet shooter. His brother is now an ensign in the navy.

8—NEVADA STATE JOURNAL   Reno, Nev., July 4, 1952

Link Piazzo Wins .20 Gauge Honors

ELKO, July 3. (Special)—Nevada's open skeet championship shoot will come to an end Wednesday, highlighted by five-man team competition in all-bore events, with teams from six Western states participating. Entries include Reno, Elko with two squads, North Island Navy Base of San Diego, Travis Air Base (Suisun-Fairfield), Phoenix, Los Angeles and Spokane.

Final firing in the all-bore windup will feature Ann Hecker, women's world skeet champ; her husband, Dick Hecker, Phoenix star; Rod Cameron, of Hollywood film fame; Alex Kerr, world's men's skeet champ.

Tuesday Link Piazzo of Reno won the .20 gauge championship after a three-way shootoff with Ann Hecker and Ralph Smith of Elko as all tied with 98x100. Piazzo hit 24-25 in the shootoff to 23's for the others. Smith cracked 24 in another shootoff with Mrs. Hecker for runner-up honors.

Some of the West's best trap shooters shared the spotlight with skeet stars as they began a two-day "in between" trip meet in conjunction with the Nevada Open. It's "in between" last weekend's Western Championships at Reno and this weekend's Sun Valley competition. Two Oregon trapshooters, Ed Winstanley of Eugene and George Jantzer of Medford, tied with 99x100 in the 16-yard championship event and Jantzer won the shootoff.

In afternoon firing Dave Burns of Elko tied Gloria Mapes of Reno in the 17-21 yard handicap group, with 49x50, and won the shootoff with 24 to Miss Mapes' 23.

Bill Cree of Long Beach, Calif., cracked 49x50 in the 21-25-yard class for the title. W. A. Davidson, Downey, Calif., had 89 for Class A doubles, while George Jantzer of Medford, Ore., won Class B doubles at 85 and Carl Collard's 81 took Class C.

In .20 gauge skeet other winners were: Class A—Jim Kelly, Phoenix, 96; second, Joe Thorne, 95. Class B—Don Heidtman, Reno, 95; Ray Hommes, Los Angeles, 86. Class C—Dorothy Stoner, Culver City, 95; Chet Fouche, Spokane, 92. Class D—Dr. H. M. Gallagher, Elko, 96; Clark Smith, Phoenix, 95. Class E—John Welch, Tucson, 82; Ed Halpin, Phoenix, 80.

As the all-bore (.12 gauge) preliminary firing began, R. W. Fore and H. P. Cady of North Island Navy fired perfect 100 rounds.

SPORTS
... Ty Cobb, Journal Sports Editor ... Phone 4121 ...

WEDNESDAY, MARCH 29, 1950   PAGE NINE

Reno Skeet Shooters Win 17 Cups At West Coast Meet in Las Vegas

Ten Reno Trap and Skeet Club members who entered the West Coast Skeet championships at Las Vegas over the weekend came home Monday bearing a lion's share of the trophies, 17 in all.

In addition to individual honors one of the local five-man teams consisting of Robert Brooks, Link Piazzo, Gordon Furst, Don Dewson and Don Heidtman placed third in team shooting with a score of 473 x 500. They trailed the El Toro Marine Base team from California which had 480 x 500 and the Hollywood Musketeers with 479 x 500. A dozen cities sent teams to the shoot.

Individual honors during the weekend gather which drew 75 skeet shooters to L-- Vegas, went to Robert Brooks, former assistant at the Reno Trap and Skeet Club, who was runner-up for hi-overall. Brooks also won trophies for the all bore championship with 90 x 100, for secon' in Class A in the 28 gauge event and second in Class A for the 20 gauge event with identical scores of 47 x 50 in each event.

Link Piazzo scored the biggest victory of the meet, a feat comparable to a hole in one in golf or a perfect game in bowling. He took three consecutive first places in Class B shooting in Saturday's program by annexing the 410 gauge with 45x 50, the 28 gauge with 47 x 50 and the 20 gauge with 47 x 50.

Don Dawson, another Renoite, took first in all-bore Class C with 95 x 100 and third in Class C 410 gauge event with 36 x 50. Manager Mike Scherupp of Reno Trap and Skeet Club won Class C championship in the 28 gauge event with 49 x 50, took third in Class C 20 gauge with 43 x 50 and annexed an all bore Class C trophy with a score of 90 x 100. Jim Stead took second in Class C in the 20 gauge competition with 47 x 50 and second in Class D in the all bore with 87 x 100.

Bino Grifantini won Class D all-bore with 91 x 100 and won a first in Class C 410 gauge with 39 x 50. Hap Albers had a first in Class E with 94 x 100.

Making the trip as representatives of the Reno Trap and Skeet Club were Robert Brooks, Gordon Furst, Link Piazzo, Don Dawson, Don Heidtman, Jim Stead, Mike Scherupp, Hap Albers, Raymond A. Smith and Bino Grifantini.

RENO BALL TEAM REACHES UTAH FOR LEGION TOURNEY
1935

Determined to knock over the Utah state champions, the Salt Lake City Rotary Juniors, and fight their way from there to a national championship, fourteen members of the Reno junior American Legion baseball team arrived in Salt Lake City today. The team left here by train yesterday afternoon, accompanied by Coaches Ralph Warren and Darrell Swope.

The players are scheduled to go through a fairly stiff workout this afternoon preparatory to a three game series. The first game will be played tomorrow afternoon and the second on Sunday. If a third game is necessary it will be played on Monday.

In high spirits as the train pulled out, the young baseball players said they were determined to stop the Utah team from the opening inning. If they are successful in defeating the Rotarians they will enter the sectional semi-finals at Denver.

Boys making the trip include: Marvin Alexander, Jack Ward, Gerald Forson, Mike Siri, Jim Flagg, Jim Shepley, Willie Curran, Jack Piazza, Edward Claxton, Bob Moore, Bob McDonald, Earl Avasino, Fran Cas- -lli and Perry Jensen.

SEEK SECTIONAL HONORS IN UTAH

Reno's junior legion baseball team, Nevada department champions, left yesterday for Salt Lake City to play the Utah champions. The boys are all enthusiastic over their chances to defeat the Utah team and go on to the semi-finals. Left to right they are (top row) —Swope, coach; Forson, Ward, Shepley, Claxton, Jensen, Curran, Cassinelli, Piazza, Warren, coach. Bottom row—Siri, Flagg, Salmon, Avansino, Moore, Alexander and McDonald.

BANKERS, M-MEN WIN GAMES IN CITY LEAGUE PLAY

Chalking up a 54-39 win over the California Avenue Grocery team in city league play last night, the First National Bank quintet set the stage for a "natural" Wednesday night when they meet the league-leading Washoe Market contingent.

Conway and Stewart of the Grocers led the scoring parade last night with twelve markers each, while Smith poured in ten points for the winners.

Continuing their steady improvement, the Reno M-Men took the measure of the Y.M.C.A. 39-33 in a closely fought game in which the Heaton brothers scored 27 points between them for the winners. Tacchino rang the hoop for eleven points to pace the "Y" quintet.

The Reno 20-30 Club handed the Savage Sentinels a 34-19 set-back with Piazzo scoring eleven points for the winners. Gulledge, with five points, led the Savage outfit.

Ringing the hoop from all angles, the Sparks Silver Dollars took the Reno Indians into camp 64-38 in a free-scoring game. Jack Streeter rang up twenty-seven points for the Dollars and Dressler scored 12 for the losers.

Tonight at B.D.B. 8:30—Nevada freshmen meet Reno Print, and at 9:30 Knights of Columbus meet Y.M.C.A. Reds. At the Northside gym, 8:30, Reno High "C" meets Camp Idlewild, and at 9:30 Reno Florists play Reno High "B".

Market vs. Bank Tonight; Printers Nose 'Y' Team

Washoe Market tangles tonight with its chief rival in the Reno Y. M. C. A. city hoop league's "A" division, playing First National Bank at 9:30 at the B. D. B. gym. At 8:30, Y. M. C. A. Reds meet Savage and Son. At Northside, Reno High "B" plays Reno Florists at 8:30, and Reno High "C" meets Camp Idlewild at 9:30.

Last night Reno Print had a close call with the Y. M. C. A., coming from behind in the last quarter to win 42-40. Curran sank 3 fast ones in the first and the "Y" led all the way, 14-8, 24-22 and 34-30 at the quarter marks. In the final period, Johns, Pierce, Motley, McGuire and Mayse all hit the hoop for the Print. Zarubi with 12 and Cassinelli with 10 led the "Y," while Pierce had 12, Motley 11 and Mayse 9 for the Print.

Knights of Columbus took another close one from Savage Sentinels, 36 to 33. The Kaycees took an early lead but in the third Hash led a Savage rally. Hill and Doyle sparked the Knights in pulling away in the final period. W. Scott had 12 for Savage, while Hill had 12 and Doyle 10 for the Kaycees.

Reno Florists slaughtered the Indians 63 to 17, holding the Braves to one goal in the first half. Alf Sorensen scored 15, Jensen 13, Kitchen 10 for the winners, with every man on the squad hitting the hoop.

The 20-30 Club nosed out Monarch Cafe in a fast contest. Score was tied at 22-all at the half, while the Monarchs led 34-31 in the third. Davis had 10, Knudsen 9 and King 8 for the Monarchs, while Piazzo scored 12 for the club, followed by Avanzino with 8.

20-30 Club Team Wins Hoop Game

Twenty-Thirty Club cagers won easily from the Reno High School "C" squad in the only city league game scheduled last night, rolling up 32 points against 20 collected by the high school team in a "C" division contest.

The high school team made a slow start and wasn't able to score a field goal in the first half. They came back in the last half to pour in eight goals, but it wasn't enough to overcome the 20-30 Club's lead.

Link Piazzo of the 20-30 Club was high point man with 13 tallies, followed by his teammate Avansino, who collected nine. R. Ward was high for the high school team with eight, followed by J. Audrain with seven.

Reno High "C"—(20)

PLAYER—	fg	ft	tp	pf
R. Ward	3	2	8	2
N. Crew	0	0	0	0
T. Audrain	0	0	0	0
Schotell	0	0	0	0
J. Audrain	3	1	7	1
Hutchison	1	0	2	0
M. Crew	0	0	0	0
Wong	0	0	0	0
Audrain	0	0	0	0
Spoon	1	1	3	1
A. Fleck	0	0	0	0
Coleman	0	0	0	0
Totals	8	4	20	4

20-30 Club—(32)

PLAYER—	fg	ft	tp	pf
Piazzo	6	1	13	1
Avansino	4	1	9	1
Graunke	2	0	4	0
Canak	0	1	1	1
Devencenzi	0	0	0	0
Russell	1	0	2	0
Ferrie	1	0	2	0
Manford	0	0	0	0
Du Pratt	0	1	1	0
Vaughn	0	0	0	0
Pierce	0	0	0	0
Totals	14	4	32	3

—Help the Red Cross—

First SeeSee Partridge Ever Shot in Nevada Bagged by Reno Couple

Thursday, October 21, 1971

Widely-known Reno sportsman Link Piazzo received a surprise when he and his wife Helen bagged a pair of game birds recently.

The two were hunting on the west slopes of Pershing County's Seven Trough Mountains when they flushed what they thought were Hungarian Partridge.

But the birds were not Hungarian Partridge. They were the first SeeSee Partridges ever shot in Nevada.

The SeeSee birds were released in April as part of the Nevada Fish and Game Department's Exotic Bird Introductions Program. The partridges are native to Afghanistan and Pakistan.

"You could easily mistake them for a "Hun" (Hungarian Partridge) or a chukar," explained Glen Christensen of the fish and game department. "We haven't closed the areas where they were released because their habitat is very closely to the habitat of chukar."

150 Released

Christensen said that 150 birds were released from three different sites. Fifty were released in the lava beds in Pershing County and the two that the Piazzos shot were seven miles from the release site.

Christensen was very pleased that the birds were in excellent condition and appeared to have no problem in fending for themselves.

"We plan to release the birds fairly extensively," Christensen said. "Of course we will get some losses this season."

The SeeSee birds will eventually be "game birds" after they have multiplied, but at present it is not open season on them.

Quick

Piazzo was impressed with the speed on the wing of the birds.

"I hear they are very good eating, but I plan to have them mounted," Piazzo said.

The birds are described as looking something like a "quail-size chukar." When they are mounted, they may be seen at The Sportsman store in Reno. Piazzo is co-owner of The Sportsman.

Torreon KO'd

HOUSTON (UPI) — Johnny "The Mad" Baldwin, an undefeated middleweight, knocked out Alfonso Aguirre Torreon, Mexico, in 52 seconds of the fifth round of their scheduled 10-rounder.

TWENTY-THIRTIANS SPREAD CHRISTMAS CHEER

Members of the Reno 20-30 Club spread Christmas cheer this week when they gathered to distribute baskets of food to families who otherwise might not have had a Christmas dinner. Some of the workers are shown above.
(Journal Photo)

This newspaper clipping shows members of our Reno 20-30 Club gathered in preparation of distributing baskets of food to needy local families who might not otherwise have a Christmas dinner. I'm at far right.

26—Nevada State Journal   Sunday, February 14, 1965

Reno Business The Sportsman Earns National Sales Honors

RENOITE LINK PIAZZO (center) received the Industry Leadership Award from C. C. Johnson Spink (left), publisher of the Sporting Goods Dealer magazine, in Chicago ceremonies earlier this month, as Dealer editor Hugo G. Autz looks on at right. Piazzo represented Reno's The Sportsman, voted the nation's outstanding small or medium-sized sporting goods retail outlet in the nation by members of the recreation industry.

Chet, Link Piazzo Win Recreation Goods Vote

The Sportsman, Reno sporting goods company owned and operated by Chet and Link Piazzo since 1938, has been selected as national winner of the Leadership Award in the sporting goods industry for small and medium-volume retailers. The award came at the hands of other businessmen in the recreation sales industry and was the fourth annual honor presented by the Sporting Goods Dealer magazine of St. Louis, Mo.

More than 775 nominations were received for the 1964 honor, naming 475 different companies, according to C. C. Johnson Spink, publisher of the magazine that sponsors the award.

Spink said the unprecedented response to the 1964 poll showed the growth and business vigor of the sporting goods trade during the year, in addition to a growing awareness of the importance of the Leadership Awards as a mark of distinction within the industry.

101 Nominations

The small or medium-volume independent retailer division drew the most nominations— 101— of the 11 classes up for balloting. The jobber category was second with 63 nominees, indicating the wholesaling trade is producing a growing number of organizations, rather than declining.

Winners in each of the 11 categories received a Sphinx statuette mounted on a pyramidal base, with the winner's name engraved on the face of the base. Presentations were made during the National Sporting Goods Association Show in Chicago.

Spink reported an impressive factor in 1964 balloting was the number of factory and jobber salesmen who nominated customers they felt worthy of recognition. An example of that factor was nominations received by 32 Winchester-Western salesmen throughout the United States.

Qualities most looked-for in the retailer field, Spink said, were: imagination, aggressive sports promotion; hard-hitting salesmanship; warm personality, adequate stocks and emphasis on quality ..merchandise rather than price-cutting.

The Sports Goods Dealer, in its special awards issue, praised the Reno operation as follows:

"Most retailers in this category (small and medium-volume) are not widely known outside their immediate trading area, but The Sportsman of Reno is an exception. The vigorous promotional policies of the brother co-owners, Link and Chet Piazzo, and their high-type merchandising operation, together with Link's trade association activities, have gained the Piazzos.

"As active exemplars of their store's slogan, 'Play More, Live Longer, the Piazzo brothers take a prominent part in nearly every sport represented in their stock, including skating, skiing, hunting, skeet shooting, fishing, bowling, softball, golf, boating, handball and squash. Tournaments, expeditions (editor's note — including Alaskan and African big game safaris), contests and other types of promotion are in progress nearly the year around."

Link has served as president of the Western Sporting Goods Association and the National Sporting Goods Association and is in his second term as past-president chairman of the national group.

The brothers opened their business in 1938, took time out for military service during World War II while their sisters, Olga and Melba ran the store. Chet served in Naval aviation and Link in the Army Air Force.

Since their return, they have expanded beyond the sporting goods business, opening the $500,000 Plaza Shopping Center in 1957 and later adding plans for a new Lakeside Village center.

Runners-up for the Category One honor were Rex Sporting Goods of Atmore, Ala., and Athletic Supply of Abilene, Tex.

Large volume independent retail winner in the national competition was Abercrombie and Fitch Co. of New York City.

COMMEMORATIVE JAPANESE POSTAL STAMPS

"Japanese Tank Corp attack, Bataan"

December 8, 1942
"Pearl Harbor under Japanese attack"

"1st anniversary of the Greater East
Asia war"

12/12/1994

Japan deserved it
Print that A-bomb stamp

I read with interest the article, "Japan opposes Atomic Stamp," wherein Mr. Hiroka of Tokyo states, "Whatever reasons there were, the use of nuclear weapons is not forgiven" (Prime Minister Muryama is also protesting).

I can give both gentlemen at least four good reasons why the bombs were dropped and the stamp should be printed:

1. Pearl Harbor — which forced us to war with Japan.

2. Bataan Death March.

3. Ended war with Japan.

4. Saved estimated 2½ million lives if U.S. was to invade Japan as planned.

Having served in the U.S. Army Air Corps for 3½ years during WWII and flown 67 missions as pilot against the Japanese in the South Pacific, I feel certain that I am expressing the feeling of not only the military but millions of patriotic Americans when I ask our Postal Service to print the "Mushroom stamp."

The stamp that the Japanese are protesting will serve to warn them and other countries to refrain from another "sneak attack" on the U.S.A.

Link Piazzo, *Reno*

War hero gets medal — 42 years late

By Don Vetter/Gazette-Journal

Reno businessman Link Piazzo's only medal from World War II had been a .25-caliber, metal-piercing bullet he wears around his neck on a thick silver chain.

It's the bullet that came within inches of Piazzo's skull as he strafed Japanese targets in the Philippines. His life was spared because the bullet lodged in the aluminum cockpit frame of his B-25 bomber instead of exploding through his cranium.

But the Department of Defense this week gave Piazzo a more conventional medal — a Distinguished Flying Cross — earned for a pair of extraordinary missions the former Army Air Corps captain flew 42 years ago in the Pacific theater.

The 69-year-old owner of The Sports-man, a Reno sporting goods store, said he

never would have gotten the medal if retired Maj. Gen. Dale O. Smith of Reno hadn't stopped into his store last summer to purchase a hunting license.

"We just got to talking — you know he was a commander in the 8th Air Force — and I told him about flying in the 5th and never got the DFC like they told me I earned," Piazzo recalled.

In the hectic final months of the war against Japan, Piazzo was discharged from the Air Corps before a general — the only person allowed to bestow the award — could pin him with the medal.

Smith got the ball rolling with some well-placed letters to the Air Force, and this week he pinned Piazzo with the Distinguished Flying Cross before fellow members of the Reno Rotary Club.

"Back then, we didn't care much about medals," Piazzo said. "We thought we

were going to get killed, so what do we need medals for? Getting the medal now, I think it means more to me."

Piazzo, who still had the letter recommending him for the reward, has a penchant for saving mementos. His office walls are plastered with photos from the war, hunting trips and special events with the likes of sports greats Joe DiMaggio, Jack Dempsey and Lefty Gomez.

At 24, Piazzo became a member of the 17th Squadron, nicknamed the "Suicide Squad."

He had to cheat on his eye exam, talk a commanding officer out of turning him into a bombardier and overcome bouts with air sickness to gain his pilot's wings.

All that to join a B-25 group that would

See WAR, page 6C

PIAZZO: Reno man's wait ends.

War medal

From page 1C

lose all its planes three times during the war and was known to strike the enemy with bombing runs only 1,000 feet above enemy fire.

"Our squadron was highly decorated in both theaters of operation, most of them posthumously," Piazzo said.

"I'll never forget one briefing we had before a run. The commanding officer addressed us in the ready room: 'Gentlemen, you're all going to die this morning.'"

But Piazzo's combination of skill and luck got him through 18 months of combat flying without a scratch. The two medal-winning episodes were examples of Piazzo's ability.

On Jan. 9, 1945, Piazzo was one of eight B-25 pilots on a mission to

support the invasion at Lingayen, Luzon, which marked the return to the Philippines of the American forces under command of Gen. Douglas MacArthur.

According to the Army Air Corps commendation, Piazzo knocked out an enemy fuel supply, a locomotive and eight freight cars. Japanese fire hit Piazzo's fuel tanks, forcing a tricky but successful return to base. It was from this flight that Piazzo collected his bullet medallion.

Then, on May 26 of that year, Piazzo flew a mission to Tarshi, Formosa.

The Japanese forces had been backed onto the 235-mile long island, which meant any bombing mission was going to be met with the very heavy enemy fire.

During the Formosa mission, Piazzo used "dangerous, but absolutely necessary tactics to avoid enemy fire," the commendation said.

Piazzo said it was more a case of dumb luck.

The target, an alcohol plant turned munitions factory, was wedged between the mountains and the sea. It was overcast, and, after the first bombing run, Piazzo flew his bomber into a rain cloud and couldn't find the mountains.

His only alternative was to make a 180-degree turn and go back the way he came, strafing the factory with 50mm machine-gun fire because his bomb bay was now empty.

"You never make two runs on the same target, but that's what I did. I guess the Japs thought no pilot would be that stupid."

Piazzo logged 300 combat hours during 67 missions. He finished his stint in Japan, setting up his squadron headquarters in Yokota, where he named the airfield control center "Reno Tower."

Thursday

January 28, 1988   35 cents

SPORTS BROADCASTING

Early days of Pack broadcasting had its ups and downs

■ **Link Piazzo:** Longtime Reno resident broadcast games of legendary Nevada teams of 1947-51 on KOH.

By Joe Santoro
RENO GAZETTE-JOURNAL

Long before Dan Gustin was behind the microphone for the Wolf Pack, there was Link Piazzo.

"We just had one station back then," the 79-year-old remembered recently. "And there was no TV. You could say we had a captive audience."

Back then was right after World War II. Piazzo brought the exploits of Wolf Pack football and basketball into northern Nevada's living rooms over KOH radio from 1947-1951.

It was a career the lifelong Reno resident all but stumbled into.

"One night during the high school state basketball tourna-

"When we screwed up, we'd just call a fake timeout or have a dog walk across the field. One time I even had a drunken sailor run across the field.'

Link Piazzo
Former Nevada broadcaster

RENO GAZETTE-JOURNAL

Monday, April 13, 1992

Piazzo family proves you can succeed in U.S.

ROLLAN MELTON

There are many new immigrants in Nevada who cannot yet speak English. Who may be confused by what now seem to be weird American customs. Who are confronted with not only a devilishly complicated new language, but who are short of money because their jobs are low-pay. If they've yet found jobs.

But things can work out, as they have for earlier Nevada immigrants. Or for those born here to immigrants.

What was, and is, vital is being given a chance to work, doing well on jobs, trying the utmost to learn English, encountering luck and hospitable timing, and finding established local people who will give them a chance. A cram-course in learning is an indispensable ally.

This leads me today to a Nevada success story that has an immigrant beginning.

Chet Piazzo, amiable Nevada entrepreneur and sportsman, was born on a Reno ranch (it was at 10th and Washington Streets), on April 6, 1917, the day America declared war on Germany, propelling us into World War I. Last Monday, I talked to him on his latest landmark date — his 75th birthday, and he was pleased to talk about his roots.

Chet, left, and **Link Piazzo.**

The parents were Italian immigrants who like many thousands of others came through New York's Ellis Island.

Once off the island, the Piazzo family headed out of New York into the West, but stalled when Santino Piazzo ran out of money at Portola and couldn't continue the train trip to San Francisco with his young wife, Emma. Instead, they came to Reno and stayed. Chet Piazzo was born, then brother Link came along on Dec. 11, 1918, a month to the day after the Amistice.

The immigrants put their elder son in first-grade at Mary S. Doten School (it was at Washington and Fifth Streets). The little boy returned home the first day, crying, "They're speaking a foreign language, Pappa." Santino Piazzo

soothed him: "They're talking American, and Chet, you now must now learn to talk American, too."

In 1938, when the Piazzo brothers were 21 and 19 years old, they used their combined savings — $1,800 — to open a little business they named the Sportsman Store. It was on North Virginia Street across from what is now the Eldorado Hotel and Casino.

As kids, they had scrapped with each other, as boys will do. But now they were irrevocably bonded by their commercial vows, and by a fierce desire to succeed. Their family was always ready to help, too — while Chet and Link fought in World War II, their sisters, Olga Dibitonto and Melba Cassinelli, managed the Sportsman until war ended and the brothers came home.

The Piazzos worked slavishly hard, hired excellent people, treated them well, gave excellent service, and had fun being with customers.

Bankers felt safe dealing with them because they were true to their word. Thus, did the Piazzo enterprise soar. If you've been around awhile, you know that The Sportsman is a blue-ribbon business in Reno. Subsequent Piazzo ventures, including three shopping centers, have also done exceptionally well.

The Piazzo family story is a thrilling Nevada success.

Such successes will be repeated in Nevada as new immigrants are given a chance to prove that impossible dreams can still come true.

Rollan Melton is a Gazette-Journal columnist.

In Gratitude for Service

LINK PIAZZO

We are very happy and proud to dedicate this Zone Basketball Tournament program to Mr. Link Piazzo. Link is a native Nevadan. He attended the Mary S. Doten Grammer School, Northside Junior High School, and Reno High School. While attending Reno High he played on the Varsity Basketball Team.

He married a Nevada girl, Helen Galbraith. Link and Helen have two sons. Craig is a sophomore at Earl Wooster High School, and Lynn is a sophomore at Colorado State University studying to be a veterinarian. Link is a member of the Reno Rotary Club.

Link and his brother, Chet, started in the sporting goods business in Reno in 1938. They expanded their business numerous times and "service" became their motto.

During World War II, Link served in the United States Air Force. He flew a B25 as a captain and squadron leader. He led the 5th Air Force in the South Pacific.

Link has donated his services as a timer for the past twenty-five consecutive years at the Northern Nevada Zone Basketball Tournaments, starting back at the new University of Nevada Gym, not long after it was built. His service has always been cheerfully given. He broadcast the University of Nevada games from 1945 to 1950.

Here are a few of the many accomplishments of this individual: he holds the first membership card in the Broadcasters & Sportswriters Association formed in 1954, and became the second President of the Association; he was president of the Western Sporting Goods Association in 1955 and president of the National Sporting Goods Association in 1962; Link along with his brother Chet, won the Sporting Goods Award for Outstanding contributions and services to the industry in 1964; he served on the Board of Directors of the National Sporting Goods Association from 1964 to 1967.

Above all, Link is a humanitarian. No one individual knows of all the people he has befriended in some way or another. He does these things quietly when needed, and they go unnoticed by most people, so, we can rightfully say that "service" to his fellowmen is one of his attributes. He exemplifies the spirit of true sportsmanship, that quality of honor that insures courtesy, fairness, and respect.

This, then, is the man to whom we dedicate this program. In behalf of the Northern Nevada Zone, we humbly say: "Thank you, Link, for everything you have done for the schools, and we wish you and your family nothing but the best in the future."

RAY CABLE
Tournament Director

An Outstanding Graduate of the Washoe County School District
Award
is presented to

Link Piazzo

by the Washoe County Teachers Association
for outstanding community service

Rita Hambleton
W. C. T. A. President

Tom Pennington
Secretary

SPORTSMAN'S TRAILS

Chet and Link Piazzo, well known local sports figures, have hosted the popular outdoors-oriented program "Sportsman's Trails" for the past twelve years. The show, produced weekly at KTVN, consists of information for all sports enthusiasts. Chet and Link, avid sportsmen themselves, also speak of their experiences and have the latest word on licenses, deadlines and tips on where to go for the best hunting and fishing. They answer questions from viewers and feature their own tried and true recipes for cooking and eating all kinds of game, plus demonstrations on the latest sports equipment. Sportsman's Trails. . .Saturday afternoons at 5:00 p.m. on KTVN.

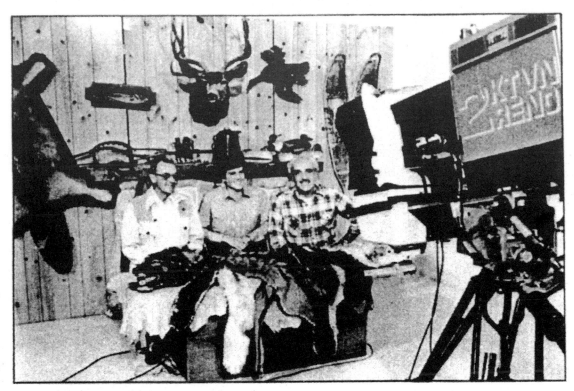

A KTVN promotional piece for "Sportsman's Trails." The show ran 28 years, from 1956 until 1984.

Soldier of Fortune Article

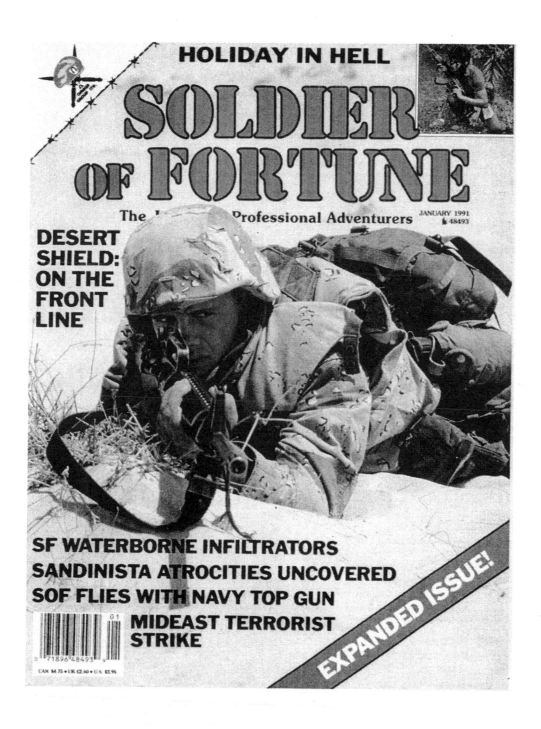

FORBIDDEN FLIGHT

THE loudspeakers boomed across the open-air theater: "Attention all personnel ... We have had a report that one of our aircraft has flown over a restricted area ... If this is true it is your duty and responsibility to report it to headquarters ... The consequences could be serious if you fail to do so ... This matter will be pursued until we find out if the report is true ... I repeat ..."

I glanced at my buddy, chuckled and said, "What are they talking about?"

It was August 1945 and our 17th Reconnaissance Bomb Squadron was flying out of Ie Shima, a small Japanese island in the Ryukyu chain. Our B-25Js had been flying in support of mop-up operations in the Philippines, making napalm strikes and strafing with our 18 .50 caliber machine guns. In addition, we were equipped for aerial photography. Good targets were getting scarce, but occasionally we caught a train or some coastal shipping. "Shipping" is a little generous, for at this stage of the war the Japanese were transporting men and materiel in anything that would float. We were also flying strikes to Formosa and mainland China.

As a radioman-gunner, my "trigger time" alternated between a .50 caliber waist gun, a Morse key, and a camera shutter. With 67 combat flights under my belt, I'd had plenty of time on all three.

Our routine all changed when the atomic bombs were dropped on Hiroshima and Nagasaki. We weren't given a lot of details on these missions, but from the scuttlebutt everyone knew that we had used a new weapon of immense destruction and that the war should soon be over. Before long we were down to the required number of hours

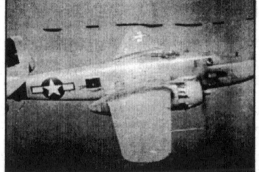
The B-25J was a versatile craft used for delivering ordnance, strafing, and aerial reconnaissance. Ordnance was usually on target — sometimes the aerial reconnaissance was not.

to keep our flight pay coming.

Then one evening our pilot, Link Piazzo, called me aside and asked if I would fly with him on a special flight the next day. Having put in all of my combat time with him, I knew Captain Piazzo as a top-notch pilot — one of the best. Sure, I'd go. Besides our co-pilot and navigator, three photographers from the squadron photo lab would go along.

I soon learned that Capt. Piazzo planned to use a scheduled recon of Sakishima Island, just north of the Philippines, as a cover mission to sneak a private peek at Hiroshima and Nagasaki. My job would be to radio position reports which would show us to be on the authorized mission.

The next day we took off with anticipation. The flight was routine and every hour I tapped a position report off to our base. My last contact put us over Sakishima, when in fact we were heading inland over the southern tip of Honshu. We were flying under 300 feet, often as low as 100 feet. Japanese coastal defense batteries pointed skyward, unattended. As we crossed the inland waters between islands we could see surfaced submarines lying at anchor. I counted

as many as a dozen in one harbor. Further inland we flew over a POW camp at about 100 feet and we thought we saw men waving from the windows. As Paul Tibbets observed in his book *Flight of the Enola Gay*, these prisoners would most likely have been executed when Japan prepared to defend her home islands against an Allied invasion. The atomic bomb saved them.

As we neared Hiroshima, the clouds thickened and smoke swirled in through the open waist windows. As prearranged, Capt. Piazzo notified me over the intercom when we approached an area that he wanted photographed, and I signaled this to the two photographers who were shooting out of the waist windows.

The putrid, sickening smoke wafting up from the destruction below became thicker inside the plane as we dropped down to 50 feet or so above the remaining rooftops. At the time we had no idea we might be exposing ourselves to deadly radiation. Captain Piazzo lowered the landing gear and flaps to drop our airspeed as low as he dared, giving the photographers the best conditions possible.

The devastation I saw gave me a feeling of total shock like I'd never experienced before and haven't experienced since. The surrounding mountainsides were scorched black and there was little left of the city itself. We could see people walking in the streets, as the sidewalks were buried beneath rubble from the demolished buildings. Every now and then we saw someone on a bicycle. People were rummaging around in the ruins and it looked like some had built lean-tos that they were living in. As we passed over, many people were looking up and waving. This gave me a strange sensa-

The B-25J's crew photographed Japanese submarines swinging on the hook off Honshu — their war ended by the bombs on Hiroshima and Nagasaki.

Army Aviators
Joyride Over Ground Zero

by Harry Hall as told to Chris Beebe

Photos Courtesy Harry Hall

tion. Were they still in shock? How could anyone wave to an enemy that had just done this to their city?

We left Hiroshima behind and flew on to Nagasaki, where the scene was much the same. The blackened slopes of the mountains gave me the impression of a great, burned-out bowl. The factory buildings in the industrial heart of the city stood like black skeletal ghosts, with dark smokestacks rising above steel girders that had been warped and twisted by the intense heat of the bomb. Unlike Hiroshima, we could see very little movement in the city. Captain Piazzo must have been getting an eyeful too, because we nearly hit one of the remaining buildings. We passed so close to one structure, it gave the camera a distorted image.

Leaving the destruction behind, we raised the gear and flaps and continued on at low altitude until we reached open water. Then we climbed to just below 10,000 feet and I tried to raise our base station on the radio. Our plane was equipped with a trailing antenna that consisted of 200 feet of copper wire with a lead weight on the end. This was reeled in and out by a small electric winch. Now as I turned the antenna switch, I saw to my dismay that the antenna reel was spinning freely, with no antenna wire. I got a sick feeling in the pit of my stomach when I realized that, in the excitement just prior to arriving over Japan, I must have forgotten to reel the antenna in. Now it was probably wrapped around the skeletal remains of a building somewhere in Hiroshima.

I reported the situation to Capt. Piazzo over the intercom and he told me to do the best I could. I switched to the shorter-range fixed antenna and tapped the Morse key. I was relieved to get an immediate response from our ground station. I sent off a bogus position report as we headed for home.

When we landed and checked in, I headed for my quarters. Later that evening

Hiroshima had only a few masonry buildings standing — and one of them probably got Harry Hall's trailing radio antenna wrapped around it.

Scorched hillsides, smoldering ruins and the skeletal remains of Japanese industry were the sight that greeted crew of phantom B-25J over Nagasaki.

one of the photographers brought a package to my tent. He told me that he had printed a set of photos, 36 in all, for each member of the crew and then destroyed the negatives. No one was to know of the flight or the photos.

I did tell our engineer-gunner and tail gunner, who had not made the flight, of our adventure, and offered them some of the photos, but with the threats being issued from headquarters regarding the rumored flight, both were hesitant to take them.

Official interest in our phantom flight soon cooled down and the issue fell by the wayside, however, because more important things were happening.

On 19 August, two Jap "Betty" bombers took off from Japan and headed for Ie Shima. Painted white with green crosses, as prearranged, they were picked up by a flight of P-51 Mustangs and escorted in. A Japanese surrender delegation disembarked and boarded a C-54 transport bound for Manila. There they were to meet with representatives of General Douglas MacArthur to finalize plans for the unconditional surrender of Japan.

Before shipping out, some of our crewmen disposed of their clandestine photos, still fearful of being caught. I brought out six prints, which I cut in half to conceal among my stationery and personal papers.

After 20 years or so, I began showing the pictures to high school classes I was teaching. I still get a thrill every time I look at these photos which, never having been published, have only been seen and enjoyed by a relative few. Today, 45 years have passed since our "forbidden flight." Maybe it's time for this small part of history to go public.

Chris Beebe is an Ohio-based freelance writer. Harry Hall recently retired from a career as an audio-visual teacher. A reunion of his B-25J crew is slated for June in Reno, Nevada.